SCHOLASTIC

Encyclopedia

of the

NORTH AMERICAN

INDIAN

SCHOLASTIC
Encyclopedia
of the
NORTH AMERICAN
INDIAN

James Ciment, PhD

with Ronald LaFrance, PhD

Scholastic
Reference

New York   Toronto   London   Auckland   Sydney

Executive Editor: C. Carter Smith
Consultant: Ronald LaFrance (Mohawk)
Project Editor: Shannon Rothenberger (Anishinabe)
Editors: Douglas Hill and Lelia Wardwell
Designer: Laura Smyth
Contributing Writer: Marlene Brill
Photo Editors: Sommer Hixson and Courtney Kealy
Production: John W. Kern
Editorial Assistant: Sara Jane Baysinger
Maps: David Lindroth

We would like to thank Lauri Brown, Katherine Ferrante, Christina Hamme, Tinisha Hawkins,
Kim Horstman, Shelley Latham, Stephen McAndrews, and Katherine Redfern.

A Media Projects Book

Photo credits are on page 224.

ISBN 0-590-22791-2

12 11 10 9 8 7 6 5 4 3 2   9   8 9/9 0 1 2/0

Printed in the U.S.A.   09

TABLE OF CONTENTS

TABLE OF CONTENTS

TABLE OF CONTENTS

TABLE OF CONTENTS

TABLE OF CONTENTS

TABLE OF CONTENTS

How to Use This Book

This book includes information about 143 groups of American Indians in alphabetical order. People who study native peoples often divide these groups into geographic categories. Eleven of these categories are also listed alphabetically. You can recognize them by the red headlines of their entries. Both kinds of entries are listed in the Table of Contents. Featured people and special topics such as Missions and Reservations also have their own entries and can be found in the Table of Contents.

Susan Billy

Pomo basketmaker Susan Billy sees her baskets as a way to connect to "all the grandmothers who have gone before me." She uses traditional Pomo techniques such as weaving bright feathers into her designs. Many Pomo basketmakers are internationally known for their work.

POMO

- LANGUAGE FAMILY: HOKAN
- LIFEWAYS: HUNTING, FISHING, & GATHERING
- LOCATION: CALIFORNIA
- THEIR OWN NAME: POMO

CALIFORNIA

There are 4,800 Pomo living in Mendocino and Sonoma counties in California. Spirituality helped the Pomo recover from the widespread slaughter and mission imprisonment of the 1800s.

How to Look Up...

WORDS IN RED mean that a separate entry on that word can be found elsewhere in the book (or that a subject is treated in the entry highlighted in red). Look up the tribe or topic in the Table of Contents and turn to the listed page. In the Index in the back of the book, page numbers in red highlight the best place to look for information on many different subjects.

A TRIBE—Look up the tribe's name in the Table of Contents and turn to the listed page. There you will find a small map that shows the region where the tribe was originally located and a Data Box that provides information on the tribe's language, traditional lifeways, present-day location, and the tribe's own name for itself. Entries describe how the tribe lived in the past, the people's traditional beliefs, and what tribe members are doing today.

IMPORTANT EVENTS AND PEOPLE—Look up the name or event in the Index in the back of the book. The Index will list the numbers of the pages on which that person or event is discussed.

PLAINS

- TRIBES OF THE REGION: ARAPAHO, ARIKARA, ASSINIBOINE, BLACKFEET, CADDO, CHEYENNE, COMANCHE, CROW, GROS VENTRE, HIDATSA, IOWA, KAW, KIOWA, MANDAN, MISSOURIA, OMAHA, OSAGE, OTOE, PAWNEE, PONCA, QUAPAW, SARCEE, SIOUX (DAKOTA, LAKOTA, NAKOTA), TONKAWA, & WICHITA

PLAINS

Native Americans have inhabited the Great Plains since A.D. 300, when they invented the bow and arrow. They roamed nearly 1 million square miles of land west of the Mississippi River and east of the Rocky Mountains. Indian settlements stretched from present-day Canada to the southern tip of Texas. Although the area contains the Platte, Mississippi, and Missouri rivers, and rugged plateaus and cliffs, most of the Plains was endless grassy prairie, home to the buffalo.

REGIONAL CATEGORIES—Look up the area in the Table of Contents. For instance: Plains. Turn to the listed page, where you will find a Data Box listing the original tribes of the region. Each entry describes the region and the tribes' history.

Maps showing Regions and Peoples, Language Families, Forced Migration, and the Loss of Land can be found on pages 210–213.

Introduction

This is an exciting time to learn about American Indian tribes. After hundreds of years of hard times in North America, many Indian tribes are becoming stronger and more independent. Our populations are growing, and many young people now return to their reservations to learn about their culture after they graduate from college. Income from new businesses is helping many tribes build schools and cultural centers. Indian children can now learn their tribe's language, art forms, and history.

Until recently, the wide variety of tribal lifeways, languages, and beliefs was not explained in most American history textbooks. Indians were placed in the past, as if their world and ways of life were dead. European-American viewpoints too often present us as a "conquered" people, or as people who stood in the way of "progress."

Unfortunately, our contact with Europeans made it difficult for Indians to survive. Our ideas of progress were different from those of Europeans. Traditional Indian weapons were no match for European guns.

Liquor supplied by Europeans brought us only pain. We did not have the natural resistance to such European diseases as smallpox, typhoid, cholera, and influenza that many Europeans had acquired over time. By 1900 our total population had been reduced by 90 percent. Some tribes were destroyed altogether, and their stories will never be told.

Forced Moves

Imagine what it would be like if strangers came to your community and forced everyone to move somewhere else. Imagine that you could carry nothing with you but your memories. Imagine that your children were forced to move again, and their children as well. What would your great-great-grandchildren know about you? And what about the great-great-grandchildren of the people who forced you to move?

That is the situation of American Indians today. Our first histories in English were written by anthropologists trying to document what they called "a dying race." Most didn't bother to ask us about our own traditions.

▶ Old Ways

In the time before Europeans came to the New World, Indians had developed ways of life that changed only gradually over the centuries. Different groups had adapted to many different kinds of climates. But Europeans introduced huge changes to the lives of the Indians. The Spanish, for example, brought the horse, which completely transformed the hunting methods of the Plains Indians.

Our other, more frequent, visitors were missionaries. They thought we should become Christians and forget our own languages and beliefs.

Today, Indian issues are changing so fast that it is a challenge to keep up with them. Many tribespeople helped us produce this book, and we thank them. To understand the full history of North America it is important to read Indian viewpoints. Our own histories go back thousands of years before Europeans arrived. Great civilizations arose here before Europeans came. To us the 500 years we have shared this continent with newcomers is very brief.

MANY PEOPLES ▼ ▼

It is very important to understand the many different tribes that are native to this land. We are as different from one another as the Spanish are from the French, or the English from the Dutch. Not only did each tribe wear different clothing and live in different types of houses but each had its own ideas of government and how men, women, and children should live together. Each group had its own name for the creator and the other powerful spirits that guided their lives. Distinct traditions of ceremonies, music, dance, stories, and prayer were central to each tribe's life. Tribes' philosophies were as different as the places they lived: oceans, deserts, prairies, wetlands, and mountains.

Although more than 500 tribes lived in the Americas at one time or another, we have created 143 separate tribal entries (and twenty other entries) for this encyclopedia. Many groups have been closely associated with each other over time and are described in the same entry. The final list was put together by consulting with tribal elders, scholars in the field, and reliable references. We made a special effort to include up-to-date information on relatively small tribes that are often left out of books on Native Americans.

In the encyclopedia we portray Indian tribes in three time frames: past, present, and future. Our most important job is to avoid creating new stereotypes or reinforcing old ones. Members of other racial groups work hard to make the public aware of stereotypes, and

STEREOTYPES

Among the stereotypes, or simplified notions, of Indians is the idea that they all wear feathered headbands and loincloths and carry tomahawks. Some Native Americans wore feathers, some wore loincloths, some used tomahawks. But it is wrong to assume that all Indians have these features in common.

And while most Plains tribes had elaborate feather headdresses, they were reserved for chiefs or elders—and for ceremonial occasions.

Another stereotype about Indians is that they were noble savages or fierce, eagle-eyed archers. Such views led people either to fear Indians unreasonably or to consider them inferior.

Stereotypes are just too simple to be true. Every human being is different, and stereotypes hide those differences. They hide reality by making everyone from a particular group seem like a cartoon version of what he or she really is, whether the person is Indian, black, white, Asian, or Hispanic.

KEEPING TRADITIONS ALIVE

Among many Indian tribes today there is a growing interest in rediscovering old traditions and ceremonies, practices that were only recently in danger of dying out.

Young people in particular are seeking to learn more about their ancestors' ways. In addition, they are concerned about such issues as the environment, poverty, and alcohol abuse among Native Americans. This poster (left), which warns of the dangers of heavy drinking, is put out by a group of Indian youth that is active on reservations and in schools.

Another issue of concern to Indians of all generations is the proper burial of ancestors' remains. These elders from the Blackfeet tribe (below) are reburying human remains that the Smithsonian Institution returned to them.

Drinking and Powwows Don't Mix

CHOOSE TRADITION NOT ADDICTION

Know the consequences of alcohol and drug abuse

A message from UNITY and the National Institute on Drug Abuse

Indian people are trying to do the same thing.

Another big job for today's Indians is convincing museums to return Indian skeletons for proper burial. It would be against the law to dig up graves in your local cemetery. Yet anthropologists have been digging up Indians for many decades in order to study them. Museums are reluctant to return our ancestors' bones, even when we have court orders. They say they need more time to study them.

The Smithsonian Institution claims that museums are holdng 600,000 Indian skeletons. According to the 1990 census, that is more than one Indian skeleton for every four Native Americans living in the United States.

There are also many objects—masks and kachina dolls, for example—that museums regard as works of art. To Indians, many of these objects are sacred and should be held by the tribes who understand them. They need to be taken care of in special ways by spiritual leaders who respect their power. Like many of our ceremonies, they are not to be photographed or displayed for entertainment. Many Indian people are going to court to get sacred objects and their ancestors' remains returned to them.

BROKEN TREATIES

Also, Indian lawyers in Canada and the United States are working to get those countries' governments to honor the treaties they made with the Indian nations. Indians made treaties to share the land, not give it away. Yet our land was taken from us, and today, even though American Indians occupy only a small part of North America, there are still many threats to our land.

According to the Council of Energy Resource Tribes (CERT), a large part of United States natural resources, such as coal, oil, and uranium, can be found on Indian lands. Indians do not trust the federal government to negotiate fairly for the use of these resources because more than 400 treaties between Indians and whites have already been broken.

RESPECTING THE EARTH & EACH OTHER

Indians have always been strongly tied to the land. The Haudenosaunee, or Iroquois (my own people), viewed the world from a turtle's back. That is because our story of the continent's creation tells about a Great Turtle who volunteered his shell for people to live on. That shell is North America, which is why some Indians call it Turtle Island.

For the Haudenosaunee, each morning began with a salutation, or greeting, that expressed thanks for a new day. A speaker greeted each person, then greeted Mother Earth, and, finally, the universe. These greetings showed how small we humans are compared to the rest of nature. Sometimes the speaker took more than an hour and a half to recite the greeting. Of course, he didn't keep track of time that way. Nature's time is very different from the time we humans read on our wristwatches, and the 20th century is merely the blink of an eye to the spirits of nature.

As you use this book to learn about the many different Indian tribes, try to think of us as changing over time, and not stuck in one place. We teach our children that, to create peace, it is necessary to accept the differences among groups of people. We believe that people's cultural differences grew out of the lands they came from, and how they learned to live there.

The world is a very delicate place, and so are all its people. We all have a rich past and present. Only through discussion and understanding can we avoid the errors of the past and make wise decisions for the future. Only that way can we make a better world for future generations.

—Ronald LaFrance PhD

DIVERSE CULTURES

There is no one Indian culture, though many Indians share cultural beliefs or practices. Each tribe's traditions—in dress, dwelling place, and way of life—were greatly influenced by the climate and landscape where that tribe lived.

Native Americans who live in the Arctic cold (like the woman at right) wear fur parkas to keep themselves warm in sub-zero temperatures. Hunters sometimes wait hours on the ice to capture seals.

Indians of the Southwest, in contrast, raise sheep. They spin wool and weave it into colorful blankets, which are used as clothing, for the home, or as a means of livelihood.

Customs also stem from religious beliefs and ceremonies. Tribal elders of the Plains traditionally wore feather headdresses, quill breastplates, and other warrior regalia for such ceremonies as the Sun Dance. These men are participating in a powwow, a festive gathering of many tribes.

ABENAKI

- **LANGUAGE FAMILY:** ALGONQUIAN
- **LIFEWAYS:** HUNTING & GATHERING
- **LOCATION:** VERMONT & QUEBEC
- **THEIR OWN NAME:** WAPANAKI

NORTHEAST

Two bands of Abenaki—Eastern and Western—lived in Maine and Vermont, respectively. Their name for themselves, Wapanaki, means Dawn Land People. Today, many of the Western Abenaki live in Quebec, to which they migrated in the 1700s, during the Northeast colonial wars. Two thousand Eastern Abenaki live in the northern Vermont towns of Highgate, Saint Albans, and Swanton.

STORIES According to legend, Tabaldak—the Abenaki creator—carved the first people from living wood. Tabaldak protects animals and plants, while the Earth (Our Grandmother) watches over people. Raccoon (Azeban) is the trickster in Abenaki tales, which were told to children on long winter nights. It was believed that spirits slept in winter and did not know they were being talked about.

The Abenaki did not hit their children. When a child was punished, his or her face was blackened with soot. The child then had to sit outside of the wigwam. Children also helped their parents fish, hunt moose, grow corn, and collect maple syrup. They also played Iroquois games such as lacrosse and snow snake.

Although the Abenaki long ago lost land to Europeans, the people are now regrouping. In the 1970s the Vermont Abenaki Self-Help Association revived traditional arts and language. The Quebec Abenaki run a museum and native center in Odanak. One important project is called "La parole aux aînés" ("The word of the elders"). Through the program, wise elders organize museum exhibits for young people.◄

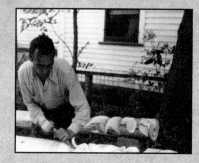

Pole Carving

Abenaki Adrian Panadis carves a tortoise in a ceremonial pole for a 1960 celebration in Odanak, Quebec.

Museum

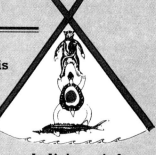

The symbol of the Musée des Abenakis d'Odanak features a bear, symbolizing courage and strength; a tortoise, symbolizing wisdom; and a sturgeon, symbolizing depth. This emblem has been the Abenaki official signature since the 18th century.

Friends

Friends and family gathered in 1995 at the Musée des Abenakis d'Odanak, the site of reunions and youth activities. Pictured in the bottom row is Martin Gill. In the second row are Isabelle Gill, Sophie Gill, and Amélie Poirier. In the top row are Olivier Lamirande and Catherine Beauchemin.

▶ Woodpecker

The Alabama tribe, one of the oldest in the Southeast, is descended from the Mississippian Mound Builders. This ivory-billed woodpecker motif was found on pottery made by ancestors of the Alabama and Coushatta Indians. They were skilled craftsmen—as the Alabama are today—but little else is known about these early tribesmen. The pot on which the woodpecker was carved served as a water bottle.

▶ Winged Serpent

Cut into other Mound Builder pottery, this winged serpent motif dates from A.D. 1200–1400. Mound Builders often buried pottery with the dead, punching holes in the bottom to allow the spirits of the pot to escape.

ALABAMA-COUSHATTA

- **LANGUAGE FAMILY:** MUSKOGEAN
- **LIFEWAYS:** HUNTING & FARMING
- **LOCATION:** ALABAMA, OKLAHOMA, & TEXAS
- **THEIR OWN NAME:** ALABAMU

SOUTHEAST

The Alabama were allied with the Creek Confederacy. They numbered about 3,000 at the time of contact with Spaniard Hernando de Soto in 1541. According to Creek legend, the Alabama are one of the region's oldest tribes. They originally lived in the southern part of the state that was later named for them. The people shared a language with their closest neighbors, the Coatsi, or Coushatta. The name Alibamu means I Clear the Thicket.

Little is known about the early Alabama. They were occasional farmers and often at war with their neighbors. They also had conflicts with the Creek because the Alabama did not follow Creek law.

FLIGHT Because of war with Europeans and other Indians, the Alabama became refugees in the 16th and 17th centuries. They finally fled to eastern Texas with the Coushatta, where they survived by hiding in the Big Thicket swamp. They received a 3,000-acre reservation along the Trinity River in Texas in the 1830s.

Today, there are three groups of Alabama: two Alabama-Coushatta groups in Texas and Oklahoma, and 400 Alabama in the state of Alabama.

That group is known for its fine cane baskets. The Texas group has a tribal museum at a reconstructed traditional village, where visitors can watch historical dramas and Friendship Dances. Since the 1930s the Oklahoma group has been associated with the Creek nation, though in 1990 it began to plan its own government. ◀

ALEUT

- **LANGUAGE FAMILY:** ESKALEUT
- **LIFEWAYS:** SEA HUNTING & FISHING
- **LOCATION:** ALASKA
- **THEIR OWN NAME:** UNANGAN

ARCTIC

The Aleut traveled from Siberia to Alaska about 9,000 years ago. The Aleutian Islands —which are named for the Aleut—extend about 1,200 miles west of Alaska into the Pacific Ocean. The islands get only about four weeks of snow annually, winters are rainy and the rest of the year is damp. The soil is far too thin for trees to grow.

WHALE HUNTS

The Aleut depended on kayaks (hide-covered canoes) for transportation, fishing, and hunting whales. Boys were carefully trained from early childhood to paddle, throw harpoons, and handle heavy spears in rough seas. To hunt whales, up to forty men would take to the sea in huge kayak-like boats known as *baidarkas.* Girls and women smoked and dried the whale meat. The Aleut used the huge whale bones to support the roofs of their rounded sod huts.

Aleut society was divided into bands and classes, and some very rich people owned slaves. Wealthy hosts gave away many presents at feasts, where masked dancers performed to honor game animals (Northwest Coast). At these times children were instructed by band leaders.

The name Aleut was first used by the Russians. The Aleut called themselves Unangan, meaning The People. In 1741, when the Russians arrived, there were about 18,000 Aleut living on the islands. Because of warfare and European diseases, there were only 1,500 Aleut left in 1820.

During World War II, first Japanese soldiers then United States soldiers took over the Aleutian Islands. The Aleut people were moved to unheated

Life Underground

To shelter themselves from severe storms, early Aleut built their houses partially underground. These houses, called *barabaras,* were shared by several families. Whale bones supported the walls and roof, which were made of earth and straw. A smoke hole in the roof also served as an entrance. People slid down a pole from the roof to the floor. Waterproof sea-mammal intestines were stretched over the windows to let in sunlight.

Sea Otter

The sea otter is a playful, highly intelligent mammal with an attractive black-and-silver coat. It is often seen floating on its back or building water slides for fun. Aleut kayakers regarded sea otters as kindred spirits and mimicked the otter's graceful movements at sea. The sea otter barely survived over-hunting by Russian fur traders in the 17th century and oil spills in the 1980s.

▶ Arctic TV

Arctic people often live in remote areas with few roads, and many of them cannot afford to make long trips. The Inuvialuit Communications Society provides native-language programming by satellite. Having their own television stations helps Arctic people to balance the influence commercial television has on children by featuring programs about their own cultures.

INUVIALUIT COMMUNICATIONS SOCIETY

canneries on the mainland. Many of them died. When the Aleut were allowed to return, they found that their villages had been destroyed. Many of their ancient sacred objects had been stolen. Aleut elders had used these sacred objects to remember stories and pass on traditions to children (Language). Without the objects, Aleut history was lost. The loss of their traditional way of life tore many communities apart. Nevertheless, traditional arts and dancing continue to enrich village life today.

In 1989 the Exxon tanker *Valdez* spilled more than 10 million gallons of oil into Alaska's coastal waters. The fish and animals the Aleut depend on for food remain contaminated. The cleanup is being continued by the Aleut people today. In 1995 Dolly Reft of Kodiak Island said, "We village people need our environment. Without it, we can't exist, can't be who we are."◀

APACHE

- **LANGUAGE FAMILY: ATHAPASKAN**
- **LIFEWAYS: HUNTING & GATHERING**
- **LOCATION: OKLAHOMA & ARIZONA**
- **THEIR OWN NAME: INDE**

SOUTHWEST

The Apache once inhabited vast stretches of the Southwest from eastern New Mexico to the northern Mexican state of Sonora. Archaeologists believe the Sarcee—ancestors of the Apache—migrated from the Subarctic to the Plains 2,000 years ago. Then, around A.D. 1200, a few bands made their way to Pueblo territory in New Mexico. By the late 1600s, there were about 5,000 Apache.

The Apache did not farm but lived in small hunting and gathering bands. They sometimes

▶ Cochise

In 1866 the United States tried to force Chiricahua chief Cochise to move from the Dragoon Mountains to the Tularosa Reservation in Arizona. Cochise refused, saying, "I have drunk of these waters and they have cooled me. I do not want to leave here." Cochise also said that bad spirits lived in Tularosa. For six years he was chased by General Gordon Granger. When he died of an illness in the summer of 1874, his sons buried him in his Dragoon Mountain home.

raided Pueblo and Zuni farms and literally made a name for themselves as warriors: Apachu is the Zuni word for enemy. The Apache called themselves Inde, or People.

They were nomadic people, so it is fitting that an Apache child's first ceremony was called Putting On Moccasins. Feasting, prayers, and gifts celebrated the child's first steps in his or her new moccasins. Soft moccasins protected the feet while also reminding the Apache of their connection to Mother Earth.

SPIRITS The Apache believe spirits, or *gans*, inhabit the high peaks of the Southwest. Gans watch over sacred places. They are called upon in the Mountain Spirit Dance to guide the Apache and cure illness. Mount Graham is the home of the gans that teach songs and dances to Crown Dancers, who still perform in brightly painted wooden headdresses. Four headdress colors are symbolic of the gans. These colors are represented by black eagle feathers, blue turquoise, yellow deerskin, and white pollen. The Apache of Arizona and New Mexico continue to guard the mountains as sacred sites.

Because the Apache shared a vast territory with other peoples, regional differences have emerged over the past few centuries. The Western Apache—including the White Mountain and San Carlos bands—resemble their Navajo and Pueblo neighbors. They became farmers. The Eastern Apache—including the Mescalero, Kiowa-Apache, Jicarilla, and Chiricahua—were more like the peoples of the Plains. They hunted bison but raided farms as well.

In fact, Apache raiding kept other tribes from settling the lands of southern Arizona and New Mexico. It also kept most Mexican farmers and ranchers out of northern Sonora. After the Civil War, the growing presence of white Americans put the Apache on the defensive. But Apache culture is rooted in a tradition of strong leadership, and

Geronimo

Chiricahua chief Goyathlay, called Geronimo by Mexican soldiers, continued the Apache warrior tradition. After his family was murdered by Mexican soldiers, Geronimo (shown here with his family) began to raid farms in Mexico. Between 1876 and 1885, he surrendered to U.S. federal agents several times. He repeatedly escaped to Mexico when he could not endure confinement on the reservation. In 1887, after Geronimo surrendered for the last time, he was exiled to a military fort in Florida. He was later taken to Oklahoma.

The Great Seal

The Great Seal of the White Mountain Apache illustrates the Creator's many gifts: waters that flow from the sacred White Mountain and the deer and elk the Apache hunted. It also shows a wickiup hut and *tus* water container, ancient aspects of Apache daily life. The lightning bolts represent the mountain spirits who guide Apache Crown Dancers in healing rituals.

Newspaper

The Jicarilla *Chieftan,* published in Dulce, New Mexico, is dedicated to the future of the Jicarilla Apache.

Shell Art

The Apalachee, like many tribes in the Southeast, etched intricate designs on shells. These snakelike figures were carved on a conch shell. Since the snake sheds its skin in the spring, it symbolizes the annual rebirth of life. Some Native Americans believed the shed skin could heal wounds and help cure the sick.

Apache warriors fought hard under the leadership of great chiefs.

Although many bands were driven into hiding in the mountains of the Southwest and Mexico, they continued to fight against intruders. It was said that Apache chief Geronimo communicated with the gans to find out where the U.S. soldiers were. When Geronimo was captured in 1887, the United States declared the Indian Wars officially ended.

Today, 28,700 Apache live on 3 million acres in Arizona, New Mexico, and Oklahoma. The Fort Apache Timber Company and several ski resorts provide most of their income. A pending Supreme Court case will probably decide whether states can tax the Apache income.

The tribe takes pride in its history of resisting outsiders. Mildred Cleghorn, chairperson of the Fort Sill Chiricahua Apache, says, "We have our heads and shoulders in the present and our hearts in the past."◄

APALACHEE

- **LANGUAGE FAMILY: MUSKOGEAN**
- **LIFEWAYS: FARMING, HUNTING, & TRADING**
- **LOCATION: NONE**
- **THEIR OWN NAME: UNKNOWN**

SOUTHEAST

The Apalachee lived on the northern Gulf Coast of Florida. They numbered about 7,000. Their name is the Choctaw word for People on the Other Side (of the river).

The Apalachee were warriors descended from the Mound Builders. In 1528 some Florida Indians told Spanish conquistador Pánfilo de Narváez that the Apalachee lived in jeweled cities. The Spanish attacked, but, as one Spanish soldier said, the Apalachee were such good fighters they "receive very little injury." However, over time the Apalachee were wiped out by diseases.◄

ARAPAHO

- **LANGUAGE FAMILY: ALGONQUIAN**
- **LIFEWAYS: FARMING & HUNTING**
- **LOCATION: WYOMING & OKLAHOMA**
- **THEIR OWN NAME: INUNAINA**

PLAINS

About 3,000 years ago, the Arapaho lived with other Algonquian-speaking tribes in the Great Lakes region of present-day Minnesota and Canada. Early Arapaho probably were farmers. Over the years they drifted southwest and adopted a Plains lifestyle. They abandoned Northeast-style wigwams for buffalo-hide tipis. The tribe also began doing the Sun Dance, which they call the Offerings Lodge. By the early 1800s, Arapaho territory spanned what is now southeast Wyoming, southwest Nebraska, eastern Colorado, and northwest Kansas.

ALLIES Different branches of Arapaho formed lasting friendships with other tribes. The Southern Arapaho allied with the Cheyenne, and the Northern Arapaho joined the Shoshone and Blackfeet. The Northern Arapaho in Wyoming hold the tribe's sacred bundles, which contain ancient, powerful objects. They are opened only on special occasions.

The Arapaho world changed when gold was discovered in Colorado in 1858. White miners and settlers flocked to the territory, sometimes clashing with native peoples. The conflict turned into a bloodbath in Colorado, and in 1864 Colonel John Chivington ordered United States soldiers to massacre a peaceful camp of Southern Arapaho and Cheyenne at Sand Creek.

After five years of fighting, Southern Arapaho surrendered their land under the Fort Wise Treaty. The treaty further separated the Arapaho by moving them to different reservations. The Southern Arapaho moved to a reservation in

▶ Bag

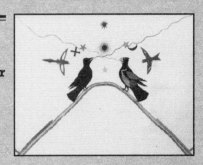

Arapaho bags were usually made of animal hide and decorated with beadwork in geometric designs. The bags were used for storing dried food, paint, small tools, or personal items.

▶ Banner

This Arapaho painted muslin banner of the sun, moon, stars, and birds demonstrates the Arapaho view of themselves as Sky People, which is what their own name means.

▶ Sun Dance

This Arapaho Offerings Lodge was photographed in Wyoming around 1900. The Sun Dance is a magnificent, four-day summer ceremony of prayer and thanks for the renewal of the people and the earth. Sun Dance rituals include fasting, buffalo hunts, flesh piercing, buffalo-tongue feasts, and a sun-gazing dance. The ceremony encourages bravery, generosity, and honesty. The lodge itself is constructed in the shape of the sun.

W. Richard West, Jr.

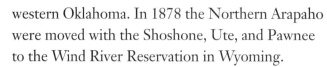

W. Richard West, Jr. (born 1943) is founding director of the National Museum of the American Indian, now part of the Smithsonian Institution. West, a member of the Cheyenne-Arapaho tribes of Oklahoma, is also a lawyer who has represented Indians before the Supreme Court.

Arapaho **BULLETIN**

CONCHO, OKLAHOMA 73022 · JANUARY, 1995   NO. 4

Newspaper

The symbol of the Cheyenne-Arapaho tribes of Oklahoma—a map of the state with a seal, arrow, and pipe—heads their reservation newspaper, the *Cheyenne and Arapaho Bulletin,* published in Concho, Oklahoma.

Cassava Cakes

The Arapaho made flour from the root of the cassava plant. The raw root is poisonous, but the Arawak learned how to grate, pound, and rinse cassava mush until the poison was washed away. The starch was then shaped into bread and cakes or dried and saved as flour. Cassava cakes were baked on a stone griddle and served with iguana or sea-turtle stew.

western Oklahoma. In 1878 the Northern Arapaho were moved with the Shoshone, Ute, and Pawnee to the Wind River Reservation in Wyoming.

The Allotment Act cost the Southern Arapaho 4 million acres of land. However, since 1965 the Arapaho have brought suits in court to win payment for their lands. So far, only one-quarter of the land has been paid for. Today, about 3,500 Northern Arapaho and Shoshone retain 2.25 million acres in Wyoming. About 3,000 Southern Arapaho are scattered throughout Oklahoma.

This dispersal has caused many troubles for the Arapaho. However, the tribe's relations with the U.S. government are improving as tribe leaders learn to negotiate with Washington. The tribe once had a small stake in oil and gas revenues in Colorado but now must find new sources of income. The Arapaho are turning to casinos and other businesses for that income. Efforts are being made to preserve Arapaho culture, language, and sacred sites.◄

ARAWAK

- LANGUAGE FAMILY: ARAWAKAN
- LIFEWAYS: FARMING & FISHING
- LOCATION: CARIBBEAN ISLANDS
- THEIR OWN NAME: TAÍNO

MESOAMERICA

About 2,000 years ago the Arawak migrated from Venezuela to the Caribbean islands in dugout canoes carrying more than 100 people. The Arawak lived in open palm-thatched houses. They collected food from the forest and sea and planted cassava, corn, and beans in large fields near the villages. The tropical climate made clothing unnecessary, and people often bathed in the warm sea. They decorated their bodies with plant dyes and gold jewelry.

The Arawak called themselves *Taíno*, which means Good People. Men leaders were called *caciques,* women leaders were called *cacicas.* Arawak leaders hosted round dances called *areitos,* during which tribe members recited creation stories and poetry and special gifts offered to Yucahu, the creator.

When Christopher Columbus arrived in 1492, he was looking for India. Columbus called the Arawak "Indians," and that name was later used for all Native Americans. The Spanish were ruthless in their quest for gold and Christian converts (Mesoamerica and Missions). By 1496 only one third of the 4 million Arawak were left.

Until recently, historians thought the Arawak were extinct. However, many Arawak had fled to the mountains. Today, 2,000 Taíno in western Cuba are direct descendants of the Arawak. In the isolated communities of Caridiad de los Indios and Rio Toa, they live in traditional family groups called *caserios* and hold Areito Dances. The University of Puerto Rico is publishing a textbook in their language. ◄

ARCTIC

- **TRIBES OF THE REGION: ALEUT, INUIT**

The Arctic region of North America stretches 5,000 miles from the Bering Strait to Greenland. Its harsh climate tests the limits of the people who live there, the Inuit and Aleut. January temperatures often drop to -40 degrees F. The land is flat, except for the Brooks Mountain Range in central Alaska. Covered in snow all winter, the ground is blanketed with grass and flowers during the brief summer. A thick layer of permanently frozen soil called permafrost lies underground. Geographers call this environment the tundra. The Inuit call it Nunavut, or Our Home.

Archaeologists disagree about when the first

► Taíno

The Taíno Nation of the Antilles was formed in the 1980s to bring organization and a sense of community to scattered Arawak descendants. Traditional dancers perform with parrot feathers and *maracas* (gourd rattles). The Nacion Taína logo is a design from an ancient petroglyph (rock drawing) of the sun.

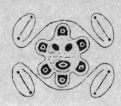

NACION TAINA

► Northern Hunters

Arctic people respected the animals they hunted, which included bowhead whales, several kinds of seals, and walruses. Whale hunts were quite dangerous, but they brought a bounty of meat. To catch seal, a hunter might wait for hours on the ice. All parts of the animals were used. Seal-skin parkas were warm and waterproof, and walrus hide made strong boats.

COZY DOMES

Snow-covered Arctic houses may have looked as though they were made of snow, but they were not. Permanent homes were stone and earth lodges, built partially underground. Whale ribs, and sometimes bones of extinct woolly mammoths, supported the roof. The central Inuit built temporary winter hunting lodges called iglus from snow and ice. Starting with a circular foundation of ice blocks, they stacked smaller blocks to create a dome at the top. A small hole was left for ventilation. Gaps in the iglu were filled in with soft snow, and the interior was lined with furs for warmth.

Summer hunting lodges were constructed from poles and hides like Northeast wigwams.

people arrived in the Arctic (Paleo-Indians). In the past, the commonly accepted theory was that the Inuit and Aleut were among the last people in the great migration from Asia, which began about 10,000 years ago. The Inuit are believed to have walked across the Bering land bridge, while the Aleut may have come later by boat.

DISPUTED ORIGINS

Many Arctic peoples disagree with this theory. They say there is evidence to show they lived here much earlier than 10,000 years ago. They also say that the idea of a more recent immigration makes white people feel better about taking Indian land. After all, if everyone is an immigrant, then the land belongs to all.

According to Inuit legend, the people once lived in a bountiful land. Then a flood picked them up and dropped them in their new home.

Arctic spirituality is closely connected to nature. Tradition held that every being has a spirit and must be treated with respect. Today, Arctic people continue to talk to animals. They thank fish for being caught and treat their house pets as guests.

Traditional Arctic people think of themselves as part of a community, not as individuals. Perhaps one reason that Arctic communities are close is that the climate has kept the food supply—and the population—small. Only about 61,000 Aleut and Inuits (28,000 in Alaska, 22,000 in Greenland, and 11,000 in Canada) inhabit an area larger than the lower forty-eight United States.

The population was even smaller 250 years ago, just after the first Europeans arrived. The Inuit called them Qallunaat, or Men with Big Eyebrows, but they were Russians who had come looking for otter, seal, and other fur-bearing sea mammals. These animals supplied food, clothing, and even shelter to the Arctic peoples, but the Russians hunted them almost to extinction. When the Aleut fought back, the Russians massacred and enslaved them. Smallpox killed still more Aleut, so that after a hundred years, fewer than 1,500 of them remained.

In 1867 Russia sold Alaska to the United States, and young native people were sent to distant boarding schools to speak English and adopt white customs. Many Arctic children forgot their native languages in the process.

Finally, in the 1930s, things slowly started to turn around for the Inuit and Aleut. In 1936 the Alaska version of the Indian Reorganization Act returned self-rule and native education to the Arctic peoples. But new pressures soon arose. During World War II, when U.S. soldiers came to Alaska, the population was more non-native than native for the first time in history. In 1959 Alaska became the forty-ninth state. In the 1960s the Alaskan Federation of Natives demanded that the U.S. return native lands.

In 1971 their efforts succeeded. The Alaska Native Claims Settlement Act (ANCSA) returned 68,750 square miles to the Aleut. In Canada the Inuit convinced the government to return 770,000 square miles, about one fifth of the whole country. The Inuit territory is now officially called Nunavut.

ENVIRONMENT The 20th century also brought environmental challenges to the Arctic. In Alaska, commercial fishing has killed nearly all the local salmon. Some control of fishing management was returned to the tribes, but salmon companies continue to defy native fishing rights. In the 1960s the United States buried 15,000 pounds of contaminated waste from an atom bomb test on Inuit land in Point Hope, Alaska. It was a secret experiment to see how radiation affects wildlife. Fish and animals got sick. So did the people who ate them. The Inuit are seeking aid, as well as a ban on nuclear tests they claim are occurring in Arctic waters.

In 1977 an organization of Arctic peoples called the Inuit Circumpolar Conference (ICC) demanded and won a share of the region's recently discovered oil wealth. Both ANCSA and the oil settlement require that Arctic villages govern

Three-Person Boat

Kayaks are made by stretching sea-mammal skins over a light wooden frame. Unlike open canoes, kayaks are covered, so kayakers don't become soaked with freezing water. A hole is left for each passenger.

Local News

Native Arctic newspapers provide people with local information, such as announcements by the Association of Village Council Presidents (AVCP), in the Yukon-Kuskowkim Delta.

Eskaleut Language

Many Inuit children learn Eskaleut in village schools until the third grade, when English is also taught. First reading lessons focus on the Eskaleut language's three vowels and on naming parts of the body.

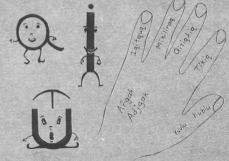

▶ First Moose

The Phillips family brought their children, Angelica and Nicholai, on their first moose hunt along the Aniak River in Alaska in the fall of 1994. Agnes Pete Phillips wants her children to learn about traditional ways, such as sharing meat with older relatives and making traditional fur clothing.

▶ Ledger Art

Before Europeans arrived, Plains Indians drew personal symbols and illustrated histories on animal hides using earth and plant dyes. When forts and reservations were built in the 1800s, Indians obtained ledger paper and colored ink. Today, these drawings—called ledger art—are collectors' items. The above drawing is from the 1873 autobiography of Running Antelope, chief of the Hunkpapa Lakota. He is killing an Arikara in an 1857 battle.

themselves as corporations. Traditional village leaders, concerned about processing oil without hurting the environment, are promoting traditional land management and local conservation.

Although snowmobiles and satellites have modernized communication, many people still travel by dog sled. Hunting is as important as ever, and villages are kept small so as not to frighten away animals. Yet the Arctic people are coming together after centuries of isolation. Getting organized has strengthened native Arctic unity and cultural pride. Children now learn native languages in tribal schools. Two major traditional gatherings, the summer trading fairs and the winter Messenger Feast, have been restored. Messenger Feasts are times of gift giving and dancing similar to the potlatches of the Northwest Coast tribes. Arctic groups also work for international native rights at the United Nations. ◀

ARIKARA

- **LANGUAGE FAMILY: CADDOAN**
- **LIFEWAYS: HUNTING & PLANTING**
- **LOCATION: NORTH DAKOTA**
- **THEIR OWN NAME: ARICKAREE OR REE**

PLAINS

Before 1750 the Arikara lived in earth-lodge villages in South Dakota. They hunted buffalo and grew crops. Relatives of the Pawnee, they often traded with Southwest tribes and with the Mandan and Hidatsa.

Over time the Mandan, Hidatsa, and Arikara migrated north to escape attacks by the Sioux. European fur traders invaded Arikara land in 1823, forcing them into North Dakota. By 1837 major smallpox outbreaks had ravaged the three tribes. Sioux attacks on the weakened tribes forced them to move up the Missouri River. In 1845 the Hidatsa and Mandan found a safer location at a bend in the river they named Like-A-Fishhook. The Arikara soon joined them there.

The 1851 Fort Laramie Treaty granted the three tribes more than 13 million acres of land. Nineteen years later the federal government established the Fort Berthold Reservation in North Dakota. By then the three tribes' reservation was only a fraction of what it had been. In the 20th century, a series of congressional orders and the Garrison Dam—which flooded the region—had reduced the tribe's land even more, to about 450,000 acres.

Today, the Arikara live on the Fort Berthold Reservation with the Mandan and Hidatsa. Although they are officially known as Three Affiliated Tribes, each tribe lives in a separate reservation community and maintains its own ceremonies, language, and crafts. The Arikara hold powwows and ceremonies year-round, and Arikara language classes are taught in the Fort Berthold College Center.◀

ASSINIBOINE

- **LANGUAGE FAMILY: SIOUIAN**
- **LIFEWAYS: HUNTING**
- **LOCATION: MONTANA, SASKATCHEWAN, & ALBERTA**
- **THEIR OWN NAME: AS'SEE NEE POI-TUC**

PLAINS

The Assiniboine, or Those Who Cook with Heated Stones, was once a tribe of 10,000 that had split from the Nakota during the 1500s. They spent winters with the Cree in the Great Lakes woodlands, tracking antelope and bighorn sheep. During summers they moved to the Plains for buffalo hunts. There they built circles of skin-covered tipis with extra-long poles extending out the top.

Assiniboine storytellers say that long ago the tribe lived where there was always snow. Then they

▶**An Arikara Family**

Photographer Edward Curtis took this portrait of an Arikara family, which he titled "Yellow Bone Woman," in 1908. The woman is wearing a breastplate made from conch shells or bone. The family was then living on the Fort Berthold Reservation, which was established in 1870.

▶**Dancer**

The Assiniboine captured eagles for ceremonial use. Eagle feathers were used to make headdresses worn in dance and battle. Edward Curtis photographed this Assiniboine making peace with the spirit of a slain eagle around the turn of the century.

Hunter and Dogs

This Assiniboine hunter was photographed with his dogs in the late 1800s. The dogs are loaded with the blankets and food the hunter will need in the wilderness.

Newspaper

The *Wotanin Wowapi* newspaper, published in Poplar, Montana, serves the Assiniboine and Sioux tribes of the Fort Peck Reservation. The newspaper's logo features a buffalo.

discovered a buffalo-skin bag containing the water of summer, but it was guarded by the people to the south. Upon hearing the news, the chief sent his fastest runners to steal the bag. As they ran away, the water spilled out, leaving green grass, plants, and flowers. The Assiniboine agreed to share summer with the southern people and asked a crane to carry the water back and forth every six months. If the crane delays either way on its journey, the people experience fall or spring.

The Assiniboine traded furs with Europeans in the 1600s. Over the next 200 years, the slaughter of the buffalo by federal soldiers brought starvation to the tribe. In 1858, when 4,000 Assiniboine died from smallpox, the tribe was reduced to fewer than 6,000 people.

DIVIDED The 1851 Fort Laramie Treaty divided the tribe into the eastern Assiniboine of Montana and the Stoneys of Saskatchewan and Alberta, Canada. The Montana Assiniboine were forced onto the Gros Ventre and Nakota reservations. With no land of their own it was difficult for the Assiniboine to remain an independent tribe. By 1890 starvation and disease had reduced the Assiniboine to fewer than 2,000.

Assiniboine elders are working to preserve their culture. Their language is now taught on the reservation and spoken during public ceremonies. The Assiniboine hold baby-naming ceremonies, sweat lodges, and the Medicine Lodge Sun Dance. On the Fort Peck Reservation today, 5,782 Assiniboine gain some income from oil, coal, and leasing land. On the Fort Belknap Agency, 2,338 Assiniboine were organized as one tribe with the Gros Ventre in 1934. The Bureau of Indian Affairs controls the reservation and has restricted Assiniboine development. Despite regional problems, Assiniboine artisans produce star-patterned quilts that are exhibited around the world. ◀

AZTECS

- **LANGUAGE FAMILY: NAHUATLAN**
- **LIFEWAYS: DIVERSE**
- **LOCATION: MEXICO**
- **THEIR OWN NAME: AZTECA**

MESOAMERICA

Mexico means The Place (*ko*) of the Meshi', another name for the Aztecs. The Aztec name comes from Aztlan, their original homeland in northern Mexico. In the 13th century, the Aztecs migrated south. According to Aztec legend, Huitzilopochtli, the god of war, told the tribe that they would know they had found their new home when they saw an eagle perched on a cactus with a snake in its mouth. They finally spotted this eagle on an island in Lake Texcoco in the Valley of Mexico. The Aztecs built their city, Tenochtitlán, there.

ISLAND CITY Tenochtitlán was a great city. It eventually covered more than five square miles of islands in the lake. Three wide bridges linked the islands to the mainland. The Aztecs built both an aqueduct to bring in fresh water and canals for transportation inside the city. They also built palaces, temples, schools, concert halls, ball courts, marketplaces, and zoos. Neighborhoods were organized into *calpulli*, with their own local councils and protective gods.

Traders and soldiers brought wealth to the city. Aztec merchants had their own legal codes, guilds, and ceremonies. Such goods as gold, jade, rubber, parrot feathers, and chocolate were traded with people as far away as Peru and the North American Southeast. At its height in the 16th century the Aztec army had over 200,000 warriors and was the largest in the world. It conquered many tribes and made them pay high taxes to Tenochtitlán. Captured enemies were used as human sacrifices.

Blood sacrifice had a powerful meaning to the

Five Suns

The five suns on this stone tablet represent the Aztec belief in the five worlds that have existed since the beginning of time. In each new world, or sun, the gods created a better race of human beings. In the first world, humans were made of ashes, then turned into fish. In the second, they were giants who became extinct. In the third, they were transformed into turkeys. In the fourth, they were men-monkeys. The Fifth Sun of Movement was the Aztecs' era.

Daily Life

These manuscript pages show two aspects of Aztec cultural life. The man and woman tying their robes together are getting married. The boy netting fish shows that Aztec children helped gather food for their families.

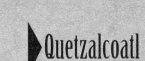

Quetzalcoatl

The feathered serpent figure in the top left of this ancient manuscript is the god Quetzalcoatl. The Aztecs believed Quetzalcoatl had given them life from his blood, then guided them to become a great people with a rich culture.

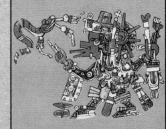

Jaguar Warriors

In this mural by García Bustos, Aztecs pay tribute to a jaguar warrior with bowls of turquoise and sacks of gold. Jaguar warriors were an elite society that served the sun god. They wore a jaguar skin in battle. The jaguar was revered by the Aztecs and Maya, and warriors tried to copy the jaguar's wise and powerful ways.

Conquistadors

This drawing illustrates the fall of the Aztecs. Spanish conquistadors entered the city of Tenochtitlán (now Mexico City) and killed thousands of Aztecs. An Aztec poet wrote, "We are crushed to the ground; we lie in ruins. There is nothing but grief and suffering in Mexico and Tlatelolco, where once we saw beauty and valor."

Fountain Sculpture

This fountain sculpture in Mexico City's main *zócalo* (square) portrays the founding of Tenochtitlán. In the 13th century, the Aztec god of war told his people that they would find their home when they saw an eagle on a cactus with a snake in its mouth. According to legend the Aztecs saw the eagle and founded a city there. The bronze sculpture and its turquoise mosaic base are a tribute to Aztec artistry.

Aztecs. They believed there had been four worlds before the one they knew. Quetzalcoatl, the feathered-serpent god, had rescued the people's bones from the fire that destroyed the last world and sprinkled them with his own blood to create the Aztecs. Aztec traditions honored Quetzalcoatl's sacrifice, though not all Aztecs approved of killing people on altars. Some saw it as power gone mad: Aztecs believed in good and evil magic, and long before Europeans came, the people of Mexico had been involved in a struggle over sorcery.

MOCTEZUMA Moctezuma II was ruler of the powerful Aztec Empire when the Spanish landed in Mesoamerica. The arrival of people from far away had been predicted by ancient Aztec prophesy. Moctezuma had a polished magnetite mirror that was like a crystal ball. According to later romanticized stories, Moctezuma saw the conquistadors riding toward Tenochtitlán on what the emperor thought were large white deer. He watched Hernán Cortés and his men advance for days before they arrived. As the Spanish came closer, Moctezuma grew more and more nervous. The Aztec poets who survived Cortés's conquest explained what happened next. Their writings in the Nahuatl language were later translated by Spanish scholars. Their beautifully illustrated poems describe the destruction of the Aztec civilization and the deaths of thousands from both war and disease.

Many *mestizo* (mixed-blood) Aztec descendants live in Mexico City today. Some have joined with descendants of other tribes in calpulli to preserve their culture and protect the environment. Indian people from North, South, and Central America often meet in Mexico City. These conferences are called the Meetings of the Eagle and Condor, symbolizing the combined powers of those two great birds. ◀

BANNOCK

- **LANGUAGE FAMILY:** UTO-AZTECAN NUMIC
- **LIFEWAYS:** GATHERING
- **LOCATION:** IDAHO
- **THEIR OWN NAME:** BAND NAMES

GREAT BASIN

The Bannock are closely related to the Shoshone. The tribe name means Grass Lodge. Bands of Bannock were usually named after the food they ate. There were, for example, Yahandeka (Groundhog Eaters) and Agaideka (Salmon Eaters).

The Bannock and Northern Shoshone—the two peoples often lived together—once ranged across southern Idaho, from the Sawtooth Mountain Range to the Snake River. Mountain streams in the territory provided salmon and trout. But the Bannock also searched the dry grasslands for wild squash and potatoes. They began to hunt bison in the 1700s, after Europeans brought horses to Idaho.

NOMADS The Bannock and Shoshone have intermarried since 1800. As nomads, the Bannock and Shoshone were loosely organized. Bannock chiefs played a small role in the tribe's affairs, except during buffalo hunts, when horsemen had to work together. At other times, councils made decisions.

After Bannock and white pioneers came to blows in the Bannock and Sheepeater Wars of 1878, the Bannock were forced to settle with the Shoshone on the Fort Hall Reservation in southwestern Idaho. Around 1900 the Bannock adopted the Shoshone Sun Dance.

The Bannock number several thousand and live mostly on the Fort Hall Reservation. Their Sun Dance, called the Offerings Lodge, is performed in the summer. The public is welcome, but the tribe asks that no photographs be taken or recordings made. The Bannock sell their floral beadwork during Fort Hall Indian Days every August.◄

▶ Fort Hall

In 1878, led by Chief Buffalo Horn, the Bannock fought a year-long war against the United States government. The Bannock lost the war and were forced onto Fort Hall Reservation. These men, women, and children were prisoners at Fort Hall.

▶ Teton Bill

Teton Bill of the Bannock tribe was photographed in traditional dress and hat on the Fort Hall Reservation in 1913.

Beaver Logo

The Beaver Tribal Council serves the three tribes of Beaver, Alaska—the Gwich'in Athapaskan (Kutchin), the Koyukon Athapaskan, and the Inupiat Inuit. The council works to improve education, employment, and health care for the village.

Grave Doll

This wooden male doll, one of the few remnants of the Beothuk culture, was found in the grave of a male child in 1886. Carved figures were part of burial ceremonies, but it is unknown whether they represented spirits or the deceased. The Beothuk believed they could communicate with their dead kin.

BEAVER

- **LANGUAGE FAMILY:** ATHAPASKAN
- **LIFEWAYS:** HUNTING
- **LOCATION:** ALASKA
- **THEIR OWN NAME:** DUNNE-ZA

SUBARCTIC

The Beaver once lived on the Peace River in British Columbia and Alberta. They hunted game and traveled in bands of related clans. Beaver society and spirituality were connected to the hunt. Each hunter shared his game with the whole band. A Beaver proverb said that a hunter who gave away meat one day would receive it another. Stories told of a long-ago time when animals ate men, instead of the other way around. Today, about 100 Beaver live in Beaver, Alaska. Others live in villages with interior Alaskan tribes such as the Kutchin and Inuit.◄

BEOTHUK

- **LANGUAGE FAMILY:** ALGONQUIAN
- **LIFEWAYS:** FISHING
- **LOCATION:** NONE
- **THEIR OWN NAME:** BEOTHUK

SUBARCTIC

The Beothuk are now extinct, but they once lived on Newfoundland. They were the first people of North America to meet the Vikings, around A.D. 1000. French fishermen often fought with the Beothuk in the 1700s. The French accused the Beothuk of stealing and hired other native peoples to kill them. The last Beothuk died in 1829, but one thing about them may live on. To keep the mosquitoes away, they painted their skin with red ocher from iron rust. It's possible that this custom gave rise to the insulting "redskin" expression for Native Americans.◄

BLACKFEET

- **LANGUAGE FAMILY: ALGONQUIAN**
- **LIFEWAYS: HUNTING**
- **LOCATION: MONTANA & ALBERTA**
- **THEIR OWN NAME: TRIBAL DIVISION NAMES**

PLAINS

The four Blackfeet nations are the Northern Peigan, Blood, and Blackfeet in Alberta, Canada, and the Southern Peigan (Pigunni) in Montana. There are 13,000 tribe members in the United States. The tribe's original hunting grounds spread from Saskatchewan to the Missouri River. Blackfeet hunted buffalo and raided the Crow, Assiniboine, and Gros Ventre.

DEER DANCE Badger Two-Medicine in northwest Montana is a sacred site to the Blackfeet. The forest there has long been used for burials, vision-quests, sweat lodges, and Sun Dances. Sweetgrass, an important medicinal plant, is harvested there. Its lovely perfume is said to attract good spirits during the Black-tailed Deer Dance. In Blackfeet legend, a deer taught the dance to a sick man. The man recovered, and the Blackfeet have performed the healing ceremony ever since.

In 1855, when many buffalo herds had been destroyed, the Blackfeet moved to reservations, where they had been promised food. Treaties reduced their reservation land. Then, in winter 1883, food supplies never arrived and about 600 Blackfeet died. Their burial grounds are known as Ghost Ridge.

In the 1890s the government banned the Blackfeet Sun Dance (Missions). The Blackfeet were able to preserve the ceremony by secretly including it in Fourth of July celebrations. The tribe restored the traditional ceremony in the 1970s. Since 1986 the Pigunni Traditionalists Association has been suing to protect Badger Two-Medicine from oil drilling. ◀

▶ Tipi

The design of this late-18th-century Blackfeet tipi in Alberta, Canada, expresses the individuality of the owner's personal vision.

▶ Moving Camp

Before horses were introduced to the Plains in the 16th century, the Blackfeet used dogs to pull their loads. Some continued this practice into the 20th century. This dog stands ready to move camp for a family in 1906.

Hampton Institute

These three Native American girls, Annie Dawson, Carrie Anderson, and Sarah Walker, were photographed fourteen months after their arrival at the Hampton Institute in 1879. Like the white doll in the chair in front of them, they reflect the values of white society. At Hampton they were taught to sew, iron, and do laundry—tasks thought to be suitable for young girls.

Strange Pilgrims

These young Indian students were dressed as Pilgrims as part of their boarding school education. When the Pilgrims first arrived in America in 1620, Native Americans taught them about hunting and planting—and helped them to survive. However, at the time of this photograph, about 250 years later, whites regarded Indian culture and knowledge as backward.

BOARDING SCHOOLS

Because European settlers considered Native Americans uneducated, they set up schools to give them a European-style education. Europeans thought it would be easier to influence Indian children if they were taken from their communities.

In the 19th and 20th centuries, American efforts to educate Indians followed the same pattern. At mission and government schools, children were not permitted to speak their own languages, worship in their own religion, or follow tribal customs. They were taught that Indian culture was backward and that American culture was superior. A common saying was, "Kill the Indian and save the man." It meant that Indians had to stop being Indians before they could become Americans.

In the early 20th century, a new education plan was tried. Native American children were sent to public schools instead of Indian schools. It was thought that if they mixed with white children, they would adopt American ways more quickly.

SELF-EDUCATION

After World War II, Indian education changed again. Native Americans demanded the right to educate their own children. The U.S. government gradually stopped forcing Indian children into boarding and public schools. Native American educators say this is important because Indian children should learn Indian ways and values. Among these values are cooperation and learning by doing instead of just listening.

In states with many Native Americans, Indian educators have created special courses of study. In Oklahoma these courses are called the Four Circles of Learning: gaining knowledge, using reason, deep thought, and insight.◀

CADDO

- **LANGUAGE FAMILY: CADDOAN**
- **LIFEWAYS: PLANTING, HUNTING, & WEAVING**
- **LOCATION: OKLAHOMA**
- **THEIR OWN NAME: HASINAI**

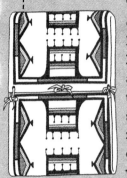

PLAINS

The Caddo are the main tribe of the Caddo Confederacy, which once united ten tribes, including the Arikara and Pawnee. The Caddo homeland stretched from western Louisiana and Arkansas to eastern Texas and Oklahoma. They built wickiups (Plains), grew corn, hunted buffalo, and wove ancient designs into cotton cloth.

GREAT TURTLE

The Drum Dance reenacts the creation of the second world. In legend, the first world was destroyed by a flood because giant monsters were eating the people. The Caddo creator, described as a voice, told the people to gather the good animals in pairs and hide with them in large hollow reeds. Then wild rains flooded the world and Great Turtle dug away at the mud beneath the monsters' feet until they drowned. When the earth dried and the people returned, the voice gave them corn, their sacred food, and told the women how to plant it.

During the 18th century, the Caddo migrated to Texas. In 1859 they joined the Choctaw and Chickasaw nations on a reservation in Oklahoma. For a century the Caddo fought to remain a tribe and keep their land. In the 1970s the United States Court of Claims granted the Caddo more than $1.2 million for their land.

In 1910 the Caddo population on the Binger, Oklahoma, reservation was only 452. Since then it has grown to more than 3,300. Most tribal income comes from oil, land leasing, and businesses owned with the Wichita and Lenape tribes. Since the 1970s elders have been working hard to record oral histories and preserve their songs, dances, and language. ◀

▶ Rawhide Container

The Caddo were nomadic, so they did not make large works of art like the totems of the **Northwest Indians**. Instead, they put their artistic skills to work decorating their clothing, tipis, and bags, such as this 19th-century painted rawhide container. The geometrically designed bags were folded like envelopes and used to carry food and possessions.

▶ Great Turtle

This turtle motif was common to Caddo pottery designs. It signifies the Great Turtle, who in ancient times saved the Caddo from man-eating monsters.

Caddo Tribal Times

▶ Newspaper

The *Caddo Tribal Times*, published in Binger, Oklahoma, keeps the Caddo informed about important news and cultural events.

Going Fishing

California Indians speared ocean fish from tule (cattail) reed boats. The lightweight boats were made of tightly tied tule reeds and sealed with tar. Indians on what is now San Francisco Bay rowed out to ocean rocks, where they gathered mussels.

Roundhouse

California tribes stacked planks and reeds to build their roundhouses.

Chemehuevi Baskets

California women decorated their baskets with feathers, shells, and colored grasses woven in hundreds of designs. Baskets ranged from thimble-sized to more than three feet tall.

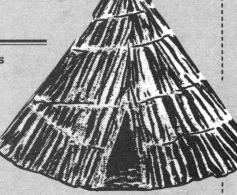

CALIFORNIA

CALIFORNIA

California slopes west from the Sierra Nevada Mountains down to the Pacific Ocean. Its 1,200 miles of forests, deserts, and river valleys is bordered by Mexico to the south and Oregon to the north. Northern California shares the mild, moist climate of the Northwest Coast. The east is like the dry, harsh Great Basin and Southwest. The sunny south has been a favorite destination since prehistoric times.

An old Maidu song goes like this: "Lively, lively, we are lots of people." And it was true. Before the arrival of Europeans, California was home to more than 300,000 people. They spoke at least eighty languages. In 1964 archaeologists found artifacts in Calico, California, that are reported to be 100,000 years old (Paleo-Indians).

Native-Californian legends say that people were created in America. California Indians have always respected the land and managed it according to natural laws. They selectively burned deadwood and carefully replanted important plants.

DANCES Concern for the environment was the focus of Californian Big Time ceremonies. Spring dances were prayers to the creator for good hunting, gathering, and fishing. In the autumn, thanksgiving dances featured giveaway feasts somewhat like the potlatches of the Northwest Coast. On these occasions, wealthy families provided the treasured dance costumes. They prepared feasts of salmon, acorns, cactus, and strawberries.

During Big Time, baskets were used not only to serve food but as sacred objects. Today, as in the past, girls learn to weave these ceremonial baskets. They gather plant fibers called Ikxareeyav (Spirit Beings) and sing to the plant spirits as they weave their baskets.

Traditionally, boys made ordinary baskets needed to carry supplies for life on the move. Because the people followed the food-gathering seasons, their clothing was as light and temporary as their houses. Plentiful food gave the people time to carve soapstone animals and create colorful, swirling rock paintings in caves.

GOLD RUSH This was the world the Spanish entered in 1542. They took over the land and tried to dominate the people by confining them to missions. They also enslaved Indians on farms, or *rancherias*. The American gold rush of 1848 flooded California with miners and settlers. During that period alone, more than 50,000 Indians were killed. By 1872 the combination of diseases and massacres had reduced the Indian population of California to below 30,000. Some tribes were completely destroyed.

The 20th century has been a time of rebuilding for California's first peoples. As late as 1930, Indians were not protected by law. They were called "Diggers" by whites who considered Indians less than human (Yana). Signs in businesses read, "No Dogs or Indians Allowed." Brave tribespeople had to fight for an end to segregation, the right to vote, and for the services the government promised when homesteaders took Indian lands.

In the 1950s many tribes lost their federal recognition without being legally terminated. They are still fighting for their land and treaty rights. There is an ongoing effort to teach ceremonies and languages, and to protect sacred land. Multitribal organizations are working with environmentalists to restore logged land and polluted salmon streams. The native peoples of California are reviving their cultures with courage and determination.◀

▶Acorns

Acorns, the seeds of the oak tree, were the most common food of California Indians. Because acorns are too bitter to eat in their natural state, they were hulled, crushed, and then washed repeatedly with warm water. The resulting meal was cooked into a sweet mush or baked into bread.

▶Deer Dance

The Deer Dance is still part of autumn Big Time celebrations for many California tribes. The elaborately decorated albino (white) deerskins symbolize birth, male power, and the spirit of the deer.

▶ Crafts

The Calusa were superb craftspeople. This painted wooden carving of a cat, shown here from two angles, is typical of their art. Below is a Calusa wolf mask, which was used in ceremonies. It and many other Calusa artifacts were found on Key Marco, an island off Florida's Gulf Coast. Objects like these are all that is left of the Calusa culture.

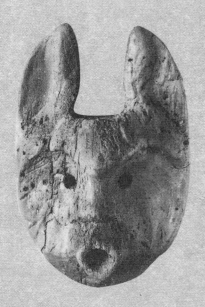

CALUSA

• LANGUAGE FAMILY: MUSKOGEAN
• LIFEWAYS: FISHING, GATHERING & TRADING
• LOCATION: NONE
• THEIR OWN NAME: CALUSA

SOUTHEAST

The Calusa once lived along the Gulf Coast of Florida from Tampa Bay to the Florida Keys. Their thatched wooden houses, called *chickees*, were built on piers in the bayous and rivers of their marshy territory. Their temples were built on mounds and were often covered with conch shells. They were far-ranging sea traders who dug a network of canals and even built islands from mounds of earth and shells.

Calusa society was quite rigid. A single chief organized the many workers needed to build the mound temples. There were three classes in Calusa society: nobles, commoners, and slaves. Slaves were usually prisoners of war. When a noble died, his servants were sacrificed to serve him in the afterlife.

The Calusa were also excellent craftspeople. Their wooden spears, clubs, and swords were beautifully carved and covered with shark's teeth set in perfect rows. They also painted wildlife scenes on wooden tablets and constructed animal heads of leather—with movable features.

DESTRUCTION Sadly, the Calusa were caught at the center of the Spanish conquest of Florida. They numbered about 3,000 people when Spanish explorer Juan Ponce de León landed on their coast in 1513. The Spanish were not welcome: The Calusa had been raided by Carib Indians in the past and were very defensive of their territory. By 1700, however, they had been virtually wiped out by disease and war. The few survivors were adopted by Florida Creek bands that later became known as the Seminole. ◀

CARIB

- **LANGUAGE FAMILY: KARIFUNA**
- **LIFEWAYS: FARMING, FISHING, & TRADING**
- **LOCATIONS: BELIZE, DOMINICA, & ST. VINCENT**
- **THEIR OWN NAME: CARIB**

MESOAMERICA

The first residents of the Caribbean islands were the Ciboney, who came from Florida around 400 B.C. (Timucua). About 400 years later, the Arawak came from South America, followed by the Carib, who adopted Arawak culture. Carib legend says the people were guided by the Master Snake. On Dominica, Carib elders journeyed to see him—a snake-shaped lava extension that juts into the sea. There, the Master Snake answered the elders' questions in dreams.

COLUMBUS

Early Carib traded by canoe with people of Mesoamerica and the Southeast. They also raided their neighbors and kidnapped Arawak women to work in their orchards. On his second voyage, in 1493, Christopher Columbus landed on Dominica. Arawak women told him the Carib ate the flesh of their captives. While the Carib were tough and independent, they were not cannibals. Nevertheless, fear of the Carib—and of the tribe's skill as warriors—kept the Spanish from invading many Caribbean islands.

Today, 3,000 Carib share a reserve on Dominica. They run a headquarters in Belize with other Carib communities. Because many of their ancestors adopted escaped African-American slaves, most Carib are of mixed race. They are led by chiefs who follow the advice of elders. Among important projects are videotaping elders, maintaining the Carib Council Library, and planting trees. Young people can join a drama and dance troupe called Karifuna or learn to build traditional dugout canoes. ◀

Hanging Out

Hammock comes from the Carib word *hamaca*. Carib Indians invented the hammock as a lightweight bed for a hot climate. They anchored Royal Palm tree trunks in the sand and thatched a roof with wide palm leaves. Open-air houses let in cool breezes while sheltering people from occasional rains.

Carib Children

Children of the Carib Reserve on Dominica look like both their Indian and African-American ancestors. They learn traditional skills, such as carving a dugout canoe from the trunk of a single ceiba tree.

▶ Indian Girls

These Carrier girls were photographed in Hazelton, British Columbia, in 1992. Fifteen Carrier bands (called Gitksan today) still live in southwest Canada.

▶ Blow Guns

The blow gun is traditionally used by the Catawba and other Southeast tribes for hunting small animals such as birds, squirrels, and rabbits. The gun is made from cane and shoots a poison dart. This early-20th-century photograph shows a Catawba man and boy each using a blow gun.

CARRIER

- **LANGUAGE FAMILY: ATHAPASKAN**
- **LIFEWAYS: FISHING**
- **LOCATION: BRITISH COLUMBIA**
- **THEIR OWN NAME: TAKULLI**

SUBARCTIC

The Carrier called themselves People Who Go Upon Water because they traded furs by canoe. Their English name comes from a unique custom: A widow carried the ashes of her late husband in a basket on her back for a year. Only then could she remarry.

Two hundred years ago, the Carrier migrated from the eastern Canadian Rockies to the Pacific Coast. There they adopted the customs of their Tsimshian trading partners. About 6,000 former Carrier in British Columbia are now called by their Tsimshian name, Gitksan.◀

CATAWBA

- **LANGUAGE FAMILY: SIOUIAN**
- **LIFEWAYS: HUNTING, GATHERING, & TRADING**
- **LOCATION: SOUTH CAROLINA**
- **THEIR OWN NAME: KATAPA**

SOUTHEAST

The Catawba live on South Carolina's Catawba River. The tribe was formed during the 1700s. The Choctaw name for them means A Division. Like their Tuscarora neighbors, they call themselves Shirt People. British traders brought the calico and ribbons the Catawba used to make their shirts. They also brought diseases, which had reduced the tribe to 100 people by the year 1900.

In this century the Catawba sued South Carolina to get land promised to them by treaty. In 1993 the 1,400 Catawba won $50 million in compensation for the land.◀

CAYUGA

- **LANGUAGE FAMILY: IROQUOIAN**
- **LIFEWAYS: HUNTING & FARMING**
- **LOCATION: NEW YORK, OKLAHOMA, & ONTARIO**
- **THEIR OWN NAME: KWENIO GWE'N**

NORTHEAST

The Cayuga are part of the Iroquois Confederacy (the Haudenosaunee). Their own name, Kwenio gwe'n, means People of the Great Swamp. In Iroquois longhouse council meetings, the tribe's title is Younger Brother. In 1660 about 1,500 Cayuga lived in the swampy area between Cayuga and Owasco lakes in upstate New York.

CLANS The four main Cayuga clans are Deer, Turtle, Wolf, and Snipe. Like other Iroquois, the Cayuga have clan mothers and hold traditional ceremonies. The Cayuga headdress, or Gustoweh, can be identified by its single feather pointing to the side.

The Cayuga allied with the British during the Revolutionary War. In 1779 American general John Sullivan ordered his soldiers to burn the five main Cayuga towns and the tribe's cornfields. Many Cayuga went to Canada, while the rest sought shelter among the other Iroquois nations. In 1807 their territory was taken by the state of New York. Since then the tribe has had no land.

Today, 500 Cayuga live on one Onondaga and three Seneca reservations. Another 3,000 reside on Six Nations Reserve in Ontario, Canada, where they are governed by hereditary chiefs. Those who were removed to Oklahoma with a group of Seneca are known as the Seneca-Cayuga. Although far from home, this tribe performs the Iroquois Green Corn Dance every summer.

Since the 1970s the Cayuga have pursued their land claims. Preserving the language is a main concern of the tribe, as is its self-government. ◀

Silverwork

Cayuga silverwork was influenced by European, particularly Scottish, designs in the late 18th and 19th centuries.

Six Chiefs

The Cayuga tribe is one of the Six Nations of the Iroquois Confederacy. These six Iroquois chiefs gathered in Ontario, Canada, in 1871. They are holding tribal wampum belts made of beads, quahogs (hard-shell clams), and freshwater shells. Wampum belts held great value for Indians and were used to ratify treaties and record important events.

The Great Law

Jake Thomas is a Cayuga chief, educator, and historian. The logo of his Learning Center in Wilsonville, Ontario, illustrates nine Cayuga clans gathered around the Iroquois Tree of Peace. All are welcome to attend Learning Center events such as Sunrise Ceremonies and recitals of the Iroquois Great Law of Peace.

Sevens

Traditionally, there were seven Cherokee clans. Each is shown on this seven-sided design next to its name in the Cherokee language. There were seven counsellors to the chief, and seven honored women took part in the government. The council house, where the government met and where the most sacred Cherokee ceremonies were held, was seven-sided. At the center of the house, as in this design, was the sacred fire that was kept burning with seven kinds of wood.

The Cherokee Language

The great Cherokee scholar Sequoya (1770–1843) invented a way for the Cherokee language to be written. He wanted the Cherokee to have a written constitution and be able to keep written records. Starting in 1809, Sequoya spent twelve years devising an eighty-six-character syllabary, or alphabet, for the Cherokee language.

The *Cherokee Phoenix,* a weekly newspaper begun in 1828 by Cherokee Elias Boudinot, carried articles in both English and Cherokee and used the Cherokee characters created by Sequoya. It was published at New Echota, Georgia, then the Cherokee capital.

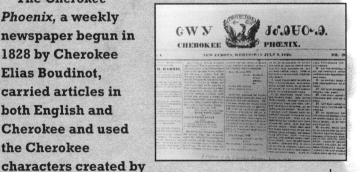

CHEROKEE

SOUTHEAST

- **LANGUAGE FAMILY: IROQUOIAN**
- **LIFEWAYS: FARMING & HUNTING**
- **LOCATION: OKLAHOMA & NORTH CAROLINA**
- **THEIR OWN NAME: KEETOOWAH**

The Cherokee are an Iroquoian-speaking people who settled in the central Southeast. They numbered about 25,000 in the early 1600s. The name Cherokee is the Choctaw word for an important Cherokee town, Keetoowah. Numbering over 300,000 in 1990, the Cherokee are the largest Native American nation in the United States today. Most live in Oklahoma, but 10,000 remain in the Southeast.

GREEN MEDICINE

The early Cherokee were farmers who lived in log houses and wore brightly dyed cotton clothing. Bean dumplings and chestnut bread were their traditional foods. The Cherokee discovered many plant medicines, including spiraea, from which aspirin is now made. According to legend, diseases were created by the animals, who were angry at humans for hunting them. The plants decided to help people by providing cures for diseases.

After the Revolutionary War, many Cherokee believed that they would have to adapt themselves to white culture if they wanted to survive. They bought land and settled on single-family farms. Because they were in the South, some even bought slaves. They built European-style towns. The Cherokee scholar Sequoya invented a written alphabet for the Cherokee language, taught many of his people to read and write, and founded a newspaper.

It was not enough. White cotton farmers wanted Cherokee land. The final blow came in

1829, when gold was discovered in northeastern Georgia. The Five Civilized Tribes (Cherokee, Choctaw, Chickasaw, Creek, and Seminole) were ordered to move to Oklahoma. The Cherokee fought the removal, took their case all the way to the Supreme Court, and won. However, President Andrew Jackson would have none of it. He said, "[Justice] Marshall has made his decision; now let him enforce it." Of course, the court had no army to enforce its decision. But the president did.

TRAIL OF TEARS

In 1838 the army and private contractors were brought in to force the 17,000 Cherokee to Oklahoma. To increase their profits, the contractors skimped on food and blankets for the tribe. The Cherokee were marched 1,200 miles in the dead of winter. So many died on the way—about 4,000 people—that they called the journey the Trail of Tears. Some, however, escaped to the mountains of North Carolina, where about 10,000 Eastern Cherokee now live on 50,000 acres.

In their new Oklahoma home, the Cherokee continued the tradition of education and hard work that had made them so successful in the Southeast. Over 140 schools were established, and the Cherokee had a higher literacy rate than their white neighbors in the 19th century.

The Great Depression struck in the 1930s, and Oklahoma became a Dust Bowl and could not be farmed. Many Cherokee were forced to move to cities to survive. Cherokee chiefs, who were appointed by the president of the United States, had little power to help their people.

Change came when the Cherokee nation reorganized itself in the 1970s. The Cherokee have again become leaders in Indian education, health care, housing, and economic development. The Eastern Band is also renowned for its crafts—baskets, beadwork, woodcarving, and pottery.◀

▶ Tahlequah Council

The Cherokee and many other tribes were forced to move to Oklahoma. In 1843 a council was held at Tahlequah, now a town in eastern Oklahoma, to form a territorial government. Representatives of sixteen tribes and of the U.S. government attended the council, which is represented in this contemporary painting.

▶ Wilma Mankiller

Wilma Mankiller (born 1945) was elected chief of the Cherokee in 1987—the first woman to be chosen chief. She was born in Tahlequah, Oklahoma.

Black Kettle

The Southern Cheyenne chief Black Kettle (1803–1868) was a famous Dog Soldier as a young man. Later, during the U.S.–Plains Indian conflicts, his band was repeatedly attacked by U.S. soldiers. But Black Kettle favored peace. He was known for stopping young warriors from raiding and for risking his life to return white captives to their families. Even after 200 members of his band were massacred, the chief continued to attend **treaty** councils. Despite his efforts, Black Kettle and his wife were killed by George Armstrong Custer's soldiers in 1868.

Dog Soldiers

Little Wolf (standing) and Dull Knife (sitting) were Cheyenne warriors who fought alongside the Sioux during the battles for the Black Hills in the 1870s. Little Wolf's band burned Fort Kearny in Montana after U.S. soldiers were forced to abandon it in 1868. In 1876 the Sioux and Cheyenne defeated Custer's Seventh Cavalry at the Little Bighorn. But after several losses, they surrendered and were moved to reservations in Montana and Oklahoma.

CHEYENNE

- **LANGUAGE FAMILY: ALGONQUIAN**
- **LIFEWAYS: PLANTING & HUNTING**
- **LOCATION: MONTANA & OKLAHOMA**
- **THEIR OWN NAME: DZI TSI STAS**

PLAINS

Before the mid-1700s the Cheyenne lived in earth lodges (Plains). Their villages, where they farmed, molded pottery, and created beads from pounded glass, were on the Mississippi River in what became Minnesota. Bands of Sioux eventually pushed the Cheyenne westward to the Black Hills of South Dakota. The name Cheyenne comes from the Lakota Sioux word Sha-hi'ye-la, meaning Different Talkers. Dzi tsi stas, or Our People, is the Cheyenne name for themselves. When the tribe began hunting buffalo on horseback, it started living in tipis. Some Cheyenne moved southward and became the Sowonia. The northern O Mi Sis were joined by a third group, the Sutaio, in 1883.

SACRED LAW The Black Hills are sacred to the Cheyenne. Noah-Vose Butte is the place where the famous Cheyenne prophet Sweet Medicine received spiritual teachings from Maheo, the creator. Maheo's Sacred Law is the basis of Cheyenne values and government. Sweet Medicine also received a bundle of Sacred Arrows from Maheo. The arrows were guarded by special keepers. Selected women taught quill and leather crafts and kept their own sacred bundles. When the bundles were properly guarded, the tribe had good health and hunting. But when the arrows were stolen by the Pawnee during a battle in 1830, bad times began. The Cheyenne lost forty-seven men in a battle with the Kiowa and Comanche.

Sweet Medicine had predicted the coming of the Europeans. He warned his people not to accept any gifts from them or to trade with the white men. The prophet had foreseen the bad effects of disease and alcohol on his people, but he could not prevent these dangers.

During the next seventy-five years, the Cheyenne suffered severe losses. An 1849 smallpox epidemic killed about 2,000 of an estimated 6,000 people. Border warfare with the Sioux, Comanche, and Kiowa killed many Cheyenne. Eventually these tribes made peace and joined with the Arapaho and Apache to fight non-Indians. In 1864, 700 U.S. soldiers massacred 200 Cheyenne men, women, and children at Sand Creek, Colorado. Although the Cheyenne and Sioux defeated George Armstrong Custer and his Seventh Cavalry at the Battle of the Little Bighorn (which the Indians call the Battle of the Greasy Grass), the tribe was weakened by disease and the slaughter of the buffalo by the U.S. military.

After several defeats, the Northern Cheyenne were moved to their current reservation in Montana. The Cheyenne and Arapaho went to a reservation in western Oklahoma. Tribal land was reduced in 1891 through the Allotment Act.

ENDURANCE Now both tribes are struggling for legal and cultural survival. The New Life Lodge ceremony was outlawed in 1907 (Missions), but the tribe preserved the ceremony by disguising it as the Willow Dance until it was again legalized in the 1970s. The Sacred Arrows have been returned and the bundle's power is renewed in a ceremony every year. Selected women's traditions are continued by the War Mothers and Quillwork societies. The 10,829-member tribe is governed by the traditional Council of Forty-Four, as instructed by Sweet Medicine.

Seven tribal elementary schools and three high schools teach the Cheyenne language and culture. The Northern Cheyenne opened Dull Knife Memorial College in 1976. ◀

Tipi

The chores of Cheyenne men and women were defined by gender. Men were responsible for hunting, fishing, and keeping the tribe safe. Women took care of raising children, cooking, and taking down and setting up tipis when the camp was moved. Putting together the tipi poles was complicated, like doing a puzzle with heavy pieces.

Indian Dancer

Dwight White Buffalo, a young Cheyenne, is dressed to perform in a modern Indian dance theater. Dance is one of the oldest Indian art forms. It is a way for Indians to express themselves and to celebrate their beliefs. Dance ceremonies were also performed before battle. The traditional outfit includes beaded armbands, sashes and belts, and a trailing feathered headdress. In earlier days such a grand headdress, or "war bonnet," would have indicated status.

Ben Nighthorse Campbell

Cheyenne Ben Nighthorse Campbell (born 1933) is the only American Indian in the U.S. Senate. He represents Colorado. Senator Campbell helped found the National Museum of the American Indian, part of the Smithsonian Institution, and in the mid-1990s he succeeded in changing the name of the Custer National Monument to the Little Bighorn National Monument. Campbell also designs jewelry, for which he has won over 200 awards. In 1964 he was captain of the U.S. Olympic judo team.

CHICKASAW

- **LANGUAGE FAMILY: MUSKOGEAN**
- **LIFEWAYS: TRADING, HUNTING, & WARRING**
- **LOCATION: OKLAHOMA**
- **THEIR OWN NAME: CHICKASAW**

SOUTHEAST

Annie Guy

The Chicasaw traditionally married outside their nation. After they were forced to move to Oklahoma in the 1820s and 1830s, the Chickasaw adopted many white customs. Annie Guy, a girl of Chickasaw and white ancestry, was photographed in European clothing and hair style.

The Great Seal of the Chickasaw

The Chickasaw officially adopted this seal in 1856. It shows Chief Tishomingo, the tribe's great leader and last war chief. Tishomingo died shortly after the Chickasaw were forced to move to Oklahoma. He was more than 100 years old. In the seal, Tishomingo is holding a bow and a shield made of deer hide stretched across a wooden frame. These stand for the tribe's determination to provide for its people. The two arrows in his right hand symbolize the two ancient branches of the Chickasaw people.

Like the Creek and the Choctaw, the Chickasaw are a Muskogean-speaking people who once lived in Alabama, Mississippi, and Tennessee. The tribe was the smallest of the so-called Five Civilized Tribes (Southeast) and numbered about 8,000 people at the time of the Revolutionary War.

The Chickasaw and the Choctaw were once one people. They are descended from the Mississippian Mound Builders. Beginning in about 750 B.C., they participated in a vast Mississippian trading and ceremonial culture that may have involved the Olmecs in Mesoamerica. However, around A.D. 1100 the group divided.

The Choctaw began to grow corn, while the Chickasaw continued to be nomadic hunters and warriors who frequently raided their neighbors— including their relatives, the Choctaw.

The Chickasaw created ceramic objects such as woodpeckers, hawks, and racoons that they used in rituals. Legends about these animals continue to be told among the Chickasaw today. Mississippian beliefs also survive in the modern Chickasaw Green Corn Dance.

WARFARE AND RAIDING

Many Native Americans died or were enslaved when Spanish conquistador Hernando de Soto attacked the southeastern tribes in 1539. To protect themselves the Choctaw and Chickasaw tried to unite, but old differences kept them apart, and they continued to raid each other. Both sides took prisoners, which led to so much intermarriage that soon there were few pure-blooded Chickasaw left.

In the 1700s the Chickasaw helped the British capture Apalachee and Timucua slaves. However, when the Chickasaw themselves were attacked by the Spanish and French, they received no help from their British allies. In the mid-1800s the United States forcibly removed the weakened tribe to Oklahoma on the Trail of Tears (Cherokee). On their 4.7 million acres of Oklahoma territory, the Chickasaw slowly began to rebuild their nation.

Although the Allotment Act of 1887 had cost the tribe all but 300 acres of land by 1922, the Chickasaw have since won back the right to govern themselves.

There are about 26,000 Chickasaw in the United States today. About 10,000 live in southern Oklahoma. Many attend tribal schools and work for tribal businesses. The Chickasaw National Recreation Area in Sulphur, Oklahoma, attracts many visitors each year.◄

CHINOOK

- **LANGUAGE FAMILY: CHINOOKAN**
- **LIFEWAYS: FISHING & TRADING**
- **LOCATION: WASHINGTON**
- **THEIR OWN NAME: CHINOOK**

NORTHWEST COAST

Early Chinook villages surrounded the mouth of the Columbia River on the Washington and Oregon coast. The Chinook were a large and powerful tribe of traders. They exchanged shells, seal oil, dried fish, and slaves with other Indians. After 1783 they traded seal skins and Indian products for European goods. The Chinook language became the trade jargon spoken by Europeans, as well as by other tribes.

Since the 1890s the Chinook have been struggling to survive. Disease reduced their original population of 15,000 to a few hundred. Settlers

▶ Linda Hogan

Linda Hogan (born 1947) is the daughter of a Chickasaw father and a white mother. A gifted poet, her work has appeared in several anthologies devoted to Native American writers. She has also published several of her own collections of poems, including *Eclipse* and *Seeing Through the Sun,* as well as a novel, *Mean Spirit.*

▶ Chinook Logo

The Chinook tribal council chose a Chinook salmon design to represent their people. Early Chinook depended on salmon fishing for survival and trading. The council members (above) celebrated their history at a 1994 dedication of a statue in Vancouver, Washington.

◀ Tony Johnson

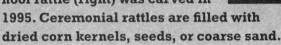

Chinook artist Tony Johnson is preserving his people's heritage by incorporating tribal designs and materials into his modern sculptures. He creates his pieces by using tribal history and artifacts as guides. This deer-hoof rattle (right) was carved in 1995. Ceremonial rattles are filled with dried corn kernels, seeds, or coarse sand.

▶ Snow Rackets

The Chipewyan Indians made snowshoes by lacing oval-shaped wooden frames with caribou hide. Snowshoes allowed hunters to track caribou in deep snow without sinking into snowbanks. Early French explorers, who had never seen snowshoes, called them "rackets." This drawing by a French baron is not accurate: It shows a European-looking Indian woman with snowshoes—but no clothes.

took over Chinook homelands without payment or treaty. The Bureau of Indian Affairs refused to recognize the Chinook as a tribe. Instead, the tribe was moved to the reservation of its traditional enemy, the Quinault tribe, on the Washington coast. In 1913 the Chinook helped organize the Northwest Federation of American Indians. Because of NFAI efforts, Congress granted money to the tribe. However, the tribe will not be paid until the federal government recognizes it.

In 1976 the state of Washington denied the Chinook their right to fish. It took six years for the tribe to regain fishing rights. Today, the Chinook and Quinault are trying to work together. The Chinook have enrolled 1,200 members in hope of gaining federal recognition. Legal fees are being paid with money from Chinook Indian Bingo and fishery work in Alaska. The Chinook community is strong, and the people continue to defend their right to be a tribe. ◀

CHIPEWYAN

- **LANGUAGE FAMILY: ATHAPASKAN**
- **LIFEWAYS: HUNTING**
- **LOCATION: NORTHWEST TERRITORIES**
- **THEIR OWN NAME: CHIPEWYAN**

SUBARCTIC

The Chipewyan once ranged across much of northeastern Canada. Today, they live around the shores of the Great Slave and Athabasca lakes and along the Mackenzie River in the Northwest Territories. They are the largest community of northern Athapaskan people, numbering over 5,000.

The Chipewyan hunted caribou for meat. The guts were dried and used as thread to stitch the skins into clothing and tents. They also used the intestines to carry dried caribou meat on long hunts. The Chipewyan developed the toboggan to carry game when hunts took them far from home.

The Chipewyan stayed out of the European fur trade (Subarctic), but they didn't escape the problems of modern civilization. In 1907 Canada offered the Chipewyan a deal, and the tribe gave up its claims to the land. They received a supply of ammunition, medicine, and five dollars spending money annually per person. European diseases killed thousands of Chipewyan. As late as 1948, a quarter of the Barren Grounds Chipewyan died from measles.

In the 1960s the Chipewyan were moved to towns along Hudson Bay, where the government offered education, housing, and health care. Life improved, but there are problems. There are few jobs in the Northwest Territories, and most families depend on hunting for food. In order to hunt on traditional lands, Chipewyan men have to leave their families for months at a time.◄

CHITIMACHA

- **LANGUAGE FAMILY:** MUSKOGEAN
- **LIFEWAYS:** FISHING, GATHERING, & FARMING
- **LOCATION:** LOUISIANA
- **THEIR OWN NAME:** PANTCH-PINUNKANSH

SOUTHEAST

The Chitimacha live in southern Louisiana. Chitimacha means, They Have Cooking Vessels. Corn and sweet potatoes were common Chitimacha foods, and the noonday sun was the most powerful force in the tribe's spiritual life.

The Chitimacha numbered 2,500 in the early 1600s, but there are only 750 of them today. The tribe was officially recognized in 1917, when Sara McIlhenny of the company that makes Tabasco sauce donated land to the Chitimacha. Today, many Chitimacha work in oil fields and sell baskets.◄

▶ Rediscovery

Chipewyan tribal conferences bring children and adults together to celebrate the rebirth of their culture. Yearly gatherings at Fort Chipewyan, Northwest Territories, Canada, help the native peoples of Canada ensure their future as nations.

▶ Basket Weaves

These three geometric patterns are traditional Chitimacha basket designs. Using split cane, Chitimacha women carefully handwove each basket, incorporating the designs into the weave. Today, tribe members still craft baskets, sometimes using these very patterns.

Chief Pushmataha

During the War of 1812, Chief Pushmataha (c. 1765–1824) refused to join other Southeast tribes in an alliance with the British. He thought it would be futile to fight the Americans, so he and Choctaw warriors fought alongside American generals. For this reason—and for Pushmataha's refusal to join Tecumseh's Rebellion of 1809–1811 (Shawnee)—the Choctaw gained a reputation as a peaceful tribe.

Allen Wright

Allen Wright (1825–1885) was born in Mississippi. His Choctaw name was Kiliahote. A white Presbyterian minister gave him his new name and took him to New York City, where Wright became a minister himself. He later returned to the Choctaw and translated their laws into English. He also prepared a Choctaw dictionary. It was Wright who suggested the name Oklahoma, meaning Red People, for the Indian Territory.

CHOCTAW

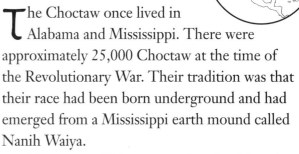

- **LANGUAGE FAMILY: MUSKOGEAN**
- **LIFEWAYS: FARMING**
- **LOCATION: OKLAHOMA & MISSISSIPPI**
- **THEIR OWN NAME: CHATA HAPIA HOKE**

The Choctaw once lived in Alabama and Mississippi. There were approximately 25,000 Choctaw at the time of the Revolutionary War. Their tradition was that their race had been born underground and had emerged from a Mississippi earth mound called Nanih Waiya.

Choctaw oral history says that the Choctaw and Chickasaw were once one group that had migrated to the Far West but had eventually returned to Nanih Waiya. Legend speaks of a magical staff that led them home. Every night, when the Choctaw made camp, the staff was placed in the ground. When they woke up, it would be leaning to the east. One morning, however, it remained upright and that is where the Choctaw settled.

FARMERS The Choctaw and Chickasaw parted around A.D. 1100, when the Choctaw settled down to farm. The Choctaw constantly developed new strains of corn and other crops. They were also well known for their peaceful ways. As members of one of the Five Civilized Tribes (Southeast), most of the Choctaw were forced to move to Oklahoma on the Trail of Tears (Cherokee) in the mid-1800s. White settlers took their land.

In Oklahoma they established a republican form of government modeled after the United States. This government continued into the early part of this century, when it was absorbed into the new state of Oklahoma.

In the 1950s the Choctaw reestablished their

traditional government. They also sued the United States for compensation after federally funded dams flooded their lands.

Christianity plays an important role in Choctaw life. Missionaries were welcomed by the Choctaw, so the Choctaw were among the first southeastern Indians to convert to Christianity. Tribal congregations sing Christian hymns in the Choctaw language.

Today, about 20,000 Choctaw live in Oklahoma. Every year they host the Choctaw Nation Labor Day Festival. The public is invited to watch the Choctaw dance, participate in traditional stickball games (similar to lacrosse), and eat Choctaw food such as corn pudding. Nearly 6,000 Choctaw live in Mississippi, about half of them on the Choctaw reservation. Around the Fourth of July, they hold their annual four-day Choctaw Indian Fair, which includes dancing, food, and the Choctaw Stickball World Series.◄

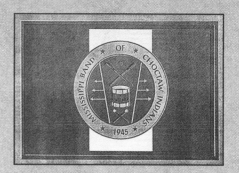

▶ Choctaw Flag

When the Choctaw were forced to move west from their homes in Alabama and Mississippi in the 1820s and 1830s, a few thousand remained in Mississippi. The Mississippi Band of Choctaw Indians adopted a constitution and this tribal flag in 1945. The drum in the center symbolizes the voice of the people. Below it are the hickory sticks used in stickball. Stickball and other games were traditionally used by the Choctaw to settle disputes.

CHUMASH

- **LANGUAGE FAMILY: HOKAN**
- **LIFEWAYS: GATHERING, HUNTING, & FISHING**
- **LOCATION: CALIFORNIA**
- **THEIR OWN NAME: LOCAL NAMES**

CALIFORNIA

With a population of nearly 20,000 in 1770, the Chumash were one of California's largest tribes. By 1865, diseases and massacres by Spanish and United States troops had reduced the Chumash to fewer than 700 people. Today, the Chumash are a prideful people. They are reviving their dances, songs, stories, and crafts. They do the Dolphin Dance in area schools. About 320 Chumash live on the Santa Ynez Reservation. Nearly 2,000 people claim Chumash descent and are seeking enrollment in the tribe.◄

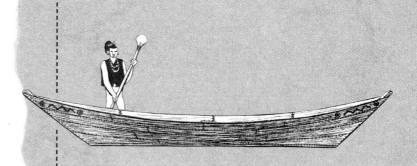

▶ Chumash Canoe

This planked canoe measured forty-one feet. The Chumash had as many as forty villages on the California coast and used these canoes to travel among them. Canoe ownership was a mark of high status.

▶ Mesa Verde

The Mesa Verde pueblo—a village of clay houses built into the wall of a cliff— in southwestern Colorado was not discovered by whites until 1888, long after its inhabitants had left. The Anasazi built and lived in the pueblo sometime between A.D. 100 and 1300. Then they disappeared— no one knows why.

▶ Kokopelli

The cliff dwellers frequently drew figures on rocks, many of which can be seen today. The figure on the right is Kokopelli, the humpbacked flute player. He may have been an Anasazi fertility symbol, and is perhaps leading someone in a dance in this drawing.

CLIFF DWELLERS

• LANGUAGE FAMILY: UNKNOWN
• LIFEWAYS: FARMING & HUNTING
• LOCATION: NONE
• THEIR OWN NAME: UNKNOWN

SOUTHWEST

The cliff dwellers, or Anasazi, were prehistoric inhabitants of the area where the states of Arizona, New Mexico, Colorado, and Utah meet today. The Anasazi do not exist anymore. Some of their traditions and arts, however, live on among the Pueblo and Hopi.

Anasazi means Ancient Ones in Navajo. The name cliff dwellers comes from their unique villages: Many Anasazi settlements were built into the sides of cliffs. They were built that way for defense and to help conserve precious land and water.

For much of their history, however, the Anasazi lived in pit houses with wooden walls and thatched grass roofs. The 60,000-square-mile Anasazi territory contains at least 30,000 archaeological sites. Humans have inhabited the region for tens of thousands of years. Continuous settlement began 12,000 years ago, and the earliest cultivated corn in the region dates to 3000 B.C.

CULTURAL STAGES

The Anasazi culture began about 3,000 years later. Archaeologists divide Anasazi history into five eras: three basket-maker periods from the beginning of the Christian Era to A.D. 700, and two pueblo stages from A.D. 700 to 1300. The first three periods get their names from the many baskets found at Anasazi sites. The next two stages are named after a new type of dwelling that first appeared at that time.

Instead of pit houses, the Anasazi began building adobe, or clay brick, structures completely above ground. Also, pottery replaced baskets as a means of storage and carrying things.

The different periods in Anasazi history are the result of changes in the environment. During the basket-maker period, the Anasazi gradually emphasized corn growing over wild plant gathering. During several especially rainy centuries from A.D. 200 to 700, large villages were built near fertile land. Baskets were used to carry corn from fields to village.

From A.D. 700 to 900, rainfall declined and the Anasazi relied on plant gathering. Because it takes many hours to dig the foundations of pit houses, archaeologists believe the Anasazi adopted pueblo construction to save labor.

PUEBLOS

During the pueblo stage, the population grew rapidly. Many people began to move into Anasazi territory, probably from Mesoamerica. Around A.D. 1100, to defend themselves and conserve land, the Anasazi moved from mesas to cliffs on the sides of mesas. They built stairways from their villages to the fields above. The stairways had random side steps that only the inhabitants knew about. At night, their enemies could not find their way down.

The Anasazi built roads from the fields to their houses and kivas. Kivas were large structures where the Anasazi performed spiritual ceremonies, ran village government, stored extra corn, and conducted trade. The Anasazi traded food and turquoise far and wide, especially during drought years. Many archaeologists believe the Anasazi even traded with the Aztecs in far-away Mexico.

The Anasazi disappeared around A.D. 1300. No one knows why. It may have been because of poor rainfall, depletion of the soil, or competition with other peoples.

Remains of Anasazi villages can be found at Mesa Verde National Park in Colorado and Canyon dc Chelly National Monument in Arizona. ◄

▶ Pottery

During the latter stages of their culture, the cliff dwellers created pottery remarkable for its durability, variety, and craftsmanship. Working with brushes made from the thin fibers of yucca leaves, they painted with such detail that they could place fifteen parallel lines in a border less than an inch wide.

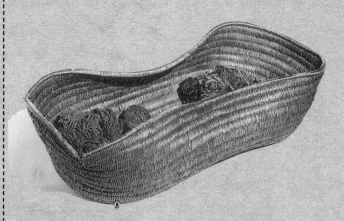

▶ Basket

Even after they began making pottery, the Anasazi continued to weave baskets. Baskets were lighter than pottery, so they were better for carrying things. They were also better for storing grains because they let in air, which dried the grains. The Anasazi could even carry water in baskets after sealing the seams with piñon gum. This basket was found in Utah and is believed to have been made between A.D. 1100–1300.

Chief Seattle

Chief Sealth (1786–1866), known as Seattle, led the Suquamish and Duwamish groups of the Coast Salish during the mid-1800s. He guided white settlers and traded furs with the Hudson's Bay Company. The city of Seattle was named after him. But in 1854 the federal government pushed Chief Seattle's people off their land. The chief refused to sign a land treaty, saying these words in a famous speech:

> *How can you buy or sell the sky? The land? The earth does not belong to man, man belongs to the earth.*

Salish Basket

Coast Salish baskets were made from spruce root and tightly coiled bundles of cedar bark dyed red, yellow, and black. They usually had a geometric design, as shown here. Some baskets were so watertight they could be used for cooking. The method consisted of dropping hot stones into a basket filled with food and water. Baskets were also used to trap fish.

COAST SALISH

- **LANGUAGE FAMILY: SALISHAN**
- **LIFEWAYS: FISHING**
- **LOCATION: WASHINGTON**
- **THEIR OWN NAME: LOCAL NAMES**

NORTHWEST COAST

The Coast Salish were once the most numerous people living along the Washington and British Columbian coasts. Traditionally salmon fishers, the tribe's 10,000 people came from several groups, including the Sliammon, Suquamish, Nooksack, Nisqually, Klallam, Lushootseed, and Quinault (Chinook). Their territory included the present sites of Seattle, Washington, and the Canadian cities of Vancouver and Victoria. Many Coast Salish remained as these cities grew.

MASKS The Coast Salish intermarried with the Nootka, Makah, and Chinook. Most of their troubles came from the Kwakiutl, who kidnapped the Salish for slaves. Kwakiutl masks influenced Coast Salish winter ceremonies. The most important dancers wore unique masks with horns and bird's-head noses. White swan feathers decorated their costumes.

Chief Seattle was among the Coast Salish chiefs who refused to sign land treaties. Resistance to reservations led to the Puget Sound Uprising of 1855. Led by Nisqually chief Leschi, Coast Salish and Yakima tribes attacked the city of Seattle.

Since the 19th century, the Coast Salish have been at the forefront of the fishing rights struggle (Red Power). The tribes are working toward self-government and preserving such traditions as the Spirit Dance and potlatch. First Salmon Ceremonies are open to the public. The Suquamish celebrate Chief Seattle Days every August with a festival.◄

COEUR D'ALENE

- **LANGUAGE FAMILY: SALISHAN**
- **LIFEWAYS: FISHING, HUNTING, & GATHERING**
- **LOCATIONS: WASHINGTON & IDAHO**
- **THEIR OWN NAME: SKITSWISH**

PLATEAU

Coeur d'alêne means "pointed heart" in French. It was an insult directed at a miserly French trader, but somehow stuck to the tribe. The Coeur d'Alene, who once ranged near the Columbia and Snake rivers in northern Idaho and eastern Washington, were at the hub of Northwest trade. In exchange for canoes, shells, and otterskins, they offered deerskins and dried grasses for basketmaking. When white traders came in the early 1800s, the tribe began to trade furs for guns and other manufactured goods.

VISION QUESTS In the 1850s the Coeur d'Alene and Kalispel went to war against white settlers who had encroached on their lands. After a few early victories, they were defeated and were forced onto a reservation with the Spokan. Many Coeur d'Alene became Catholic when Christian missionaries came to their region (Missions and Northeast). However, their cultural traditions—which include an important role for children—continue. Children go on vision quests when they reach puberty.

Today, the Coeur d'Alene are a powerful voice in Northwest Indian affairs. Tribe members are leaders in Idaho state government. They are working to restore natural areas that were destroyed by uranium mining. They also run one of the largest farms in Idaho, a model for other reservations. The tribe has won back hunting and fishing treaty rights for its members. That means they are allowed to use more effective traditional nets and traps to catch salmon. ◀

▶ Coeur d'Alene Boy

Dave Garry, a Coeur d'Alene, posed in a traditional costume on the Flathead Reservation in Montana in 1913.

▶ Sherman Alexie

Sherman Alexie (born 1967) grew up on the Spokan–Coeur d'Alene reservation in Wellpinit, Washington. By the age of twenty-one, he was already becoming a major literary figure. His recent fiction includes *The Lone Ranger and Tonto, Fistfight in Heaven,* and *Reservation Blues.* In an excerpt from his 1992 poem *Powwow,* Alexie both protests uranium mining on tribal land and expresses pride in Indian endurance:

*today, nothing has died, nothing
has changed beyond recognition*

*dancers still move in circles
old women are wrapped in shawls
children can be bilingual: yes and no*

*still, Indians have a way of forgiving
    anything
a little but more and more it's memory
    lasting longer
and longer like uranium just beginning
    a half-life*

Quanah Parker

Chief Quanah Parker (1845–1911) was the son of a Comanche chief and a captive white woman. In 1874 Quanah led the battle to save Texas buffalo herds from extermination by white hunters. Parker lost faith in Comanche spirituality when he thought it had failed his tribe in battle. After his surrender in 1875, Parker became a successful businessman. His faith was revived when he joined the Native American Church.

NATIVE AMERICAN CHURCH

The Native American Church was established in Oklahoma in 1918 by followers of the peyote religion. Peyote religion is centered on the sacramental use of the peyote plant, a small cactus with psychedelic properties. The dried buttons of the plant are eaten for their healing and teaching powers. Peyotists formed the Native American Church to protect their religious ceremony from attack by Christians who considered it pagan and from the U.S. government, which wanted the use of peyote outlawed. The all-night peyote ceremony practiced by the Comanche is also known as the Half-Moon Ceremony. It includes drumming and singing sacred songs, praying, eating peyote, smoking tobacco, and having breakfast, with a talk by the roadman, or leader, and perhaps a reading from the Bible.

COMANCHE

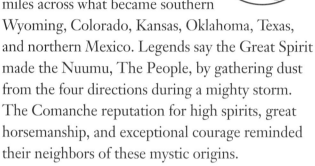

- **LANGUAGE FAMILY: UTO-AZTECAN NUMIC**
- **LIFEWAYS: HUNTING**
- **LOCATION: OKLAHOMA**
- **THEIR OWN NAME: NUUMU**

PLAINS

Comanche buffalo hunters once roamed hundreds of miles across what became southern Wyoming, Colorado, Kansas, Oklahoma, Texas, and northern Mexico. Legends say the Great Spirit made the Nuumu, The People, by gathering dust from the four directions during a mighty storm. The Comanche reputation for high spirits, great horsemanship, and exceptional courage reminded their neighbors of these mystic origins.

The Comanche were the only Numic-speaking tribe to live solely on the Plains. They traded widely because their Shoshone dialect was understood by most of their neighbors. Historically, the Comanche were a division of the Shoshone of southern Wyoming. The Sioux and other Plains tribes forced the Shoshone into the mountains as they pushed the Comanche farther south.

WAR Comanche warriors battled Spaniards in Mexico as far south as Durango during the 18th and early 19th centuries. They also attacked Spanish missions in Texas. At first they had friendly relations with Americans. Then the Comanche launched a war against Texans who had driven them from their sacred hunting grounds. The war lasted forty years.

The first treaty between the Comanche and the United States government was signed in 1835. Plans for a reservation began thirty years later under the 1867 Medicine Lodge Treaty. But the Comanche and their allies, the Kiowa and Apache, fought removal. In 1876 Comanche chief Quanah Parker finally surrendered his people at the Kiowa Agency in Oklahoma. By 1908 the U.S. had sold or given away the reserved land to non-Indians.

Today, there is no separate Comanche reservation, though the tribe has a headquarters north of Lawton, Oklahoma. Since 1900 its population has grown from about 1,500 to 8,500. About 60 percent of the Comanche live near Lawton, with the rest scattered across the United States. The tribe manages itself according to the 1975 Indian Self-Determination Act. The University of Oklahoma is helping to preserve the Comanche language.

The Comanche still perform many traditional ceremonies. A yearly homecoming powwow with the Kiowa and Apache recalls how Comanche warriors returned to camp. Dancers perform Litte Pony Society and Medicine dances in vibrant costumes with fine feathers and beadwork. Tribe members play a traditional handgame that involves tricky hand movements, singing, and gambling.◄

▶ LaDonna Harris

LaDonna Harris (born 1931), a Comanche from Oklahoma, has long advocated social welfare programs, civil rights, and Indian self-government. She helped found, and later became president of, Americans for Indian Opportunity, a powerful force in the economic development of Indian communities.

CREE

- **LANGUAGE FAMILY: ALGONQUIAN**
- **LIFEWAYS: FISHING & HUNTING**
- **LOCATION: QUEBEC & MONTANA**
- **THEIR OWN NAME: ANISHINABE**

SUBARCTIC

The Cree were made up of independent hunting and fishing bands that spoke a common language. These bands covered great distances by canoe and toboggan in search of game. Their own name, Anishinabe, is also used by the Ojibwa. The two tribes consider themselves to be one group. Their language is similar and they share spiritual beliefs. Most Cree live farther north than the Ojibwa, around Canada's Hudson and James bays.

The Cree were and are great believers in spirits and dreams. Children who had powerful

▶ Around the Fire

The French fur traders who came to Canada in the 1600s profited from their ties with Cree hunters, who taught them how to survive in the rugged northern wilderness. The Cree received firearms, tools, cloth, and other trade goods in exchange for beaver pelts.

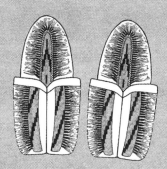

Makisina

The word *moccasin* comes from the Cree word *makisina*, which means shoe. Cree women decorated caribou or moose-hide moccasins with dyed porcupine-quill embroidery. The design faces the weaver, so it must be personally pleasing.

Cree Unity

Cree national unity is symbolized by their buffalo-shield and bear-track seal. The Cree-owned Hawk radio station is part of a growing Native American communications network devoted to Indian issues.

dreams might become healers. Some healers worked in a shaking tent, which was a narrow, hide-covered lodge. After everyone had fasted and prayed in a sweat lodge, helpers tied the healer's hands and feet with leather thongs. The healer was then hung from the roof of the shaking tent. People waited outside the tent, where they heard the voices of spirits and watched the tent shake. Sometimes animal sounds and sparks of light came from the tent. When the healer came out, he or she would tell the people what the spirits had advised.

REBELLION

In 1885 the Cree, Ojibwa, and Métis rebelled against hunting restrictions imposed by the Canadian and U.S. governments. After the rebellion, the famous Cree chiefs Poundmaker and Piapot were arrested. They were found innocent and released, but Canadian soldiers took revenge against the Cree. Chief Rocky Boy fled to Montana with his people, where he joined the Little Shell Ojibwa. The tribe, called the Chippewa-Cree, received its Montana reservation in 1915.

With more than 75,000 people, the Cree are the largest Indian nation in Canada. Many live in northern Quebec, where a huge hydro-electric project flooded 7,500 square miles of James Bay, Cree and Inuit territory, in 1975. Quebec plans to build an even larger dam. Because Quebec is seeking independence from Canada, the provincial government is ignoring national Indian treaty rights.

Cree leaders continue to travel and speak about James Bay. In 1991 Grand Chief Matthew Coon Come said, "I am only one among many people who believe in speaking for Mother Earth, for who can speak better than the ones who have lived with the animals and are tied to the land?" International environmental groups are actively supporting the Cree. Their studies show that completion of the dams will damage the environment (Subarctic).◄

CREEK

- LANGUAGE FAMILY: MUSKOGEAN
- LIFEWAYS: FARMING
- LOCATION: OKLAHOMA
- THEIR OWN NAME: MUSKOKE

SOUTHEAST

The Creek once lived primarily in present-day Georgia and Alabama. They considered themselves one people, though the Creek were a confederacy of more than 300 villages that spoke six different languages. Early Natchez, Seminole, Shawnee, and Yuchi tribes were part of the confederacy. The name Creek was given to the Muskoke by European colonists because of the many creeks in the territory. The Creek numbered 22,000 around the time of the Revolutionary War.

Traditionally, Creek villages were either "white towns," devoted to peace ceremonies, or "red towns," developed for warfare. Each of the 300 towns had a chief and several clan leaders. Chiefs were elected and could be removed, and all decisions were made by the unanimous consent of the people. Chiefs met twice a year in a national council. However, any town could ignore council decisions it didn't like. Even individuals were free to make decisions for themselves. However, Creek society was mostly peaceful and without disputes: There were no civil wars, and murder was rare.

STOMP DANCE

Creek traditions include the Green Corn Ceremony, which is still held today. Each village builds a mini-forest of brush and bushes around the rectangular dance grounds. A sacred fire burns there. For several weeks the Stomp Dance is done from about midnight until dawn. Then people purify themselves by fasting, scratching their skin with thorns, and drinking the Black Drink, an herbal beverage containing caffeine.

In the 1820s the Creek and the other so-called

▶ Tomochichi

Tomochichi (1650?–1739) was an important Creek leader. He was friendly with the English settlers in America and visited England in 1734, where he met the English king and queen He is shown here with his nephew, who is holding a pet eagle.

▶ The Creek Seal

Muscogee is another name for the Creek. In this seal, created in 1885, the letters *I. T.* stand for Indian Territory (Oklahoma). Since the Creek are farmers and some of them adopted Christianity, there is also Biblical symbolism on the seal. The plow refers to a Biblical prophecy: "Behold, the day comes, saith the Lord, that the plowman shall overtake the reaper." The sheaf of wheat stands for Joseph's dream in the Bible of "finding sheaves in the fields."

Joy Harjo

Joy Harjo (born 1951) is a Creek poet originally from Tulsa, Oklahoma. She has won many awards for her poetry and taught at the University of New Mexico. She currently lives in Santa Fe, New Mexico, where she writes poetry and plays saxophone in the band Poetic Justice. Harjo's poetry speaks of her many identities:

I am from Oklahoma. But that isn't my
*   only name.*
I am Creek and other
Oklahoma/Arkansas people. I am
a woman, many women. The namings can
*   go on and on …*

Plenty Coups

Chief Plenty Coups was part of a Crow delegation that went to Washington, D.C., in 1880 at the request of President Rutherford B. Hayes. The Crow leader traveled by train for the first time, describing the machine as a big black horse that "ran so fast that every time he stopped, he puffed." In Washington, the president talked with Plenty Coups about building a railroad through his hunting ground. The chief at first resisted, but agreed to the plan after he returned home and consulted with his people.

Five Civilized Tribes (Cherokee, Choctaw, Chickasaw, and Seminole) were forced to move to Oklahoma. The Lower Creek became Christian; the Upper Creek remained committed to traditional spirtuality and the Green Corn Ceremony. Sadly, the Creek tradition of tolerance did not survive the migration, and the Green Corn War of 1917 broke out between the two groups for control of the tribal government.

For years the struggle kept the Creek government powerless. In 1970 a federal law gave new powers to the Lower Creek government, even though they are outnumbered by the more traditional Upper Creek. Of the 30,000 Creek in the United States today, approximately 10,000 live on reservations in Oklahoma.◄

CROW

- **LANGUAGE FAMILY: SIOUIAN**
- **LIFEWAYS: FARMING**
- **LOCATION: MONTANA**
- **THEIR OWN NAME: ABSAROKA**

PLAINS

The Crow, or Bird People, were once part of the Hidatsa tribe along the Missouri River in what became South Dakota. In 1776 Chief No Vitals had a vision that told him to take his people west into the Rocky Mountains. There they would find the sacred tobacco whose seeds would protect them and give definition to their customs through the Tobacco Society.

Two groups, the River Crow and Mountain Crow, formed after leaving the Hidatsa. By 1800 the Crow had settled along rivers in southern Montana and northern Wyoming. They planted corn

61

and tobacco until Europeans brought horses in the mid-1700s. The Crow became known for their high-quality horses and fancy riding gear. A family's status was tied to the number of horses and buffalo skins it owned. Decorated rawhide shields reflected higher powers and the deeds of their owners.

Before the 1800s the Crow numbered about 9,000 people. Then smallpox outbreaks reduced the population to less than 5,000. Clashes with gold hunters, settlers, and ranchers led to the signing of the 1851 Fort Laramie Treaty, which set aside 38.5 million acres for the Crow Reservation. But the Crow received only a small part of their land, along with harsh restrictions designed to eliminate their traditions. They were forbidden to hold giveaway feasts or Sun Dances, take more than one wife, sell horses to one another, leave the reservation without consent, or practice traditional medicine (Plains).

PEACE The great chiefs Plenty Coups and Medicine Crow had visions that told the Crow to make peace with the whites. They fought alongside American soldiers against the Sioux and Cheyenne. Chief Plenty Coups traveled to Washington several times to negotiate with the government. But it was only after his death that controls on Crow traditions were lifted. The Sun Dance was resumed in 1941.

Today, most of the 8,500 Crow speak the Crow language. A respected spiritual leader names babies and offers prayers. Besides basketball, Crow teenagers play a traditional handgame and hold arrow-throwing tournaments. Rodeos showcase their colorful beaded costumes with traditional geometric forms and floral designs.

Education and economic independence remain the biggest challenges. Coal and grazing land provide some employment, though the tribe is struggling with the state of Montana over land use. Many Crow perform such traditional work as painting, jewelry making, and beadworking. ◀

Grasshopper's Daughter

Grasshopper's Daughter, a young Crow girl, was photographed in an elk's-tooth dress around 1910.

Dean Bear Claw

The Film and Video Center of the American Indian was established in New York City in the early 1980s to support Indian film makers. Crow film maker Dean Bear Claw is shown here with his son Francis in 1993. His work includes the award-winning *Warrior Chiefs in a New Age* and *Native Visions, Native Voices*.

Grey Eagle

Grey Eagle of the Dakota tribe was photographed in front of his lodge in Minnesota at the turn of the century. He is wearing the traditional Sioux dress of hide leggings and a fringed, beaded top. The U.S. flag sewn into his tipi was placed there as a sign of peace.

John Trudell

Dakota musician John Trudell was the national chairman of the American Indian Movement (AIM) from 1974 to 1980 (Red Power). He turned to poetry and music following the death of his wife and children in a trailer fire in 1979. Trudell mixes politically conscious lyrics with both traditional and contemporary musical styles. He feels music is a way for Indians to assert their presence in the world: "The whole American trip is to keep the Indians in the past....When I see...indigenous peoples experimenting with the electric sound and the traditional sounds, to me this is...a natural survival thing." Musician Jackson Browne produced Trudell's albums *Graffiti Man* and *Johnny Damas and Me.*

DAKOTA

- **LANGUAGE FAMILY: SIOUIAN**
- **LIFEWAYS: HUNTING, FISHING, & PLANTING**
- **LOCATION: NORTH & SOUTH DAKOTA & MINNESOTA**
- **THEIR OWN NAME: DAKOTA**

Dakota is the name of four eastern Sioux tribes of South Dakota—the Mdewakanton and the Wahpekute (both also referred to as Santee), the Sisseton, and the Wahpeton. Originally from the Southeast, these tribes migrated in prehistoric times and settled in hunting, fishing, and planting villages in eastern Minnesota. In the Dakota language, Minnesota means Waters that Reflect the Sky. After Ojibwa Indians came to their territory in the 1700s, the Dakota scattered westward across Minnesota.

SACRED PIPES The Dakota name means Friend in a dialect of the language the tribe shares with the Lakota and Nakota. Besides language, the tribes share the Sacred Pipe ceremonies (Plains). The pipes used in this ceremony are carved of pipestone, a soft red stone that is found near Pipestone, Minnesota. Ancient Dakota rock art marks the pipestone quarry, and legends say the stone was formed from the blood of the Dakota people.

As a result of the 1862 Sioux resistance to white settlers in Minnesota, most Dakota either fled to Canada or were expelled from Minnesota. Dakota who were not involved in the war stayed on their assigned land but received no government benefits.

Today, about 20,000 of the 30,021 enrolled Dakota live in North and South Dakota, Minnesota, Manitoba, and Saskatchewan. Modern Dakota are trying to preserve their heritage by speaking their language. They revived the Sacred Pipe and Sun Dance ceremonies in the 1980s. Some have adopted Christianity. The church in Granite Falls, Minnesota, conducts services in both Sioux and English. ◄

FILM: NATIVE AMERICANS IN THE MOVIES

The history of Native Americans in the movies is almost as old as the history of movies themselves, and Hollywood's view of Indians has generally reflected America's attitudes.

Such early films as *Kit Carson* (1903) and D.W. Griffith's *Battle at Elderbush Gulch* (1913) depicted Indians as savage warriors who attacked innocent whites for no reason. Sometimes—as in Griffith's film *The Redman and the Child* (1908)—Native Americans were shown as noble primitives who were doomed to extinction.

From the 1930s through the 1950s, the movie Western reached its peak in popularity. Such directors as Howard Hawks and John Ford often portrayed Indians as honest and courageous, though easily misled. John Ford's *She Wore a Yellow Ribbon* (1949) and *Rio Bravo* (1959) are good examples of this.

NEW ATTITUDE

The Civil Rights movement (Red Power) and growing environmental awareness of the 1960s created a new attitude about Indians, which was reflected in the movies. Arthur Penn's *Little Big Man* (1970) focuses both on Native American culture and the massacre of Native Americans. A breakthrough film was Kevin Costner's *Dances with Wolves* (1990). It contrasted whites' destruction of the environment to Native Americans' protective attitudes. Yet this film still focused on a white star.

A recent TV documentary called *500 Nations* is trying to correct this problem. In its four episodes, Native Americans recount history from their point of view.◄

Jim Thorpe

This photograph of Jim Thorpe (1888—1953) was taken in 1934, just after he was cast in Sylvia Sidney's film *Behold My Wife*. An Olympic athlete and Hollywood actor, Thorpe was a full-blooded Sac and Fox. He is dressed as he appeared in the Sidney film.

Nathan Chasing His Horse

Nathan Chasing His Horse is a young Lakota from South Dakota. He is best known for his role as Smiles A Lot in Kevin Costner's film *Dances with Wolves*. He has also worked with United National Indian Tribal Youth (UNITY) to promote sobriety. His anti-alcohol posters for the group declare, "Choose tradition, not addiction."

The Honored Horse

Flathead children learned to ride soon after they learned to walk. The tribe loved horses and decorated them with beautiful collars, saddles, blankets, and bridles. For festive gatherings such as this powwow in 1900, girls wore deerskin dresses studded with elk's teeth.

D'Arcy McNickle

Flathead tribe member D'Arcy McNickle (1904–1977) was an early activist for Indian self-government. He authored poetry books as well as anthropology texts, including *Native American Tribalism,* and became known as the father of Native American literature.

Coloring Book

Educational coloring books for children illustrate tribal knowledge, such as the uses of wild plants, in both the Salish and Kutenai languages.

Mother Earth gives us many plants that taste good and make us well when we are sick.

Na ka-amak namatikɬapni kikɬis.

ɬes x̣ecli ̓ɬ spe n̓am

FLATHEAD

- **LANGUAGE FAMILY:** SALISHAN
- **LIFEWAYS:** HUNTING
- **LOCATION:** MONTANA
- **THEIR OWN NAME:** SALISH

PLATEAU

The Flathead lived in the Plateau region, where they hunted small game, gathered plants, and fished. Many of their neighbors shaped their babies' heads to a point with wicker braces. The Flathead did not, and their English name probably comes from Europeans' stories about the other, "pointy-headed," tribes in the region.

HORSES When Europeans brought horses in the 1700s, the Flathead expanded to the Plains and hunted buffalo. This created conflicts with the powerful Blackfeet.

The Flathead maintained their rich spiritual life in war and peace. The Jump Dance brought health and good fortune to those who danced. The Spirit Dance included singing and dancing to assure a fruitful spring. These dances are still performed at powwows.

The Flathead wished to live peacefully with whites. They signed a treaty giving up most of their land in 1855. The tribe finally received payment for the land in 1980. The federal government tried, unsuccessfully, to end the Flathead's tribal status in 1954. Today, the Flathead are members of the Confederated Salish and Kutenai Nation. Some of their Kalispel relatives share their 1.2-million-acre reservation in western Montana. The mountainous reservation borders the National Buffalo Range, which attracts tourists and provides work for some of the 6,000 tribe members. The tribe runs the large KwaTaqNuk resort on Flathead Lake. Visitors can also join classes, demonstrations, and tours at the People's Center in Polson, Montana. There, tribe members share their experience of living harmoniously with nature.◀

GREAT BASIN

- **TRIBES OF THE REGION:**
  BANNOCK, PAIUTE, SHOSHONE, &
  UTE

GREAT BASIN

Vast, dry, and sparsely populated, the Great Basin includes Nevada, Utah, and parts of Oregon, Idaho, Wyoming, and Colorado. Bound by the Rockies to the east and the Sierra Nevadas to the west, the region gets its name from the fact that its few rivers flow inward, not to the sea.

Most of the Great Basin is flat and high, with elevations above 5,000 feet. The only wide river is the Humboldt in northern Nevada. The nearly lifeless Great Salt Lake in Utah is the largest body of water. Brutally cold in winter and extremely hot in summer, the region averages only ten inches of precipitation a year.

SMALL BANDS Conditions are harsh, yet the Great Basin is home to several tribes, including the Bannock, Paiute, Shoshone, and Ute. Farming is difficult in the Great Basin, so the people were hunter-gatherers. They ate small mammals, as well as lizards, fish, and even insects, but plants provided most of the food: piñon, mesquite beans, agave paste, berries, wild onions, and carrots. People wandered widely for their food, some bands of Shoshone and Paiute traveling as far as California. Great Basin tribes carried their supplies and developed basket making to a fine art.

A 12,000-year-old medicine wheel is the oldest record of humans in the Great Basin. The National Park Service maintains the site in central Wyoming and reserves it for native ceremonies during equinoxes (the first days of spring and autumn) and solstices (the first days of summer and winter).

In the 1840s Europeans began crossing the region heading for California and Oregon. Few

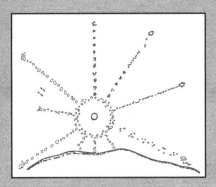

Medicine Wheel

Medicine wheels are ancient Indian spiritual sites. Typically, rocks and boulders were used to form a central ring with radiating spokes. The medicine wheel drawn here is in north-central Montana. Riverbank erosion has destroyed about half of it, but some medicine wheels still measure up to eighty feet in diameter.

GOSHUTE INDIAN RESERVATION
NO TRESPASSING
BY NON INDIANS
ILLEGAL TO ENTER, FISH, HUNT,
TRAP OR CAMP ON THIS PROPERTY
WITHOUT PERMISSION

Keep Out

This No Trespassing sign, photographed in 1971, was meant to keep non-Indians off the Goshute Indian Reservation in Nevada and Utah. Great Basin Indians want to protect their hunting grounds and the purity of their water supply. They were afraid outsiders would spoil their land.

GHOST DANCE

The Ghost Dance was based on dances of the Paiute World Renewal Ceremony. Dancers decorated their deerskin shirts with signs received in visions. Suns, moons, stars, and birds were the most common symbols. In the 1880s, traveling Arapaho leaders brought the Renewal Dance to the southern Plains. Wovoka, a Paiute prophet (above), had a vision predicting the dance would bring the buffalo back to the Plains.

Other prophets spoke of the disappearance of the whites and the return of dead relatives. News quickly spread to the northern Plains and California, and people began performing the Ghost Dance and watching it performed (below). They wanted only to communicate with their dead relatives and find their old traditions again, but white settlers did not understand. They thought the Ghost Dance was a war dance. Finally, the U.S. Army moved nearly half its troops to the Sioux reservations in 1890, and about 200 unarmed Lakota Ghost Dancers were killed at Wounded Knee.

stayed, except for the Mormons, who established a colony in Utah. Despite the sparse settlement, the United States government began to force Great Basin peoples onto reservations in the 1860s. Many people died there.

GHOST DANCE

In 1889 a Paiute prophet named Wovoka reintroduced an old spiritual rite known as the Ghost Dance. He told people that if they returned to the old ways, they would be reunited with lost loved ones.

The Ghost Dance spread to the Plateau, Plains, and California tribes. Native Americans quickly adopted the Ghost Dance, but U.S. military leaders had it banned. When Sioux on the Wounded Knee Reservation continued to dance, they were gunned down in 1890 in the last Native American massacre of the 19th century. The dance has regained popularity in recent years.

Sheep raising has been a main occupation of Great Basin people since the 1600s. Because sheep tend to cause erosion by overgrazing, the tribes are developing other ways of making a living. This is difficult because they compete with cities for resources. Los Angeles and Reno use much of the available water. In recent years the Shoshone have had troubles from uranium mining in Wyoming. Although they have protested to protect their health and sacred sites, they are still in danger.

With 50 percent of the tribal populations under the age of eighteen, education is important. Some tribes have taken over local schools to improve the quality of education. Elders are concerned that young people are not learning tribal culture. The tribes are providing language instruction, and federal grants pay for community centers where young people can find identity and pride in their heritage.

Most spiritual leaders in the region mix traditions such as the Sun Dance with Christianity and the Peyote Religion (Plains and Comanche). The Paiute still hold most of their traditional ceremonies. ◀

67

GROS VENTRE

- **LANGUAGE FAMILY: SIOUIAN**
- **LIFEWAYS: FARMING**
- **LOCATION: MONTANA**
- **THEIR OWN NAME: AH-AH-NEE-NIN**

PLAINS

French fur traders (Subarctic) renamed the Gros Ventre when they traded with the tribe by the Gros Ventre River in present-day Wyoming. The river's name translates as Big Belly in English. Before Europeans arrived, the Gros Ventre had separated from their Arapaho relatives and moved north into Montana. There they allied with the Blackfeet, who called them the Atsina.

The Gros Ventre call themselves Ah-ah-nee-nin, which means White Clay People. According to legend, their creator, Worldmaker, made the tribe from white clay to keep himself company. Worldmaker gave them a Flat Pipe and Feathered Pipe and taught them their Pipe ceremonies.

DISEASES

Because they had been created from the land, the Gros Ventre were opposed to selling their land. But by 1885 European diseases had reduced the tribe to 964 people. Federal commissioners representing the Pegasus Gold Company told the tribe they would all be dead in two years if they didn't sell their land. The Gros Ventre gave in and were paid $360,000 for their sacred mountains.

In 1888 there were only 576 Gros Ventre left. They were given the Fort Peck Reservation in Montana but had to share it with the Assiniboine, their traditional enemies. Today, the Gros Ventre and Assiniboine are working out their differences. They have united against the Pegasus Gold Company, which they say poisoned the water and caused health problems for the tribes. The Gros Ventre tribe has 2,900 members and is legally changing its name back to Ah-ah-nee-nin.◄

► Warriors

The Gros Ventre were mighty Plains warriors and allies of the Blackfeet. Gros Ventre warriors posed for this photograph in 1908, overlooking a tipi village in northern Montana, where the tribe had resettled after the Indian Wars.

► James Welch

Celebrated writer James Welch (born 1940) is part Blackfeet and part Gros Ventre. In his book of poetry *Riding the Earthboy 40* (1971) and his novels *Winter in the Blood* (1974) and *The Death of Jim Loney* (1979), he portrays how Indians often feel separated from contemporary America. His historical novel *Fools Crow* (1986) tells the story of a Blackfeet family and incorporates Indian legends.

Eagle Crest

Haida mothers gave their clan names and totem crests to their children. The main clans were Raven, Eagle, Frog, Beaver, and Bear. The Eagle crest, sewn in red flannel on a dance shirt, shows the bird's internal organs.

Totem Tatoos

Johnnie Kit Elswa, a Haida from Skidegate, British Columbia, displayed his tatoos in 1886. A brown bear on his chest and dogfish on his wrists illustrate events in his clan's history.

Robert Davidson

Robert Davidson is a Haida sculptor who carves contemporary works using traditional tribal subjects and materials, such as the cedar-wood salmon totem he carved in 1993. In 1969 a Davidson totem was the first pole to be raised in Masset, Queen Charlotte Island, in nearly a century.

HAIDA

- **LANGUAGE FAMILY: HAIDA**
- **LIFEWAYS: FISHING & TRADING**
- **LOCATION: ALASKA, BRITISH COLUMBIA, & WASHINGTON**
- **THEIR OWN NAME: HAIDA**

NORTHWEST COAST

The Haida homelands are the Queen Charlotte Islands in British Columbia and Prince of Wales Island in Alaska. Dense forests there bore some of the tallest cedar trees along the Northwest Coast. The Haida carved cedars into canoes, boxes, rattles, and totem poles. Their woodcarving skills became known throughout the region. The neighboring Tlingit and Tsimshian traded candlefish oil and woven blankets for painted Haida canoes.

In 1869, English merchants built a Hudson's Bay Company trading post on Haida land. By 1915, 90 percent of the 5,000 Haida were dead of European diseases, leaving only 588 people. Although the population has increased to 1,805, canneries and large lumber companies have replaced most island villages.

CITY DWELLERS
Today, most Haida live in Seattle, Washington, and Hydaburg, Alaska. Others live in Vancouver, Skidegate, and Massett in British Columbia. Hydaburg was founded as a Presbyterian mission town in 1880 (Tsimshian). Many Haida were drawn by the prosperous lumber mills, but some still prefer to follow ancestral ways, gathering their food from the land and sea.

Since 1936 the Haida have lobbied for a reservation in Alaska. The plan was blocked by the Alaska salmon industry, which wants no competition. After more than thirty years of lawsuits, the Haida and Tlingit received land payments in 1970. The funds have been used to include traditional Haida knowledge in the Alaska public school system. ◄

HAVASUPAI

- **LANGUAGE FAMILY: HOKAN**
- **LIFEWAYS: HUNTING, GATHERING, & FARMING**
- **LOCATION: ARIZONA**
- **THEIR OWN NAME: HAVASUPAI**

SOUTHWEST

The Havasupai's ancestors are believed to have come from Arizona's Red Butte. It is sacred to the Havasupai, whose name means People of the Blue-Green Water. The tribe still grows peach trees on the canyon floor. Their annual Peach Festival attracts many visitors, as do their Grand Canyon tours. The 565-member community has survived European diseases and conflicts with white ranchers. Today, its health is threatened by uranium mining on Red Butte. The legal struggle to protect the sacred site has awakened young people's interest in traditional ceremonies.◄

HIDATSA

- **LANGUAGE FAMILY: SIOUIAN**
- **LIFEWAYS: FARMING & HUNTING**
- **LOCATION: NORTH DAKOTA**
- **THEIR OWN NAME: HIDATSA**

PLAINS

The Hidatsa—whose name means Rows of Lodges—once lived in three earth-lodge villages at the mouth of Knife River in North Dakota. The tribe migrated up the Missouri River and settled near the Mandan to the west and Arikara to the south. While Hidatsa men hunted, women planted corn, squash, and beans, singing special songs to make them grow. Old men of the village raised tobacco for ceremonial smoking. Hidatsa boys were expert eagle catchers who waited in special pits to grab the birds by their legs. Eagle feathers had special

► Baskets and Trays

The Havasupai commonly used striking geometric designs on their baskets, trays, and pottery.

► Joe Rava

Havasupai Joe Rava was 103 years old when this photo was taken in 1913. He is wearing a vest and cap adorned with traditional Navajo silverwork.

► Buffalo Bird Woman

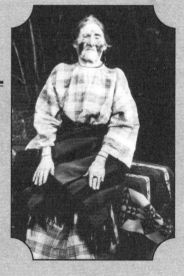

By 1926, Hidatsa elder Buffalo Bird Woman was living a very different life from the one she had lived as a young girl. She no longer lived in an earth lodge but in a house with a chimney and stove. Her son had gone to a white man's school and learned to read and raise cattle. She missed the Hidatsa tradition of singing to the corn as it was hoed. She said, "Our Indian life, I know, is gone forever."

Carlos White Shirt

Hidatsa Carlos White Shirt (left, with Navajo Elaine Bilstad and Inuit Eric Schweig) had a featured role in the 1992 film *The Broken Chain,* the story of the Iroquois Confederacy.

Walpi Pueblo

Walpi Pueblo, photographed in 1879, was a typical Hopi pueblo community. Dancer's Rock, on the left, was important for ceremonies in which Hopi dancers dressed up as spirits (*kachina*) and prayed for rain and vegetation in the dry region.

ceremonial powers (Plains). Hidatsa girls did the Skunk Dance when warriors killed Sioux enemies.

Gradually, the villagers moved again to find more fertile soil and to hunt buffalo. Their migration quickened after smallpox spread through the tribe in 1837. A Hidatsa medicine man named Missouri River guided the Hidatsa, Mandan, and Arikara to Like-A-Fishhook village in 1845.

The 1851 Fort Laramie Treaty granted the three tribes 13 million acres of reservation land. By 1870 a series of presidential orders had dramatically reduced their land. In 1954 the tribes lost more land to the Garrison Dam (Arikara), which separated clans and forced many members to move off the reservation.

The Hidatsa opened a casino in 1993, and the Hidatsa Center revived the War Bonnet dances. The Hidatsa, Arikara, and Mandan are legally called the Three Affiliated Tribes.◄

HOPI

- **LANGUAGE FAMILY: UTO-AZTECAN NUMIC**
- **LIFEWAYS: FARMING**
- **LOCATION: OKLAHOMA & ARIZONA**
- **THEIR OWN NAME: HOPI**

SOUTHWEST

Like other Pueblo peoples, the Hopi have farmed and lived in adobe villages since prehistoric times (Cliff Dwellers). Hopi means Peaceful, Kind, Truthful People. Hopi territory in Arizona and New Mexico—surrounded by Navajo lands—is twice-blessed. First, Oklahoma's Black Mesa, a sacred ground to both Hopi and Navajo peoples, is at the edge of their traditional lands. Second, because they were just out of reach of Spanish missions, the Hopi were able to keep their customs and beliefs, and also escape war with European settlers.

71

The Hopi have one of the richest cultures and faiths in North America. Masau-u is the Great Spirit who taught the people how to live. The Hopi are proud to say that the only treaty they ever made was with Masau-u, when they promised to take care of the land. Their spiritual societies follow laws written on ancient stone tablets. The Hopi believe we are living in the Fourth World. The first three worlds were destroyed when people began to believe in technology more than spirituality. Hopi prophecy states that unless people protect the environment, a Great Purification will destroy the earth again.

Respected Hopi elder Thomas Banyacya spoke at the United Nations in 1993. He said, "In every continent there are human beings who are like you but who have not separated themselves from the land and from nature.... If we return to spiritual harmony and live from our hearts, we can experience a paradise in this world." He invited world leaders to sit in kivas with Hopi elders and learn their ancient secrets of survival and balance.

CEREMONIES Today, the 7,360 Hopi live in thirteen pueblos on three mesas. Dances are performed at the Hopi Cultural Center in Second Mesa. They do the Bean Dance in February, the Water Serpent Ceremony in March, and the Home Dance in July. In the Home Dance, men wear huge pointed kachina masks and dance from dawn into the night.

While tourists are welcome at many dances, traditional Hopi oppose the sale of the popular kachina dolls. Real kachina dolls are carved of cottonwood tree roots, painted, and dressed according to traditional rules. They are used to teach Hopi children about the spirits. The Hopi believe these dolls are too sacred to be sold. Imitation kachina dolls are widely available, but the Hopi feel that the imitations are insulting to the spirits.

Conflict between traditionalists—who want to avoid white ways—and the business-minded Tribal

KACHINA

At the core of Hopi spiritual life is the *kachina,* or spirit. Kachina are the powerful spirits of the dead. They take the forms of plants, birds, animals, and even humans. Over 250 kachina bring the rain and ensure good crops and continued health.

Although a few kachina are strong enforcers of Hopi law, most are friendly. During kachina ceremonies, dancers dressed as kachina spirits bring gifts of kachina dolls for children. These dolls are then hung from house rafters so the children can learn their names and what powers they have.

Kachina may come and go, depending on the needs of the Hopi. In modern times, new kachina have visited the Hopi to help them deal with such 20th-century problems as unemployment.

Unlike the Hopi creator, Masau-u, the kachina are not worshipped. But they are respected, which is why there are so many Kachina ceremonies in the Hopi calendar. Ceremonies begin at the winter solstice (the shortest day of the year, in December) and end just after the summer solstice (the longest day, in late June). The Hopi believe that the mountain-dwelling kachina temporarily inhabit the dancers who impersonate them. After the dance the kachina return to their homes in the San Francisco Mountains to the southwest.

Butterfly Whorls

This Hopi girl, photographed around the turn of the century, wears her hair in butterfly whorls. This characteristic hairstyle indicates that she is old enough to marry.

David Risling

In 1967 Hupa tribe member David Risling (born 1921) read that most teachers' understanding of Native American history was based on Hollywood Western movies. With other concerned Indian parents, he successfully worked for accurate teaching of Native American history in schools. He designed the first Native American Studies program in the country, and co-founded the first Indian-run college, where students study traditional culture as well as academic subjects.

Council have divided the Hopi people through much of this century. For example, traditionalists protest the council's leasing Black Mesa to a coal company. Since 1966, mining in areas shared by the Hopi and Navajo has caused pollution, as well as conflict within the tribes. But the Hopi are united in the struggle to retrieve sacred objects taken to museums without tribal consent.

Education is a major concern of the Hopi. To keep children in school, Hopi biology professor Frank Dukepoo started the National Native American Honor Society in 1981. Indian students in the fourth grade or above who have had perfect grades for one semester may join. Dukepoo has given awards to more than 1,200 children in public ceremonies. He says the awards celebrate the Hopi belief in "hard work, high expectations, treating people nice, and being driven by the Great Spirit."◄

HUPA

- **LANGUAGE FAMILY: ATHAPASKAN**
- **LIFEWAYS: FISHING & GATHERING**
- **LOCATION: CALIFORNIA**
- **THEIR OWN NAME: NATINOOK-WA**

CALIFORNIA

The Hupa's original name was the same as their valley, Where the Trails Return. Presently, the 4,300-member tribe is located on twelve square miles of ancestral land in northwestern California. Their Takimildin Village is an ancient spiritual center. An 1849 treaty gave the Hupa the largest reservation in California. But, since 1861, federal land restrictions have created conflict with the neighboring Yurok. In 1978 the government seized Hupa timberland, which the tribe wants back. Forest management involves the people's deepest spiritual and environmental commitments.◄

HURON

- **LANGUAGE FAMILY:** IROQUOIAN
- **LIFEWAYS:** HUNTING, FARMING, & TRADING
- **LOCATION:** OKLAHOMA & QUEBEC
- **THEIR OWN NAME:** WYANDOTTE

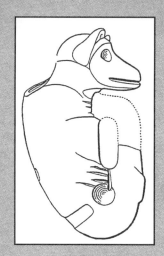

NORTHEAST

The Huron are descended from Great Lakes tribes called the Wyandotte (Island People). In 1590, four Wyandotte tribes formed a confederacy in what is now Ontario, Canada. They became great traders among the Northeast tribes. Canoeing lakes and rivers from the Subarctic to the Southeast, they came into conflict with the powerful Iroquois. A Huron called the Peacemaker devised the Great Law of Peace, which united the Iroquoian-speaking tribes.

Competing European fur traders arrived in 1609 and opened new conflicts among the Iroquoian tribes. The Wyandotte sided with the French, who called them Huron.

MISSIONARIES War began when the Iroquois joined the English against the French and Huron. Traders brought alcohol, which confused people, and guns, which made killing easier. European diseases killed half the Huron. Missionaries tried to convince the tribe that its traditional beliefs did not work. Soon the Huron fled to Quebec and Ohio.

Those who went to Ohio were forced to Oklahoma by the United States Army in 1857. They settled in Wyandotte, near the Seneca-Cayuga. Their tribal status was terminated in 1956, but they regained it after a struggle in 1978. Today, the 3,617-member tribe is known as the Wyandotte. It has many programs to help elders and students. Its historians are publishing books and building a museum and library to preserve Wyandotte culture. Every year, the tribe joins the Miami to celebrate Indian Heritage Days. ◄

Pipe

This Huron animal pipe is made of gray and purple slate. Pipe smoking was usually part of a ritual or ceremony. Huron spiritual belief was based on a supreme female deity and other life-giving gods. The Huron also believed there were two sides to the soul, and the goal of one's existence was to unite the two sides.

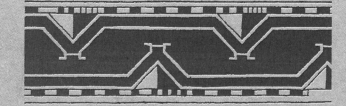

Moosehair Embroidery

The Huron decorated jewelry and clothing with dyed moosehair embroidery. These floral motifs show how Huron designs were influenced by the French and Dutch, who arrived in the 17th century.

Snow Spirits

Inuit healers wore masks such as the seal spirit mask (right) during ceremonies called Messenger Feasts. Animal spirits helped healers cure sickness, predict the future, and change the weather. Helper spirits such as the *palraiyuk* (below) and the creature on the left were invisible to all but healers.

Family Dog Sled

Inuit families raised Huskies to pull their loaded sleds across the tundra. In the 1880s a pack of three or more dogs would pull large loads over long distances. Today, dog teams are being replaced by snowmobiles, but the dogs are still trained for the sport of dog-sled racing.

INUIT

- **LANGUAGE FAMILY: ESKALEUT**
- **LIFEWAYS: HUNTING & FISHING**
- **LOCATION: NORTHWEST TERRITORIES, GREENLAND, & ALASKA**
- **THEIR OWN NAME: INUIT**

ARCTIC

Arctic people are often called Eskimos. This name is wrong. Eskimo was the name given to the Inuit by their southern neighbors, the Athapaskan peoples (Subarctic). It means Eaters of Raw Meat, and was meant as an insult. The Arctic people call themselves Inuit, which means The People. They inhabit a huge territory, from Greenland to western Alaska, and are divided into two subgroups: the Yup'ik, who live on Alaska's Pacific coast, and the Iñupiat, who live along the Arctic coast of Alaska, Canada, and Greenland. The two groups speak different dialects of the same language. The real difference between them, however, concerns their environments.

FORESTS Western Alaska does not freeze over in winter. Like the Aleut, the Yup'ik hunt such sea mammals as seals, whales, and walruses from their boats year-round. Also, forests stretch to the sea in many parts of Yup'ik territory—such thick forests that the Yup'ik must hunt by canoe. They use logs to build their homes.

Each village traditionally had a community house, where festivals and ceremonies were held during the long winter months. Around the end of October, the Yup'ik held a Halloween-like event. Two men would put on ragged clothing and silly masks and beg food from the women. Then they would feast on the food with the other men.

Storytelling was another important part of Yup'ik life. Women and girls did the storytelling, using a carved wooden blade called the story-knife to draw illustrations in the dirt or snow. Symbols for such interrelated words as *man* and *hunt*, or *woman* and *basket* formed a unique written language.

The other Inuit, the Iñupiat, live in a colder place. Their Arctic coast home is ice-bound all winter. Waiting for seals at their breathing holes in the ice is the only kind of hunting that goes on during the long winter nights. The absence of wood leads the Iñupiat to build their famous iglus, an Inuit word that means "house of ice."

CEREMONIES AND SPIRITS Perhaps because their environment is so bleak, the Iñupiat have an especially rich spiritual life. They believe that each person has not one but three souls. One is an immortal spirit that leaves a person's body when he or she dies and goes to live in the spirit world. The second, known as the "breath of life," ceases to exist at death. And the third, or name-soul, is reborn when babies are named after their deceased relatives. This gives children strength to survive infancy. It guards adults against the many dangers of Arctic life.

The Inuit have also developed ways of protecting themselves from modern dangers. In recent times, Arctic resources such as gold, oil, whales, and salmon have attracted companies from the United States, Canada, and other countries. These companies have not always respected the Arctic environment or the rights of native people. The Inuit have formed groups to defend themselves in court. They have won land and a share of the region's wealth.

While efforts to protect hunting grounds continue, new sources of income are used to teach native language and traditions to young people. Inuit preschoolers learn Eskaleut as their first language. By elementary school, they can do tribal dances. Traditional Inuit community houses have been created as places where young people can learn life skills from elders. ◄

▶ Hood Pouch

In 1912, Inuit girls and women still carried the babies of the family in the hoods of their traditional parkas. This kept babies warm and nearby, while the women had their hands free to go about their daily chores.

▶ Susan Aglukark

Susan Aglukark (born 1967) is a popular Inuit musician who successfully combines tribal identity and urban topics in her songs. Aglukark, whose Inuit name means Scarred from Burns, is called the Arctic Rose. She was the first Inuit to sign with a major recording company, and she hopes her success will encourage self-confidence in Arctic youth.

Joe Vetter

Joe Vetter, an Ioway Indian, was photographed in 1903 wearing a bear-claw necklace and holding a tomahawk. Bear claws were hard to get, so they were especially valuable. They were typically made into chiefs' necklaces.

Mohawk Chiefs

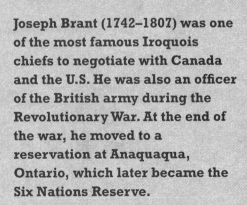

Chief Tiyanoga (c.1680–1755) went to London in 1710, sent there by British colonists who wanted him and the king of England to form an alliance to fight the French in North America. Near the end of his life, Tiyanoga fought at the Battle of Lake George in the French and Indian War.

Joseph Brant (1742–1807) was one of the most famous Iroquois chiefs to negotiate with Canada and the U.S. He was also an officer of the British army during the Revolutionary War. At the end of the war, he moved to a reservation at Anaquaqua, Ontario, which later became the Six Nations Reserve.

IOWAY

- **LANGUAGE FAMILY: SIOUIAN**
- **LIFEWAYS: PLANTING, HUNTING, & TRADING**
- **LOCATION: KANSAS, NEBRASKA, & OKLAHOMA**
- **THEIR OWN NAME: PAXOJE**

PLAINS

The Ioway lived in what is now Iowa, Minnesota, and Missouri. They lived in clans, planted corn, and hunted buffalo. After the Civil War, the federal government divided the tribe, relocating one group to White Cloud, Kansas. The rest were moved to Perkins, Oklahoma. Today the tribe is resisting a proposed toxic waste dump on its burial grounds. In the 1970s the combined 2,455 Ioway received $8 million in a land claims settlement. The tribe holds a yearly rodeo and makes the ribbonwork that adorns powwow dancers.◀

IROQUOIS

- **LANGUAGE FAMILY: IROQUOIAN**
- **LIFEWAYS: HUNTING, TRADING, & FARMING**
- **LOCATION: NEW YORK & QUEBEC**
- **THEIR OWN NAME: HAUDENOSAUNEE**

NORTHEAST

Six nations form the Iroquois Confederacy: the Onondaga, Mohawk, Cayuga, Seneca, Oneida, and Tuscarora. All except the Tuscarora are descended from corn-growing people called Owasco, who lived between the Hudson River and Lake Erie from A.D. 100 to 1300. The Tuscarora are Iroquoian-speakers from the Southeast. (They joined the Iroquois after fleeing war in the Southeast in 1722.)

Iroquois spiritual leaders say the Owasco were given the first plant, the sacred tobacco, by the

creator. Long ago, people discovered the bones of dinosaurs, and the ancient Iroquois Alligator and Turtle dances were devoted to these extinct animals.

The confederacy is governed by the Grand Council of Chiefs. Each nation's chief is invited to the council by messengers carrying strings of wampum beads. A chief tries to have a "good mind," which means he must be wise and kind. If he fails in this, the clan mother talks to him. After three warnings the clan can remove him if he doesn't listen to her.

The Iroquois hold thirteen different ceremonies each year. The largest are the Midwinter Renewal and Green Corn Harvest ceremonies. The sacred foods eaten at these gatherings are called the Three Sisters: corn, beans, and squash. Strawberry Thanksgiving is celebrated when strawberries come up in the spring. It reminds the Iroquois of the creator's gift of health and that the path to the Sky World (in the afterlife) is lined with strawberries.

GAMES During the ceremonies children play such traditional games as lacrosse and snow snake. Snow snakes are sticks, spears, or miniature canoes that are raced down icy trenches in snowy hillsides. Lacrosse and snow snake are Iroquois national sports. The Iroquois believe one can judge a society as good or bad by the way children and old people are treated. Their sachem, or prophet, Handsome Lake warned that troubled times begin when elders and children are not respected. He also predicted that pollution would endanger the world.

At the time Europeans arrived, Iroquois influence spread from Canada to the Carolinas and from Maine to the Mississippi River. The confederacy's democracy was based on peace, justice, sharing, and the equality of all people. Men and women had equal authority. The confederacy influenced the English colonists' Albany Plan of Union and the United States Constitution. Using an Iroquois expression, Thomas Jefferson referred

The Longhouse

Haudenosaunee means People of the Longhouse. Although the Iroquois lived in wooden longhouses, the word *longhouse* means much more than a type of dwelling. The Iroquois consider all of New York to be their longhouse, and each nation represents a different door.

The Clans

Three clans—Turtle, Wolf, and Bear—are common to all Iroquois nations. Members of different tribes consider themselves family if they are in the same clan. Clan membership is inherited from the mother's family. Clan mothers are the teachers and guardians of ceremonies.

The Tree of Peace

The Iroquois were united by the Peacemaker and his Great Law of Peace (Huron). When he handed down his law, the Iroquois buried their weapons under the Tree of Peace. The Great Law says all life is equal, and that by protecting plants and animals, people protect themselves. The law requires that leaders consider the effect of their actions on the seventh generation to come.

▶ Bridge Crossing

Although the Jay Treaty of 1794 ensured the Iroquois freedom to trade and travel across the U.S.-Canadian border at the Saint Lawrence Seaway, it was not until 1969 that the Canadian government actually recognized these rights. Each year the Indian Defense League honors the victory with a march across the bridge at this border.

▶ Chief Masseslow

Masseslow, chief of the Kalispel tribe at the end of the 19th century, was a Catholic convert. By the mid-1800s, several Catholic missions had been established in Kalispel territory.

▶ On Horseback

Kalispel Indians were photographed on horseback and in traditional dress in 1914. When the Lewis and Clark expedition met the Kalispel in 1805, the tribe counted 1,600 people in three bands. Today, descendants live on a reservation in Usk, Washington, just north of Spokane.

to the Constitution as a "tree of peace."

Nevertheless, after the Revolutionary War, George Washington sent soldiers to "extinguish" those Iroquois who had fought with the British. Between 1778 and 1780, soldiers burned Iroquois villages and cornfields, slaughtered men, raped women, and forced the people onto reservations.

The Iroquois have survived wars, European diseases, the loss of their lands, and the banning of their ceremonies. Today, they are a politically conscious nation with 60,000 members. They maintain tribal unity and self-rule, issue their own passports, and publish several newspapers. They use state and federal courts to fight for land rights, stop highways, end mining on burial grounds, and retrieve sacred objects from museums. Iroquois parents are working to reform school systems and educate their children traditionally. Iroquois spiritual leaders travel the world to speak out for the rights of native peoples everywhere. ◀

KALISPEL

- **LANGUAGE FAMILY:** SALISHAN
- **LIFEWAYS:** FISHING
- **LOCATION:** WASHINGTON & MONTANA
- **THEIR OWN NAME:** KALISPEL

PLATEAU

The Kalispel are also known as the Pend d'Oreille, French for Earring, because both men and women wore large shell earrings. Their homeland lies along the Pend Oreille River in northeast Washington State and southeast British Columbia. Salmon was their main food and the center of their spirituality. In 1887 some Kalispel were moved to the Flathead Reservation in Montana. Today, 250 Washington Kalispel run a cooperative fish-and-game store. Like their Northwest Coast neighbors, they sponsor an annual potlatch. ◀

KAW

- **LANGUAGE FAMILY: SIOUIAN**
- **LIFEWAYS: FARMING**
- **LOCATION: OKLAHOMA**
- **THEIR OWN NAME: KONZA**

PLAINS

Originally known as the Konza, the Kaw are related to the Sioux. Before 1600 they migrated from the Ohio Valley to the Kansas River. When Kansas was organized as a territory in 1854, white settlers moved in. Chief Al-le-go-wa-ho fought to hold onto Kaw land in the 1860s. But by 1873 the tribe had been forced onto a reservation in Oklahoma.

Today, about 1,700 Kaw own tribal businesses in Oklahoma. They built a Supreme Court building and ceremonial center in 1992. The Kaw prefer to keep their spirituality private, yet they still perform the Grass Dance at yearly powwows (Shoshone). ◄

KICKAPOO

- **LANGUAGE FAMILY: ALGONQUIAN**
- **LIFEWAYS: FARMING, HUNTING, & GATHERING**
- **LOCATION: OKLAHOMA, TEXAS, KANSAS, & MEXICO**
- **THEIR OWN NAME: KICWIGAPAWA**

NORTHEAST

Before 1667 the Kickapoo lived around Lake Michigan with their Sac and Fox relatives. By 1862 the federal government had moved the tribe to Kansas. Some Kickapoo fled to Mexico. U.S. soldiers forced half of them back to Oklahoma, but most escaped and returned to Mexico. Today, they are associated with small Kickapoo groups in Texas and Oklahoma. Their language is no longer spoken, but many of the 600 Kansas Kickapoo practice other native traditions, such as the Potawatomi Drum Religion and the Southeast Green Corn Dance. ◄

▶ Mon-Chonsia

Kaw chief Mon-Chonsia was painted by Charles Bird King, probably early in the 19th century. He is wearing a colorful turban and a peace medal given to him on a trip to Washington, D.C.

▶ A Battle

This drawing of Kickapoo in combat in southwest Texas was made around 1872. The Kickapoo warriors, on horseback and throwing long spears, are distinguished by their long hair plaits. The Kickapoo often raided in Texas in response to anti-Indian policies. The men with guns are either Texas rangers or U.S. soldiers.

Cradleboards

Native American women often used cradleboards—a kind of backpack—to secure their infants while they attended to other things. Each cradleboard was individually decorated. This early-20th-century photograph of a Kiowa mother shows how beautifully decorated the Kiowa cradleboards are. Toy cradleboards, such as the one this Kiowa girl held in an 1890 photograph, were popular among children.

Sitting Bear

This 1870 photograph shows Sitting Bear, a Kiowa warrior. After his son was killed in 1870, Sitting Bear gathered up his son's bones and carried them around with him wherever he went. This was because he could not return to his homeland to bury his son. In 1871 Sitting Bear was arrested for raiding a U.S. Army wagon train. He was killed while trying to escape.

KIOWA

- **LANGUAGE FAMILY:** UTO-AZTECAN
- **LIFEWAYS:** FARMING
- **LOCATION:** OKLAHOMA
- **THEIR OWN NAME:** KA'I-GWU

Kiowa settlements once lined rivers from what is now Montana all the way to Oklahoma. The oldest records show Kiowa living near present-day Virginia City, Montana. Their legends speak of a migration to the lower Plains during the 1700s. The tribe probably numbered about 3,000 at that time, and was divided into ten different bands.

The Kiowa's own name for themselves means The Principal People, perhaps to distinguish the tribe from its neighbors. Frequent battles with the Cheyenne, Arapaho, and Sioux forced the Kiowa to migrate toward the southwest along the Arkansas and Red rivers. During the early 1800s the Kiowa made peace with the Cheyenne and Arapaho. Then the Kiowa united with the Comanche, and together the two tribes raided frontier settlements in Mexico and Texas, capturing horses they traded with other Plains tribes.

TREATIES AND REVOLTS

The Kiowa's first treaty with the U.S. government came in 1837. They signed the Medicine Lodge Treaty in 1867, and by the next year the Kiowa had been completely driven onto the Kiowa-Comanche-Apache Reservation. Although the Kiowa-Apache were said to be friendly to whites, the tribes joined the Comanche from 1874 to 1875 for one last, unsuccessful, revolt against the United States. The tribes surrendered at the Kiowa Agency in 1876.

In 1900 the federal government claimed more than three-quarters of the 2.5-million-acre Kiowa reservation. By then, war and disease had reduced the Kiowa to about 1,165 people.

The Kiowa value their traditional arts and customs. A group of young Kiowa painters known as the Kiowa Five exhibited at the 1927 American Federation of Arts Convention and the 1928 European International Art Festival. During the 1930s, Kiowa and Cheyenne women formed the Woman's Heart Society to revive beadwork and moccasin making. Today, well-known Kiowa artists include T.C. Cannon and Mirac Creepingbear. Several Kiowa artists recently illustrated the tribe's history with ten huge murals that enrich the Kiowa Nation Culture Museum in Carnegie, Oklahoma.

The largest Kiowa settlement in Oklahoma— 9,000 people—is near Carnegie. The Kiowa hold an annual homecoming powwow with the Apache and Comanche, re-creating the traditional celebration that was held when warriors returned from battle. ◀

KLAMATH

- **LANGUAGE FAMILY:** PENUTIAN
- **LIFEWAYS:** FISHING & GATHERING
- **LOCATION:** OREGON
- **THEIR OWN NAME:** AUKSNI

PLATEAU

The Klamath (People of the Lake) lived near the headwaters of the Klamath River in northern California and southern Oregon. Three regions meet here—the Plateau, California, and the Great Basin. The Klamath shared traits with the peoples in these regions. Like Great Basin and California peoples, they gathered roots and wild potatoes. Like Plateau peoples, they fished for salmon and migrated from winter earth lodges to summer homes, or wickiups, of matted reeds (Plains).

Like their Modoc neighbors, the Klamath

▶ **N. Scott Momaday**

N. Scott Momaday (born 1934) is the son of a Kiowa father and a Cherokee mother. A professor of English at Stanford University, he has been awarded both a Guggenheim fellowship and a Pulitzer Prize for fiction. Among his many works are *The Way to Raining Mountain*, *The Gourd Dancer*, *The Names*, and *Angle of Geese and Other Poems*.

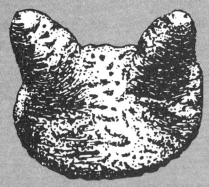

▶ **Muller**

This two-horned grinding stone, or muller, made from lava slabs was used by Klamath women to grind the shells of wokas seeds, a common food of the region. The women held the horns and crushed the seeds with the flat underside of the muller. The pulp of ground wokas seeds was boiled to make a gruel. Wokas seeds were also dried and roasted.

▶ Woodpecker

The woodpecker was very useful to the peoples of California for, among other things, its fine bones and feathers. Men often wore the feathers in their hair, while women used the bones for necklaces and earrings. Sometimes, the Klamath even used sharpened bones to pierce their noses.

▶ Kutchin Council Seal

The Kutchin seal features a caribou, the tribe's namesake. Council gatherings begin with a prayer recited by an elder in the Gwich'in language. For example:

O Great Spirit
Make me wise, so that I understand
the things you have taught my people.
Let me learn the lesson you have hidden
in every leaf and rock.
I seek strength, not to be greater than my
brother
but to fight against my greatest enemy—
myself.

respected verbal skills and chose leaders and healers for their speeches. Male leaders ran the group's daily affairs. Healers were spiritual leaders and were often women. Today, healers lead Thanksgiving ceremonies celebrating roots and suckerfish (Umatilla).

In 1869 the Klamath and Modoc were forced onto a single reservation. The Modoc rebelled. The Klamath did not, and managed to hold on to their land when the 1887 Dawes Act would have divided it. Valuable Ponderosa pine on Klamath land supported the tribe for many years. But because of the Klamath's timber wealth, the federal government terminated the tribe in 1954. Most of the people had to sell their reservation land to pay taxes. After years of hard work, they regained tribal status in 1986, but did not regain their land. Today, the 2,700 Klamath teach their children beadwork and basket making for sale at powwows. Children study native-language textbooks to ensure that the language will continue to be used.◀

KUTCHIN

- **LANGUAGE FAMILY:** ATHAPASKAN
- **LIFEWAYS:** HUNTING & FISHING
- **LOCATION:** ALASKA
- **THEIR OWN NAME:** GWICH'IN

SUBARCTIC

The Kutchin name means People of the Deer, because the tribe traditionally followed the herds. Today, most Kutchin still hunt, but they have settled in villages with other Athapaskan people (Beaver). There are few roads in eastern Alaska, so most people travel by plane, boat, or snowmobile.

Each village has a school, so children do not have to go far from home. Village elders advise leaders and lead ceremonies such as the potlatch. In the 1960s the Kutchin group Our Land Speaks worked with Arctic groups to regain land from the U.S. government.◀

KUTENAI

- **LANGUAGE FAMILY: KUTENAI**
- **LIFEWAYS: HUNTING**
- **LOCATION: IDAHO, MONTANA, WASHINGTON, & BRITISH COLUMBIA**
- **THEIR OWN NAME: KUTENAI**

PLATEAU

The Kutenai hunted deer and buffalo on the plateaus of Idaho, Montana, Washington, and British Columbia. This traveling lifestyle explains why today's Kutenai are spread out on seven reservations in these areas. Like their Flathead neighbors, the 2,000 Kutenai held on to their language and ceremonies. They are independent people and prefer to keep their spirituality private. In 1974 the Idaho Kutenai filed a land claim by sending a "declaration of war" to President Gerald Ford. He granted them a town-sized reservation in Bonners Ferry, Idaho. ◄

KWAKIUTL

- **LANGUAGE FAMILY: WAKASHAN**
- **LIFEWAYS: FISHING**
- **LOCATION: BRITISH COLUMBIA**
- **THEIR OWN NAME: KWAGIUTL**

NORTHWEST COAST

There is only one true Kwakiutl tribe. It lives on northern Vancouver Island. Kwakiutl means Beach on the North Side of the River. For years historians have mistakenly called thirty British Columbia tribes the Kwakiutl. That's because these people all spoke a Wakashan dialect called Kwakwala.

The Kwakiutl and Nootka shared ceremonies and often intermarried. They also raided their southern neighbors, the Coast Salish, for property and slaves. In summer each band built rows of small

Salish Kootenai College

Before 1980 many Kutenai children dropped out of school. In 1977 the Flathead Reservation tribes founded Two Eagle River School and Salish Kootenai College. The college offers academic and vocational associate degrees and a bachelor's program in human services. About fifty Indian students graduate from there each year.

Clan Ceremony

Kwakiutl dancers wore masks representing the totem spirits of their clans. According to legend, Kwakiutl ancestors learned the dances from the spirits themselves. In one story, Chief Wakiash was carried off by a large raven to a village of spirits in human form. The surprised spirits gladly shared their totem dances and songs with the chief, who then taught them to his clan.

Kwakiutl Visions

Today's Kwakiutl Band Council has chosen a tribal logo of a frog atop a copper eagle (above). Copper art was symbolic of high status. The mask below represents the fearsome sea monster Sisiutl, whose two heads search for those who cannot control their fear. Legends say that those who stand their ground when they face Sisiutl will be bestowed with magic and will never be alone again.

A Dress of Shells

This Lakota girl is wearing a deerskin dress that is decorated with cowrie shells. Cowrie are small marine creatures that live in warm waters. The Lakota may have gotten these shells through trade with Native Americans from the Southeast.

wooden cabins along the steep, rocky coast to be close to good fishing. The area was famous for large clams, fine salmon, and many berry patches. A wealthy tribe, the Kwakiutl gave elaborate potlatches and built large winter homes.

In 1849, Kwakiutl bands settled by a British fort to trade, but by 1862 smallpox and disputes with the British had cost many lives. About 2,000 Kwakiutl were moved to reserves in 1880.

Today, 144 Kwakiutl live on the Fort Rupert Reserve. Another 297 tribe members live nearby. The tribe runs hatcheries and a shipyard. In 1980 the tribe opened two musems to house potlatch items returned from an Ottawa museum. Once, 99 percent of students did not finish high school, but that changed when the band opened a tribal school in 1979. Children who learn the Kwakiutlan language, dances, art, and history often continue their educations at community colleges. ◄

LAKOTA

- **LANGUAGE FAMILY: SIOUIAN**
- **LIFEWAYS: HUNTING**
- **LOCATION: NORTH & SOUTH DAKOTA**
- **THEIR OWN NAME: LAKOTA**

PLAINS

The Lakota are part of the Sioux nation that migrated to the source of the Mississippi River around A.D. 1000. After their traditional enemies, the Ojibwa, received French guns in the early 1700s, the Sioux were forced to the Plains.

When the Sioux moved to the Plains, the Lakota occupied the buffalo country of what became South Dakota, Montana, Wyoming, and Nebraska. Lakota claim South Dakota's Black Hills as the home of their Great Spirit.

The Lakota include seven bands: Hunkpapa, Miniconjou, Oglala, Brule, Sans Arcs, Oohenunpa, and Sihasapa. Until the 1800s the Lakota bands built tipis, hunted buffalo, and fought the Crow and Pawnee. In the 1830s whites began traveling through Lakota country to Oregon and California, disrupting the Indians' way of life.

RED CLOUD Oglala chief Red Cloud's protests against the Bozeman Trail through Indian territory resulted, in 1863, in the Red Cloud War. By 1868 some Lakota had agreed to stay close to Fort Laramie in present-day Wyoming or on the Great Sioux Reservation in western South Dakota. They agreed to do this because the war had deprived them of food and clothing. Red Cloud held out and eventually got the Bozeman Trail closed.

During the 1870s white prospectors flocked into the Black Hills looking for gold. Colonel George Custer led government troops to protect them. The soldiers slaughtered the buffalo and tried to push the Sioux onto reservations. The Indians were horrified that sacred land could be mined. Oglala chief Crazy Horse and Hunkpapa chief Sitting Bull led 3,000 Lakota and Cheyenne to defeat Custer at the famous Battle of the Little Bighorn.

Under the 1887 Dawes Act the Sioux lost 100 million acres of land. Medicine men Short Bull and Kicking Bear encouraged the Ghost Dance to protect their people (Great Basin). Settlers' fears of the dance contributed to the Wounded Knee Massacre, where, in December 1890, Big Foot's band of 260 unarmed Lakota men, women, and children were slaughtered on South Dakota's Pine Ridge Reservation. By then, bands of Lakota lived on six different reservations in North and South Dakota and one in Saskatchewan, Canada.

Today, Lakota still honor their veterans as strong warriors. Lakota men volunteered in World War I, World War II, the Korean War, and Vietnam. When they returned, the Lakota held

▶ Custer

George Armstrong Custer's wagon train was photographed crossing sacred Sioux hunting grounds in South Dakota in 1874. His presence there was a violation of the Fort Laramie Treaty of 1868, which guaranteed the Sioux exclusive rights to their Black Hills lands. Two years later, the Sioux War of 1876 broke out, and Custer was killed at the Little Bighorn.

▶ Mary Crow Dog

The Lakota writer Mary Crow Dog was born in 1953 on the Rosebud Sioux Reservation. Before her marriage to the Sioux medicine man Leonard Crow Dog, her name was Mary Brave Bird. She gave birth to a child during the siege of Wounded Knee in 1973. Her book *Lakota Woman* tells about the hardships of reservation life. Her latest book is called *Ohitaka Woman*.

Sacred Circle

A common sight on the reservation, the four directions symbol is key to Lakota spiritual practice. Each direction—north, south, east, and west—is linked to a particular spirit. The symbol is often made of wood, bent into a circle and sometimes adorned with feathers or porcupine quills. This photograph, taken by a Lakota boy in North Dakota, shows a four directions symbol attached to the rearview mirror of his parents' car, probably to offer protection to the family.

qʷidiččaʔa·tx̌i·c
"People of the Cape
it is theirs . . .

hu·ʔiya·p qʷa·bito·wis
hu·ʔe·yʔukʷi·
. . .bringing it back the
way it was long ago."

Makah

The Makah language, part of the Wakashan language family, was spoken by the Makah people, who lived on Cape Flattery in northwest Washington State. Teachers at the Makah Cultural and Research Center in Neah Bay, Washington, teach the Makah language to future generations. The words above are part of the Makah Museum's motto.

ceremonies that included gift-giving, songs, Sun Dances, and cleansing in sweat lodges. Later, in the 1970s, Lakota activists became leaders in the Red Power Movement.

In 1990 the Lakota completed the Big Foot Memorial Ride. Every year, riders repeat the journey Big Foot and his people made in 1890 before they were massacred. The Lakota believe that by doing this they help heal the spirits of those who were killed more than 100 years ago. The youngest Big Foot Memorial rider, Wanbli Numpa Afraid of Hawk, was eight years old when he completed the ride.

Today, about 59,000 Lakota live on one of six reservations or hold jobs in major cities. The Pine Ridge Reservation has the largest Lakota population—23,000 Oglala. Most residents there work in small businesses and casinos.◀

LANGUAGE

The Native Americans of North America spoke more than a thousand different languages before Columbus arrived. Except for South America, no continent had so many different languages. Many of these languages are still spoken today.

Like languages everywhere, Indian languages can be grouped together by similar vocabulary, sentence structure, verb forms, and other things. Two languages may be from the same family, but if speakers of those languages cannot understand each other, then the languages are considered different.

Most related Indian languages are spoken by people who live near each other. But that is not always the case. For example, most Athapaskan languages are spoken in the Canadian Subarctic. Yet the Navajo are an Athapaskan-speaking people who live in the Southwest United States.

Language Families

Region	ARCTIC				
Language	Eskaleut				
Tribe	Aleut				
	Inuit				

Region	CALIFORNIA				
Language	Athapaskan	Hokan	Numic	Penutian	Ritwan
Tribe	Hupa	Chumash	Luiseño	Maidu	Yurok
		Pomo		Miwok	
		Yana		Wintun	
				Yokuts	

Region	GREAT BASIN				
Language	Uto-Aztecan	Uto-Aztecan Numic			
Tribe	Ute	Bannock			
		Paiute			

Region	MESOAMERICA				
Language	Arawakan	Karifuna	Mayan	Nahuatlan	Unknown
Tribe	Arawak	Carib	Maya	Aztecs	Olmecs
				Toltecs	

Region	NORTHEAST	
Language	Algonquian	Iroquoian
Tribe	Abenaki	Cayuga
	Kickapoo	Huron
	Lenape	Iroquois
	Mahican	Mohawk
	Maliseet	Oneida
	Massachusetts	Onondaga
	Menominee	Seneca
	Miami	Susquehannock
	Micmac	Tuscarora
	Mohegan	
	Montauk-Shinnecock	
	Nipmuc	
	Ojibwa	
	Ottawa	
	Passamaquoddy	
	Pennacook	
	Penobscot	
	Peoria	
	Pequot	
	Potawatomi	
	Shawnee	
	Wampanoag	
	Wappinger	

Region	NORTHWEST COAST					
Language	Chinookan	Haida	Salishan	Tlingit	Tsimshian	Wakashan
Tribe	Chinook	Haida	Coast Salish	Tlingit	Tsimshian	Kwakiutl
						Makah
						Nootka

PLAINS

Language	Algonquian	Athapaskan	Caddoan	Siouian	Uto-Aztecan	Uto-Aztecan
Tribe	Arapaho	Sarcee	Arikara	Assiniboine	Kiowa	Numic
	Blackfeet		Caddo	Crow		Comanche
	Cheyenne		Pawnee	Gros Ventre		
	Sac and Fox		Tonkawa	Hidatsa		
			Wichita	Ioway		
				Kaw		
				Mandan		
				Missouria-Otoe		
				Omaha		
				Osage		
				Ponca		
				Sioux		
				Dakota		
				Lakota		
				Nakota		
				Winnebago		

PLATEAU

Language	Kutenai	Penutian	Sahaptian	Salishan	Uto-Aztecan
Tribe	Kutenai	Klamath	Nez Perce	Coeur d'Alene	Shoshone
		Modoc	Palouse	Flathead	
			Umatilla	Kalispel	
			Warm Springs	Spokan	
			Yakima		

SOUTHEAST

Language	Algonquian	Iroquoian	Muskogean	Siouian	Yuchi
Tribe	Powhatan	Cherokee	Alabama-Coushatta	Catawba	Yuchi
			Apalachee	Lumbee	
			Calusa	Quapaw	
			Chickasaw		
			Chitimacha		
			Choctaw		
			Creek		
			Natchez		
			Seminole		
			Timucua		
			Tunica-Biloxi		
			Yamasee		
			Yazoo		

SOUTHWEST

Language	Athapaskan	Hokan	Penutian	Tanoan	Unknown	Uto-Aztecan	Uto-Aztecan	Uto-Aztecan
Tribe	Apache	Havasupai	Pueblo	Pueblo	Cliff Dwellers	Yaqui	Numic	Pintan
	Navajo	Mojave	Zuni				Hopi	Pima
		Yavapai						Tohono O'odham
		Yuma						

SUBARCTIC

Language	Algonquian	Algonquian & French	Athapaskan
Tribe	Beothuk	Métis	Beaver
	Cree		Carrier
	Montagnais		Chipewyan
	Naskapi		Kutchin

Most Indian cultures were oral. They did not have a written language, so tribal elders kept track of their people's history and verbally passed on knowledge from generation to generation. Most Indians trace their history back many generations and have much knowledge about their world.

But oral culture, though often powerful, can also be fragile. If a single generation fails to pass on the wisdom of the tribe, it may be lost forever. This frequently happened when wars and European epidemics killed a tribe's eldest members. Today, many Native Americans are rediscovering their lost culture. Native American historians have searched out their tribal elders and have set up schools to pass the wisdom on to their children.

Some Native American cultures did have written language. The Aztecs and Maya, for example, used a complicated system of symbols that stood for words. Some of these symbols were carved into pyramids and told the history of royal families. ◄

LENAPE

- **LANGUAGE FAMILY:** ALGONQUIAN
- **LIFEWAYS:** FARMING, HUNTING, & GATHERING
- **LOCATION:** WISCONSIN, OKLAHOMA, & ONTARIO
- **THEIR OWN NAME:** LENNI-LENAPI

NORTHEAST

The Lenape are famous for writing the oldest history book in North America, the Walam Olum, or Red Score. It is a tribal record carved on reeds. British colonists named the Lenape the Delaware, after the Delaware River. Actually, the Lenape tribe was a confederacy that had settled most of what became Delaware, New Jersey, Pennsylvania, and southern New York. The other Algonquian-speaking tribes of the Northeast recognize Lenape territory as their place of origin. That is why they still call the

kish	=	**girl**
quil-se	=	**boy**
we-seena-low	=	**come eat dinner**
pon gose con	=	**sugar**
pannick	=	**potatoes**
no wana con	=	**bread**
nip pea	=	**drink**

▶ Peoria

The Peoria spoke a language similar to that of the Miami. Both languages were part of the Algonquian language family. Unfortunately, no scientific study of the Peoria language was conducted before it became extinct. All that is known about it is what was recorded by 17th- and 18th-century missionaries—including the words above.

"Those who were strong and those who had power came away, separating from those who remained living there."

"When all were friends Wolf Man was chief; and he was the first of these."

"...persons floating in from the east; the Whites were coming."

▶ Walam Olum

The Walam Olum, the sacred record of the Lenape, is carved on reeds. The story begins with the creation of the sun and stars and traces the tribe's great migration over a frozen sea. The two figures (above left) represent the powerful ones who migrated. The central figure represents Wolf Man, who was chief "when all were friends." The boat (right) is titled "People floating in from the east. The whites are coming....Who are they?"

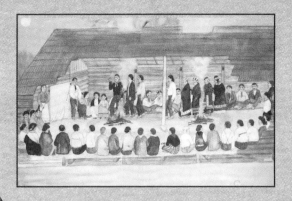

▶ Big House

Shawnee Earnest Spybuck painted this watercolor of a Lenape vision recital in 1912. During the ceremony, a narrator moves around two central fires in a Big House, a log cabin–style longhouse (Iroquois) while telling about his experiences with supernatural beings. The ceremony, which can last as long as twelve nights, includes prayers, fasting, dancing, and drumming.

▶ Indian Rights

In 1937, Luiseño Indian Rights Association members joined delegates representing 100 California tribes. They successfully lobbied California Congressman Harry R. Sheppard, who sponsored a bill giving them greater access to federal courts for land-claim suits.

Lenape tribe Grandfather.

The main Lenape clans were Turkey, Wolf, and Turtle. Big House, their Thanksgiving Ceremony, has been revived in Wisconsin. The twelve-day ceremony includes a venison feast, the lighting of a sacred fire, and prayers to Misinghalikun—the spirit of game animals.

Today, the largest Lenape community is in eastern Oklahoma, where about 10,000 are members of the Cherokee Nation. Another 1,000 Lenape in western Oklahoma form the only federally recognized Delaware tribe in the United States. There are some Lenape living among the Wisconsin Stockbridge-Munsee tribe (Mahican), and about 1,500 live in Ontario, Canada, with the Cayuga.

In 1992 the Lenape formed the Delaware Nation Grand Council, which helps organize powwows and baby-naming ceremonies. Most Lenape are members of the Native American Church (Comanche).◀

LUISEÑO

- **LANGUAGE FAMILY: NUMIC**
- **LIFEWAYS: HUNTING & GATHERING**
- **LOCATION: CALIFORNIA**
- **THEIR OWN NAME: LUISEÑO**

CALIFORNIA

The Luiseño formerly comprised local bands that roamed 1,500 square miles of coastal southern California. The tribe's name comes from the mission at San Luis Rey. The federal government did not recognize tribes it called Mission Indians. However, the Luiseño won a land-claim suit in 1891 and had become successful fruit growers by 1910. Today, they are in court again because dams have diverted their water supply. Programs are being developed for elders, schools, and libraries for the 1,650 tribe members, who honor their traditions in private ceremonies.◀

LUMBEE

- **LANGUAGE FAMILY:** SIOUIAN
- **LIFEWAYS:** FARMING & HUNTING
- **LOCATION:** NORTH CAROLINA
- **THEIR OWN NAME:** LUMBEE

SOUTHEAST

The Lumbee live in a swampy area on the North Carolina–South Carolina border. They settled there just south of Cherokee lands after losing their former land to the Iroquois.

Whites didn't want their swampy land, so the Lumbee were not forced to leave with other Southeast tribes. They have survived without a reservation of their own. Today, about 50,000 Lumbee live in Robeson County, North Carolina. They contribute to Pembroke State University's Native American Resource Center and publish a newspaper. ◀

▶ Routing the KKK

The Ku Klux Klan (KKK) is an extremist organization that is hostile to minority groups such as African-Americans, Native Americans, Catholics, and Jews. In January 1958 the Lumbee drove the KKK out of Robeson County, North Carolina. Charlie Warriax and Simeon Oxendine displayed the KKK flag they seized at that time.

MAHICAN

- **LANGUAGE FAMILY:** ALGONQUIAN
- **LIFEWAYS:** HUNTING, FISHING, & FARMING
- **LOCATION:** WISCONSIN
- **THEIR OWN NAME:** MUH-HE-CON-NE-OK

NORTHEAST

Muh-he-con-ne-ok means People of the Waters that Are Never Still. That water is the Hudson River, where the 4,000 Mahican were fur traders until diseases and colonial wars reduced them to 500 people by 1700 (Subarctic). They joined a Massachusetts mission village, but were forced west in 1783. Today, about 1,500 Mahican and Lenape descendants live on the Stockbridge-Munsee Reservation in Bowler, Wisconsin. In the 1970s they built a museum and library, and have since revived their twelve-day Thanksgiving Ceremony (Lenape). ◀

▶ Club

This fish-shaped wooden club with an iron blade was used by fur-trading Mahican to kill and skin beavers and otters. It was given to a white traveler in the late 18th century at the present-day Stockbridge-Munsee Reservation.

Bear Power

The Maidu, like many tribes, perform Bear dances to honor the bear because it is considered a splendid animal and a powerful guardian spirit. When hunters properly honored a bear's remains, it was traditionally believed that the bear's spirit would be reborn.

Killer Whale

The killer whale is the logo of the Makah Museum, symbolizing the tribe's respect for the whale. Before going fishing, the Makah often waited for the killer whale to drive fish close to the shore.

MAIDU

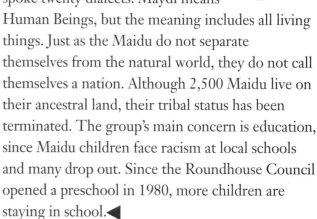

- **LANGUAGE FAMILY: PENUTIAN**
- **LIFEWAYS: HUNTING & GATHERING**
- **LOCATION: CALIFORNIA**
- **THEIR OWN NAME: MAYDI**

The Maidu were divided into three regional groups that spoke twenty dialects. Maydi means Human Beings, but the meaning includes all living things. Just as the Maidu do not separate themselves from the natural world, they do not call themselves a nation. Although 2,500 Maidu live on their ancestral land, their tribal status has been terminated. The group's main concern is education, since Maidu children face racism at local schools and many drop out. Since the Roundhouse Council opened a preschool in 1980, more children are staying in school. ◄

MAKAH

- **LANGUAGE FAMILY: WAKASHAN**
- **LIFEWAYS: SEA HUNTING & FISHING**
- **LOCATION: WASHINGTON**
- **THEIR OWN NAME: QWIDICA**

The Makah's name for themselves is difficult to write in English letters. One of the tribe's challenges is that there are only about twelve people left who speak Makah fluently, though tribal educators are working with elders and young people to preserve the language. The word Makah is Klallam for Generous People. The Strait of Juan de Fuca separates the Makah of Washington's Olympic Peninsula from the Nootka of southwest Vancouver Island. Both groups were whalers and shared important ceremonies to attract whales and protect their hunters at sea. Many whale songs were required for a hunt. As they paddled their canoes, whalers sang these powerful songs of prayer, which came to them in their dreams.

In the mid-1800s, European traders brought diseases that killed more than half the Makah population. The Makah Reservation was formed in 1855, but the current reservation is smaller than the pre-treaty Makah territory. Because of the depletion of natural resources—especially fish—by outside commercial ventures, there is high unemployment among the Makah and many move away to find work. Today, about half of the 2,200 Makah live on the reservation.

In 1970 the Makah received a gift from a storm. The storm exposed a 400-year-old Makah village at Ozette. From beneath the mud, 55,000 objects were excavated and preserved. The tribe's Cultural and Research Center created a museum to display the objects. Since 1979 more than 250,000 visitors have come through its doors. ◀

trade
xuʔuya·

▶ Living Language

In 1978 the Makah developed a written language program with workbooks for teaching in the classroom. The Makah Cultural and Research Center in Neah Bay, Washington, records tribal songs and stories from the few elders who speak Makah.

MALISEET

- **LANGUAGE FAMILY: ALGONQUIAN**
- **LIFEWAYS: HUNTING & FISHING**
- **LOCATION: MAINE & NEW BRUNSWICK**
- **THEIR OWN NAME: PASTIMOKATIYEK**

NORTHEAST

The Maliseet and Passamaquoddy divided their Maine homeland by fishing grounds. Maliseet territory had more pollack, so the tribe called itself after that fish. Maliseet children could fish and guide canoes by age ten. In winter they heard stories about Turtle the clown and Snowshoe Hare the trickster. Today, 3,000 Maliseet live in Canada and Maine. In 1980, 560 Maliseet received land in a settlement they shared with the Penobscot and Passamaquoddy. Today, Maliseet community centers are teaching children the tribe's language and culture. ◀

▶ Community Gathering

On Corpus Christi Day in 1887, a group of Maliseet gathered at Kingsclear, New Brunswick, in Canada. Maliseet woodworking skills are evident from their finely constructed homes and carved canoes. The man at the center of the photograph is holding a carved paddle.

A Mandan Home

This painting shows the interior of a Mandan chief's lodge. The family is gathered around the hearth, where a fire was often lit under an opening in the roof. Mandan lodges were made of logs, branches, grass, and clay. Horses and other animals were sometimes kept in the lodges. Mandan lodges and domesticated animals were owned by women.

Mato-Tope

This 1830 painting shows Mandan chief Mato-Tope, whose name means Four Bears. Mato-Tope was himself a skilled painter. The eagle-feather headdress he is wearing is often used in American popular culture to symbolize the American Indian, but it may have originated with the Mandan and their Arikara and Hidatsa allies. Mato-Tope is also wearing bison horns and a long shirt of ermine skin. He died during the great smallpox epidemic of 1837.

MANDAN

- **LANGUAGE FAMILY:** SIOUIAN
- **LIFEWAYS:** FARMING
- **LOCATION:** NORTH DAKOTA
- **THEIR OWN NAME:** MANDAN

PLAINS

About 8,000 Mandan once occupied earth-lodge villages on the shores of the Heart River near present-day Mandan, North Dakota. They hunted buffalo and grew corn, beans, and squash. Their allies were the Arikara in central South Dakota and the Hidatsa to the north. The Mandan were known for pounded glass beads and figures.

In 1837 smallpox reduced the tribe to about 130 people. Survivors fled up the Missouri River and founded a village called Like-A-Fishhook. The 1851 Fort Laramie Treaty assigned the Mandan, Arikara, and Hidatsa more than 13 million acres of land in Montana, Wyoming, and North Dakota. By 1870 settlers had taken all but about 1 million acres of it. The three tribes then officially united as the Three Affiliated Tribes.

FLOOD In 1954 the U.S. Army Corps of Engineers dammed the Missouri River, flooding the reservation. The tribes' ranchers and farmers were forced onto less fertile land. The Mandan never recovered. Mandan clans were divided by the reservoir and many people moved to cities. Today, only a few of the 6,000 reservation Mandan are farmers or ranchers, and half of the 900,000-acre reservation has been leased to non-Indians. Some Mandan work for the tribal or federal governments. They hope that their new casino will provide more jobs.

Members of the three tribes often intermarry, yet the Mandan have their own language and customs. Their annual Twin Buttes Celebration highlights Mandan activities such as War Bonnet dances, beadwork, and quilting. ◀

Massachusetts

- **LANGUAGE FAMILY:** ALGONQUIAN
- **LIFEWAYS:** FARMING, FISHING, & GATHERING
- **LOCATION:** BERMUDA
- **THEIR OWN NAME:** MASSACHUSETTS

NORTHEAST

Massachusetts means By the Great Hill, after the Blue Hills along the Massachusetts coast. The Massachusetts tribe is related to the Nipmuc and Mahican and followed Algonquian customs (Northeast). They fished and grew corn, beans, and squash. Smallpox killed most of the 4,000 Massachusetts before 1620. The remaining people joined mission villages, where they lost their traditions. Some were shipped to the Caribbean as slaves. Today, some Indians of Massachusetts and African-American descent live in Bermuda.

Modern-Day Massachusetts

The Pharaoh family (above) of the Massachusetts tribe posed for a photographer in Bermuda, as did this young Massachusetts girl (left). The Massachusetts have been in Bermuda for 350 years.

Maya

- **LANGUAGE FAMILY:** MAYAN
- **LIFEWAYS:** FARMING, GATHERING, & FISHING
- **LOCATION:** MEXICO & GUATEMALA
- **THEIR OWN NAME:** LOCAL NAMES

MESOAMERICA

The Maya lived in mountainous regions of what is now Guatemala and Mexico, as well as lowland regions of present-day Belize and Honduras. In Huehuetenango, Guatemala, people started growing corn in 2600 B.C. Members of the twelve Mayan groups began migrating north into Mexico about 800 years later.

Mayan civilization reached its peak in about A.D. 300. Adopting ideas from the Olmecs, the Maya built incredible cities—Tikal, Chichén Itzá, Copán, and Palenque—without wheelbarrows,

Rabbit Scribe

The Mayan rabbit god, shown here as a scribe on an 8th-century painted vase, is using a brush pen to write in a volume bound in jaguar hide. The book recorded important events such as marriages, deaths, and wars.

Mayan Sculpture

This ancient stucco sculpture was found in Palenque, a grand city of palaces and temples built around A.D. 600. The architectural designs there included latticed roofs and stucco sculptures. Astronomers there tracked the movements of the stars and planets from the palace tower.

Ceiba Tree

Ceiba trees grow quite large, with enormous trunks, leafy branches, and bell-shaped, crimson flowers. Some ceibas even grow brown pods filled with a silky substance that can be used to make a fiber called kapok. Mayans may have valued the ceiba for its fine bark, beautiful flowers, and fiber-bearing fruit.

shovels, or oxen. They created sophisticated calendars and a written language, and they independently invented the idea of zero.

The Maya also wrote history books on tree-bark paper. The Spanish burned most of the books, but two important texts survived—the Chilam Balam and the Popol Vuh. Both of these books include stories of the origin of the universe, formed by the gods Plumed Serpent and Heart of the Sky. They say that people were created from ground corn, with water added to make their blood (Mesoamerica).

OVER-POPULATION ▼▼▼ While the great period of Mayan achievement was over by A.D. 900, the last great city, Mayapán, did not fall until about 1450. Historians do not know why the cities declined, though over-population is a possible reason.

Today, more than 4 million Maya live much as their ancestors did, growing corn, beans, and chilies on farms called *milpas,* where everything is owned by the community. Many Maya speak no Spanish at all. Both men and women wear long, loose tunics and have long hair. They still gather in the old temples for month-long renewal ceremonies dedicated to Hachakyum, the creator. There they drink *balche* tea prepared in a sacred canoe, burn incense in gold pots shaped like human faces, and pray. When they emerge from the temple, they are painted with sacred jaguar spots.

The Maya survived colonization because, unlike the Aztecs, they had no central city to conquer. Their cities were mostly ceremonial centers, and the people farmed on scattered sites in dense forests. It took Spanish conquistadors 200 years to fully infiltrate the forests, and by the time they did, most of the Maya had slipped away. Although some things have not changed, the Maya feel the effects of a shrinking rain forest and the intrusion of grazing cattle and oil drilling on their lands. Mayan elder Chank'in Viejo says, "Every time a tree is cut down, a star falls from the sky."

A rebellion started in Chiapas in 1970 when the Mexican government began allowing private plantations to take over Mayan milpas.

In her autobiography, Quiché Maya Rigoberta Menchú—who won the Nobel Peace Prize in 1992 for leading the struggle for her people's land rights—describes life as a migrant worker on large plantations. The native people have no civil rights and are treated like serfs. They live in unhealthy conditions and are often victims of abuse by landowners.

In the 1980s the Guatemalan government forced millions of Mayan families into armed camps called model villages. More than 20,000 Maya were killed there. Many Maya fled to Mexico, where they joined their relatives in Chiapas. Together, they are fighting to keep their land and to be able to hold fair elections. ◄

► Helping Out

Today, Mayan children help their parents earn a living. This girl in an Oaxacan churchyard is selling woven crafts made by the women in her family. She is wearing a traditional handmade dress decorated with delicate embroidery. The boys in the fishing village of Puerto Escondido, Mexico, show traits of several tribes, as well as some Spanish ancestry. They join men in small fishing boats each morning to catch fish such as red snapper, which they sell to local restaurants.

MENOMINEE

- **LANGUAGE FAMILY: ALGONQUIAN**
- **LIFEWAYS: HUNTING, GATHERING, & GARDENING**
- **LOCATION: WISCONSIN**
- **THEIR OWN NAME: OMENOMENEW**

NORTHEAST

The Menominee call themselves Omenomenew, or Wild Rice People, because they harvested rice near the Great Lakes in what is now central Wisconsin and northern Michigan. Like other Algonquin of the Northeast, they built bark-cabin villages in winter and wigwams of reed mats in summer. The two main clans, the Thunderers and Bears, built different lodges for sweating, dreaming, and fasting. With the Ojibwa, they share Ma'nabush and Ma'nido spirit ceremonies.

The Menominee believed that children and

► Menominee Family

Before Europeans arrived, the Menominee constructed villages of bark cabins. Hide lodges served as temporary shelters while the Menominee hunted or traveled. This Wisconsin Menominee family was photographed in the early 1900s.

► Embroidery

When French fur traders arrived in the 1700s, they brought sewing materials that the Menominee used to create their elegant floral embroidery.

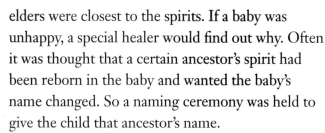

▶ Ada Deer

Menominee Ada Deer (born 1935) is best known for leading the fight for federal recognition for her tribe. The U.S. government passed an act terminating the Menominee in 1953, thus plunging the tribe into poverty. In 1970 Deer and others created Determination of Rights and Unity for Menominee Shareholders (DRUMS). After three years of hard lobbying, their land was restored. In 1993 Deer became the first woman assistant secretary of the interior in the Bureau of Indian Affairs.

▶ Pottery Stamps

Mesoamerican Indians decorated their pottery by pressing carved wooden stamps into wet clay. The Olmec corn stamp (above) from Veracruz, Mexico, illustrates the importance of corn in the region. Legends say that people were created from ground corn. Aztec stamps from Oaxaca depict the powerful jaguar god (above left) and a parrot trader (below).

elders were closest to the spirits. If a baby was unhappy, a special healer would find out why. Often it was thought that a certain ancestor's spirit had been reborn in the baby and wanted the baby's name changed. So a naming ceremony was held to give the child that ancestor's name.

After the colonial wars, the tribe received a 10-million-acre reservation, which was reduced to 233,900 acres by allotment. There the tribe survived hunger, European diseases, and Franciscan missions (Northeast). By 1908 the Menominee had profited from their timber resources. As a result, they lost their tribal rights in 1953. It took 20 years of work to get back federal recognition. During that time the tribe had to sell land to pay taxes.

Today, 7,100 Menominee have rebuilt their economy. Their forest management is a model for the country. Menominee College teaches the native language and is helping to preserve the tribe's clan stories and Big Drum ceremonies (Potawatomi). ◀

MESO-AMERICA

• TRIBES OF THE REGION: ARAWAK, AZTECS, CARIB, MAYA, OLMECS, & TOLTECS

MESOAMERICA

Mesoamerica—Central America—connects the continents of North and South America. Meso means "middle" in Greek. The area discussed in this book also includes Mexico and the Caribbean islands, which lie to the east. Three ranges of the great Sierra Madres Mountains dominate Mexico, and the Tropic of Cancer divides the country into a temperate north and tropical south. Northwest Mexico is desert country. The central highlands are cool and dry, while the southern rain forests are lush and steamy. Mexico's southern beaches are among the most famous in the world. Equally luxurious are the white sands of the tropical Caribbean islands, which are the forested tips of a submerged mountain chain.

The earliest archaeological sites found in Mesoamerica are around 10,000 years old. Before 1492 there were 25 million people living in what is now Mexico. At least 9 million lived on the Caribbean islands. More than 230 different languages were spoken. Cultures varied from nomadic hunter-gatherers to city-states. A vast network of roads connected the cities of the Maya and Aztecs with the Inca Empire in Peru.

CORN AND TURTLES

Corn was, and remains, the region's most important crop. In fact, corn was developed in Mesoamerica and spread to the north and south. Ancient stories told how the gods created the first people from ground corn. This versatile grain came to play an important part in tribal ceremonies throughout the Americas.

The island Arawak tribe hunted sea turtles. According to legend, the Arawak ancestor Deminan gave birth to the turtle that became the world. Turtle creation legends are widespread in the Northeast. What is unusual is that Deminan was male and the turtle grew out of his back.

The first Mesoamerican people to leave important signs of their passing were the Olmecs. Beginning in about 1500 B.C., they built cities on the eastern coast of Mexico, cities that became the model for future Mesoamerican civilizations. For thousands of years, empires rose and fell in the Valley of Mexico. They all featured large pyramids, precise calendars, and written histories. Mayan cities flourished in the jungles of the Yucatán Peninsula from A.D. 400 to 900, during which time the Maya made discoveries in astronomy and calendar-keeping that had never been equaled.

The Aztec city of Tenochtitlán, which lies under present-day Mexico City, was among the

PYRAMIDS TO THE STARS

Mesoamerican Indians built pyramids as great temples to their gods. The enormous stone pyramids were built in city centers, in dense rain forests, and atop mountains—all without wheels or pack animals. The Aztec pyramid built for Emperor Tizoc has a temple at its peak. Thousands of captives were sacrificed to the sun god on the temple's altars. Aztec priests cut out the victims' hearts and rolled the bodies down the pyramid's steep steps. The victims' blood was offered to stone statues of the god.

Mayan pyramids were built to align with the stars and the positions of celestial lights on the horizon. Star charts guided complex time and calendar computations, and prophets and rulers depended on astronomy for their information.

The Big Picture

Long ago a Mayan artist captured coastal village life in a detailed mural. Fishermen take in bountiful catches as a market bustles on the shore. In the town square, villagers barter for products from the farms and forests. The swirled shapes overhead represent speech. The seated elders may have been

reciting stories such as that of the Four Quarters, in which magic bees "kept watch over the temples of the green turtle and of the deified fathers of cities."

Zapata

Emiliano Zapata (1879–1919) was a powerful Indian leader of the Mexican Revolution from 1910 to 1917. After dictator Porfirio Díaz had given the Indians' land to wealthy farmers, Indians rallied under Zapata's slogan, "Land and Liberty." In 1911 Zapata's warriors held the city of Cuautla and blocked the southern road to Mexico City until Díaz fled the country. In 1914 Zapata and his comrade Pancho Villa occupied Mexico City, but could not reach an agreement with the new president, Venustiano Carranza. Carranza's army trapped and killed Zapata in 1919, and his grave has never been discovered. But his spirit lives on as a symbol of freedom for all Mexican Indians.

largest cities in the world in 1500.

Ancient prophesies foretold the coming of white people in 1519. They also foretold the eventual disappearance of the civilization the strangers would build. Because the Spanish arrived in the same year the god Quetzalcoatl was predicted to return, Aztec king Moctezuma II eagerly awaited them. Many of his subjects had seen a darker vision and had fled north. They joined the Yaqui, Yuma, and Tohono O'odham tribes in the high Sierra Madres. Together, these northern tribes resisted Spanish rule until it ended. Meanwhile, Hernán Cortés and his Spanish conquistadors destroyed the Aztec civilization by a combination of warfare and diseases such as smallpox and typhoid.

Across the Gulf of Mexico, Christopher Columbus had already received a royal reception from the Arawak in 1492. But the Spanish soon brought slave catchers, and in 1510 Arawak *cacique* (chief) Hatuey led the first native peoples' resistance. When he refused to convert to Christianity, the Spanish burned him alive. Weakened by disease and slavery, 90 percent of the Caribbean natives died as a result of the conquest.

LAS CASAS The Spanish conquest of Mesoamerica was long and bloody, but far from complete. Their brutality was documented by Spanish priest Bartolomé de Las Casas in 1552: "They [the colonists] are still acting like ravening beasts, killing, terrorizing, afflicting, torturing, and destroying the native peoples, doing all this with the strangest and most varied new methods of cruelty."

Unlike other Europeans, the Spanish did not relate to the native peoples as nations. They did not negotiate trade or political alliances. Instead, the Spanish demanded goods and labor as tribute called *encomienda*. They forced the Indians to build massive churches and pay taxes called *repartimientos*.

Remnants of the encomienda system remain in modern Mexico. Indians can grow corn on shared land they won in the Mexican Revolution of 1910, but they are still at the mercy of wealthy landowners and their private police forces.

Today, 25 million Mexicans are directly descended from one of the 230 Mesoamerican tribes. But most Mexicans are proud of being *mestizo* (mixed race), not full-blooded Indian. Many people celebrate Indian symbols and legends, but the Mexican government did not recognize Indian nations until the 1980s.

Although there have been three Indian presidents of Mexico, the native people have had a hard journey. They continue to survive poverty and military repression. Most have subtly blended their spirituality with Catholicism, but some remain traditional. Native Mesoamericans are organizing themselves with new pride and determination. Cuna leader Marcial Arias García spoke for these natives at the United Nations in 1993: "What we want is to be the leaders in the solutions of our problems."◄

▶ History Mural

This mural by García Bustos inside Oaxaca's Palacio de Gobierno portrays the long and extraordinary history of Mexico. Beginning with ancient Indian gods and legends, the mural depicts events until the late 19th century. In the center, the revered Indian president Benito Juárez (1806–1872) is quoted: "Peace is respect for the rights of others ."

MÉTIS

- **LANGUAGE FAMILY: ALGONQUIAN & FRENCH**
- **LIFEWAYS: TRAPPING & TRADING**
- **LOCATION: BRITISH COLUMBIA, ALBERTA, & SASKATCHEWAN**
- **THEIR OWN NAME: MÉTIS**

SUBARCTIC

The first Métis were the offspring of French fur-trappers and Cree, Ojibwa, or other native women of the Subarctic. Their name, Métis, is French for half-breed. Métis children usually learned the Algonquian language from their mothers. When they grew up, many became trappers like their fathers.

Métis communities spread throughout Canada, and even along the Yukon River in Alaska. As traders and trappers, the Métis carried news from village to village. They called this network the "bush telegraph" or the "moccasin telegraph."

▶ Crossbloods

Catherine Lafferty of the Mackenzie District Métis poses with her children, James and Edward, around 1912. Her baby wears a European lace bonnet but is snuggled in a traditionally beaded, moss-filled hide bag.

Foster Children

The Métis have always been protective of their people and culture. In recent years they have protested Canadian agencies that place Indian children with non-Indian foster and adoptive families without consulting the tribes. The Métis Child and Family Services Society of Alberta, Canada, advertises for Indian families to provide children with foster homes where a common heritage is observed.

WANTED

Metis and Indian families to provide temporary care to children of Aboriginal descent, aged 0 - 18 years. If you are energetic, enthusiastic and love children we would welcome your application.

IF NOT YOU, THEN WHO?

For further information, contact:
Metis Child & Family Services Society
10437 - 123 Street, Edmonton, Alberta T5N 1N8
452-6100

Little Turtle

Miami war leader Little Turtle resisted American expansion west of the Ohio River. Armed with British guns, Little Turtle led a Great Lakes tribal confederacy in battle against General Arthur St. Clair in 1791. The Indians killed 623 U.S. soldiers and lost only twenty-one men. They celebrated their victories by stuffing the mouths of the slain soldiers with dirt—to symbolize the whites' greed for land. The confederacy was defeated at Fallen Timbers in 1794. This defeat would have been minor, but the British locked the retreating Indians out of Fort Miami.

In 1869 the Canadian government divided Métis land into square-mile grids. The Métis could not hunt or trap outside their squares. The Métis, however, needed to follow the game, and when the government refused to change its orders, the Métis went hungry. In the 1870s and 1880s, they rebelled twice (Cree). The Canadian army crushed both uprisings, capturing and executing Louis Riel, leader of the Métis, in 1885. The government then gave each Métis family 240 acres to farm. But the Métis were not farming people, so many of them lost their land to European immigrants.

Today, the Métis number between 500,000 and 1 million. Their unusual heritage entitles them to few of the benefits offered to other Indian peoples. They are presently forming tribal councils to work with other Indian nations. Métis musicians are known for their fiddle music and songs sung in both French and Algonquian.◄

MIAMI

- **LANGUAGE FAMILY: ALGONQUIAN**
- **LIFEWAYS: HUNTING & FARMING**
- **LOCATION: INDIANA & OKLAHOMA**
- **THEIR OWN NAME: TWA-HI-TWA-HI**

NORTHEAST

The Miami tribe originally lived along the St. Joseph and Wabash rivers in present-day Indiana. The tribe was actually a confederacy of five bands. Each band had a chief who was chosen by the village chiefs within the bands. War chiefs were chosen for their bravery. Peace chiefs were chosen for their negotiation skills.

Both young boys and girls were trained for adulthood by their elders. For boys, this included learning to provide for one's family by making stone tools, hunting, and defending the village.

Girls were taught by their grandmothers and aunts how to prepare animal hides for clothing and how to plant and harvest food. When adults, they might be chosen to serve on the Women's Council, which had the authority to prevent wars.

The most famous Miami war chief was Little Turtle. From 1780 to 1794, he led the Miami and confederated Great Lakes tribes in a series of victories over American troops until the confederacy was defeated at the Battle of Fallen Timbers.

In 1846, the Miami were divided, and 327 members were moved to Kansas. Known as the Western Miami, they were moved to Ottowa County, Oklahoma, in 1867.

There are approximately 6,000 members of the Eastern Miami, whose tribal headquarters are located in Peru, Indiana. Here they maintain a day care center, substance abuse programs, food programs for the elderly, and own a 40-acre spiritual ground, Seven Pillars in the Mississinewa River.◄

MICMAC

- **LANGUAGE FAMILY: ALGONQUIAN**
- **LIFEWAYS: HUNTING & FISHING**
- **LOCATION: MAINE & NOVA SCOTIA**
- **THEIR OWN NAME: ELNU**

NORTHEAST

Micmac hunters and fishers traveled by canoe in Maine and Nova Scotia. They were among the first Native Americans to meet Norsemen, in A.D. 1000. Since 1700 the Micmac have been allied with the Penobscot, Passamaquoddy, and Maliseet in the Wabanaki Confederacy. The Micmac nation includes more than 25,000 members in Canada and northern Maine. In 1991, Micmac of Presque Isle, Maine, received tribal status and land settlements with the other Wabanaki tribes.◄

► Speech of the Animals

The Miami are members of a secret Ojibwa medicine society, the Midewiwin. According to Miami legend, members were first taught the ceremonies by sacred animals such as the fox, deer, and turkey. The Speech of the Animals describes the rules of the Midewiwin:

"We saw you much afflicted and were disposed to relieve your troubles.... Conduct every part of the ceremony with gravity and secrecy and [let] no one condemn it or ridicule its proceedings."

► Mi'kmaq Family

The Micmac filmmaker Catherine Anne Martin made a documentary about traditional Micmac parenting called *Mi'kmaq Family*. Sponsored by the National Film Board of Canada, Martin's film provides a slice of life in a Nova Scotia Micmac community. The film opens with the birth of her second son, Thomas, and contains advice on child rearing from elders. A grandmother sings a child to sleep in Micmac, and a grandfather takes a child on a tour of the forest. Martin says, "In the Micmac community we're all a family. We're all connected."

CHRISTIAN COLONIZERS

North American Spanish Catholic missions were built in California, Florida, the Southwest, and Mexico, while French Catholics and English Protestants settled mainly in the Northeast.

Acoma Pueblo Indians (above) gathered for a feast day at the Saint Esteban del Rey Mission in New Mexico in 1890. Two men and two women are shown carrying a statue of a saint from the church to the feast-day dancing grounds. Southwestern Indians included their own dances and art forms in Catholic ceremonies. The Santa Barbara Mission in California (below) is typical of mission architecture.

MISSIONS

Missions are the churches and related buildings built mainly by Spanish colonists in the Americas. Almost every exploring party—particularly the early ones—included priests or ministers. Many of these people spread the idea that Indians had no religion and had to be converted. (For more about French Catholics, see the Black Robes feature in Northeast and Reservations.)

INQUISITION The Spanish missionaries who began arriving in America after 1492 came from the culture of the Inquisition. During the Spanish Inquisition (1478–1834) thousands of people were burned alive in Europe because they were not Catholic. The Spanish missionaries' attitudes toward Indians were shaped by these events. The Spanish demanded that the Indians convert. But they also made them slaves and ordered them to pay tribute. A few priests—including Bartolomé de Las Casa—defended Indian rights (Mesoamerica). But authors of government documents opposed them, saying that nonwhite peoples were not human and had no souls. Therefore, it was acceptable to kill and enslave them.

Some Spanish priests created uniquely self-sufficient missions using the labor of captive Indians. Mission crops and products were either sent to Spain or used for trade with Europeans. The main mission industries were soap, leather, wool, wrought iron, food, and wine production.

Spain—which claimed the Americas from the Northwest Coast to the tip of South America—built missions in Florida, the Southwest, California, and Mesoamerica. The Florida missions built in 1544 lasted for 100 years, until they were destroyed by the British. By then the missions of the Southwest had become very strong, and about 60,000 Zuni, Hopi, and Pueblo had been baptized.

They held their traditional ceremonies in secret, at the risk of beatings and execution. Outrage at this treatment led to the Pueblo Rebellion of 1680. The tribes destroyed several missions, killed 400 Spaniards, and drove the rest into Mexico—temporarily.

ESCAPES

In the early 1800s, the Chumash and Luiseño frequently escaped from California missions, but the people were usually recaptured. A few California tribes are still listed as Mission Indians by the Bureau of Indian Affairs (BIA). That's because these tribes lost their land while they were confined in missions from 1769 to 1820. During that period, disease, starvation, and brutality greatly reduced the native population of the Southwest and California. Spain was forced to abandon its missions in the 1820s, after Mexico won its independence.

From the 1880s to the 1940s, after the region had become part of the United States, the BIA used missionaries "to foster a competitive, individualistic, economic mentality" among the Indians. That statement comes from a 1923 document encouraging priests and ministers to restrict Indian dancing. Although the U.S. Constitution requires separation of church and state, Native Americans were not protected from government interference in their religions.

Two generations of Indian children were forcibly removed from their families and sent to church-run boarding schools. Any attempt by children to speak their native languages or maintain tribal traditions was severely punished. It wasn't until the 1970s that Indian ceremonies were legalized. Today, tribes are reviving the ceremonies, but much information has been lost. Some tribes hold workshops to help people heal from the loneliness and abuse they suffered in mission schools.◄

BLENDING BELIEFS

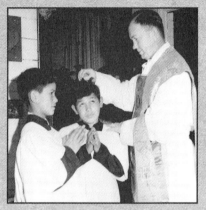

Many Ojibwa Indians converted to Christianity—as these boys did. However, the Ojibwa also developed a strong spiritual society, the Midewiwin, which met in secret during the night to promote native religious beliefs. By 1930 most missionaries had caught on to the society and left Ojibwa reservations.

Many Native Americans were curious about Jesus, whose miracles sounded like those of Indian prophets. These people adapted Christianity to their own beliefs. Blackfeet priest Joseph F. Brown (left) was ordained on the Flathead Reservation in 1948. There are about 250 Indian priests and ministers today.

Some Indians were drawn by church music and composed hymns in their own languages. Others created Christian images in their tribal art styles, such as this portrait of Jesus by a Nootka artist.

▶ Three Plains Chiefs

This 1908 painting shows chiefs from three related **Plains** Indian tribes. From left to right are a Missouria, an Otoe, and a **Ponca** chief.

▶ Old Eagle

Old Eagle, an Otoe chief, was photographed wearing a bear-claw necklace and a medallion with a picture of Abraham Lincoln. The medallion was a gift to him when he visited Washington, D.C.

▶ Chief Greg Sarris

Greg Sarris is chairman of the Coast Miwok tribes and a professor of English at U.C.L.A. He is also the author of *Grand Avenue*, ten linked short stories about the lives of urban Indians and their interactions with other people.

MISSOURIA-OTOE

- **LANGUAGE FAMILY: SIOUIAN**
- **LIFEWAYS: HUNTING & FARMING**
- **LOCATION: OKLAHOMA**
- **THEIR OWN NAMES: NIUTACHI & WAT OTA**

PLAINS

Otoe historians say the tribe migrated from the Southeast to the Great Lakes with the Missouria. A conflict later split the tribes, and the Otoe moved to Nebraska. Defeated by the Sac and Fox and Osage, the Missouria rejoined the Otoe in 1796. In 1882 the U. S. government moved the tribes to Oklahoma. Today, 1,550 Otoe-Missouria live in Red Rock, Oklahoma. ◀

MIWOK

- **LANGUAGE FAMILY: PENUTIAN**
- **LIFEWAYS: HUNTING, GATHERING, & TRADING**
- **LOCATION: CALIFORNIA**
- **THEIR OWN NAME: MIWOK**

CALIFORNIA

The three central California Miwok territories were major targets for Spanish missionaries, Russian traders, and American gold rushers. As a result of disease, starvation, and killings, the Miwok population of 8,000 had fallen to 700 by 1860.

Today, 3,400 Miwok people are alive and well. Court battles to attain federal recognition are long and costly, but a cultural revival is under way among the Miwok. Children are eagerly learning the Miwok language, dances, and songs from elders. The Maidu and Pomo join the Miwok in their Big Time Celebrations. ◀

MODOC

- **LANGUAGE FAMILY: PENUTIAN**
- **LIFEWAYS: HUNTING & FISHING**
- **LOCATION: OREGON & OKLAHOMA**
- **THEIR OWN NAME: MO ADOK**

PLATEAU

The Modoc got their name from their northern neighbors, the Klamath. In the language they share, Mo Adok means Southerners. The Modoc once lived in the Cascade Range along the present-day California-Oregon border. Mount Shasta (Wintun) is sacred to both tribes.

The Modoc are respected for being among the last people of the Far West to resist white settlement. In 1864 they were ordered to give up their lands and move onto the Klamath reservation in eastern Oregon. But younger warriors fought back. In 1873, at the end of the Modoc War, 150 people were removed to Oklahoma.

DREAM DANCE Meanwhile, Modoc on the Oregon reservation developed new spiritual practices. To combat the white man's diseases, they introduced the Dream Dance. The dance was a way to act out visions from the dreams of sick persons. Without dance, they believed, the disease would kill the victim.

In 1909 some Oklahoma Modoc returned to the Klamath reservation. Others stayed near Miami, Oklahoma, where they farmed and some became Christians. The Modoc lost their tribal status with the Klamath in 1954. By 1978 the two Modoc tribes had won back their status by working with the Klamath, Peoria, Ottawa, and Huron. Today, about 1,000 Modoc live in Chiloquin, Oregon. Another 200 live in Miami, Oklahoma. Tribe historians are recording the Modoc language and family histories. Modoc travel to Northwest Coast ceremonies and Oklahoma powwows, where they join the Creek Stomp Dance.◀

▶ Captain Jack

Modoc leader Kintpuash (c. 1838–1873) was nicknamed Captain Jack because of his habit of wearing a military jacket with brass buttons. Captain Jack was willing to settle on a reservation, but only if it was in Modoc territory, not among the Klamath, as the U.S. government intended. In 1872 he led a band of Modoc to the California Lava Beds and held off the U.S. Army for a year. In 1873 he was captured and hanged.

Before he died Captain Jack said, "I want no more war. You deny me the right of a white man. My skin is red; my heart is a white man's heart; but I am a Modoc. I am not afraid to die....When I die, my enemies will be under me."

▶ Michael Dorris

Writer Michael Dorris (1945-1997) was Modoc on his father's side. He brought national attention to fetal alcohol syndrome, or birth defects caused by a mother's drinking during pregnancy. This problem is widespread on reservations. Dorris's 1989 book *The Broken Cord* was based on his experiences with his adopted son, who was a victim of fetal alcohol syndrome. Dorris wrote many works of fiction, some with his wife and writing partner, Louise Erdrich (Ojibwa).

St. Regis Seal

The seal of the St. Regis Mohawk, designed by Mohawk artist Gesso Thomas, contains motifs important to Mohawk culture. The main Mohawk clans—Bear, Turtle, and Wolf—are represented across the center. (The bird, a snipe, stands for other people who live on the Mohawk reservation.) The people around the turtle represent the Circle of Destiny, which protects all people. The pine tree on the turtle's back is the Tree of Peace (Iroquois). At the top is a Gustoweh, or feather hat. Its feathers indicate a man from the Mohawk nation.

The Eastern Door

As the easternmost tribe in the Iroquois Confederacy, the Mohawk are known as Keepers of the Eastern Door. The *Eastern Door* is also the name of the weekly newspaper published in the Kahnawake Mohawk Territory.

Akwesasne School

The Mohawk call the region through which the St. Lawrence River flows Akwesasne, meaning Land Where the Partridge Drums. The Akwesasne Freedom School was founded in 1979 by Mohawk parents worried that their language and culture were dying out. At the school, Mohawk culture is taught along with reading, writing, math, science, and history. Some of the symbols of the St. Regis seal can be seen on the school's insignia.

MOHAWK

- **LANGUAGE FAMILY: IROQUOIAN**
- **LIFEWAYS: HUNTING, GATHERING, & FARMING**
- **LOCATION: NEW YORK & ONTARIO, CANADA**
- **THEIR OWN NAME: KANIENGEHAGE**

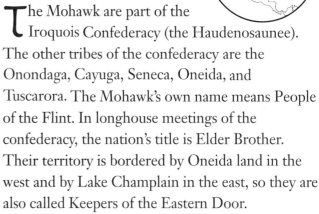

NORTHEAST

The Mohawk are part of the Iroquois Confederacy (the Haudenosaunee). The other tribes of the confederacy are the Onondaga, Cayuga, Seneca, Oneida, and Tuscarora. The Mohawk's own name means People of the Flint. In longhouse meetings of the confederacy, the nation's title is Elder Brother. Their territory is bordered by Oneida land in the west and by Lake Champlain in the east, so they are also called Keepers of the Eastern Door.

The Mohawk have three clans: Turtle, Bear, and Wolf. Their traditional headwear, Gustoweh, has three upright feathers (Seneca). Mohawk villages were stockaded and were so large that Dutch explorers called them castles when they first saw them in 1634.

Although most Mohawk remained neutral during the Revolutionary War, American soldiers burned Mohawk villages because some Mohawk had fought on the side of the British. By 1791 New York State had taken all but six square miles of Mohawk land.

LAND CLAIMS

Today, about 13,400 Mohawk in New York and Canada govern themselves by a traditional chiefs' council. They have filed several land claims against New York State, arguing that the state broke a 1790 federal law when it took Mohawk land.

Since 1950 Mohawk have also blockaded roads and bridges to claim treaty rights. In 1977 the Mohawk community of Ganienkeh was built on land reclaimed from the state.

The Mohawk are leaders in Indian education. In 1968 they built the first Indian library on a U.S. reservation. The Akwesasne Freedom School teaches the Mohawk language as well as Mohawk culture and history to elementary school children. In fact, the tribe was the first in the United States to start and run a program to teach its native language to children. The Mohawk also publish several newspapers.

In the 20th century, many Mohawk have worked in the construction industry, building skyscrapers and iron and steel bridges. Akwesasne Mohawk have helped build practically every major steel project in North America, a source of pride for the Mohawk tribe. Mohawk women's sweetgrass baskets are world famous. Many Mohawk still attend traditional longhouse ceremonies.◄

▶ Peter Blue Cloud

Peter Blue Cloud, a Mohawk of the Turtle Clan, lives in California. After retiring from ironworking, he became the editor of a local magazine called *Coyote's Journal*. He has also written poetry and stories of his own. Some of his books include *Elderberry Flute Song, Coyote and Friends,* and *Back then Tomorrow.*

MOHEGAN

- **LANGUAGE FAMILY: ALGONQUIAN**
- **LIFEWAYS: HUNTING, FARMING, & GATHERING**
- **LOCATION: CONNECTICUT**
- **THEIR OWN NAME: MAINGAN**

NORTHEAST

Around 1600 the Mohegan moved from their New York homeland to Connecticut. The Mohegan name for themselves means Wolf in Algonquian. Like other Algonquins, they were sometimes led by female chiefs (Ojibwa).

Today, the tribe is trying to get back some of the land it lost to English settlers in the 1600s. The 980-member tribe gathers in Uncasville, Connecticut, for its annual Wigwam Powwow and Green Corn Ceremony (Southeast).◄

▶ Chief Uncas

In 1637 Mohegan chief Uncas (1588?–1683?) led warriors in a joint attack with colonial settlers on a **Pequot** village near present-day West Mystic, Connecticut. At least 300 men, women, and children were killed in the attack, the opening round of the Pequot War. In the next 250 years, whites would often take advantage of Indian rivalries like the one between Uncas and the Pequots.

Moshe

This portrait of Moshe, a Mojave girl, dates to 1903. Life was hard for Moshe and her friends at the turn of the century. Malnutrition and horrible living conditions contributed to the spread of fatal diseases among Native Americans. In 1907 tuberculosis alone caused 90 percent of all deaths in the Mojave tribe.

Last Smoke

Montagnais Indians still perform ancient hunting ceremonies, such as honoring animals with sacred tobacco. In 1925, before skinning a bear, this Montagnais woman filled a pipe to put it in the animal's mouth. After a bear is butchered and cooked, the men must eat the head first, making sure they finish it all at one sitting.

MOJAVE

- **LANGUAGE FAMILY:** HOKAN
- **LIFEWAYS:** HUNTING & FISHING
- **LOCATION:** ARIZONA, NEVADA, & CALIFORNIA
- **THEIR OWN NAME:** AHA MACAV

SOUTHWEST

The Mojave lived in huts and fished the Colorado River from reed rafts. They also grew corn, beans, pumpkins, and melons. Legendary prophet Avi kwa'ame, revered by all Hokan-speaking peoples, is supposed to live in the Mojave Mountains. Mojave means People Who Live on the River, and the Mojave still live on the Colorado—but on a fraction of their ancestral land. They believe in the power of dreams to see the future. In Parker, Arizona, the Mojave have a museum. The Aha Macav Society teaches the Mojave language.◀

MONTAGNAIS

- **LANGUAGE FAMILY:** ALGONQUIAN
- **LIFEWAYS:** HUNTING & FISHING
- **LOCATION:** QUEBEC & NEWFOUNDLAND
- **THEIR OWN NAME:** INNU

SUBARCTIC

Like their Cree neighbors, the Montagnais traveled in small hunting bands. They followed game by canoe in the summer and by snowshoe in winter. They and their close relatives the Naskapi called themselves the Innu. They considered themselves to be one people. Their territory, Nitassinan, or Our Land, included what is now Quebec, Labrador, and Newfoundland. They believed their world was created by Kuekuatsheu, the wolverine, from undersea mud and rocks. Their world was unchanged until the late 10th century, when they may have been attacked by

Vikings. Montagnais legend says the tribe chased the Vikings away in A.D. 1003.

The Innu were given the name Montagnais by the French in the early 1600s. In French, *montagnais* means "of the mountains." The French sent Jesuit missionaries to live with the Montagnais and teach them how to be "civilized" (Northeast). As Father Paul Le Jeune wrote, this wasn't easy. The Montagnais laughed at white men for blindly obeying their captains. They also thought whites were too hard on their children. Montagnais rarely punished their children and hardly refused them anything.

Today, about 10,000 Montagnais and Naskapi belong to the Innu Association in Labrador. Most still depend on their annual hunts for survival. Since 1987 the Montagnais and Naskapi have been protesting against low-flying European supersonic military jets that practice bombing on their hunting grounds. They are also fighting to reclaim land flooded by Canadian dams (Subarctic). ◄

MONTAUK-SHINNECOCK

- **LANGUAGE FAMILY: ALGONQUIAN**
- **LIFEWAYS: GATHERING, FISHING, & WHALING**
- **LOCATION: NEW YORK**
- **THEIR OWN NAME:**
  MEANTAUKETT-SHINNECOCK

NORTHEAST

The Montauk-Shinnecock gathered clam shells on Long Island—the source of wampum for the whole Northeast. They hunted whales, then manned the first commercial whaling ships in the 1670s. The tribe's original population is unknown, but there were only 180 Montauk-Shinnecock by 1900. Today, the tribe holds an annual open house in June and is building a museum in Southampton, New York. ◄

▶ Innu Couple

This photograph of Philomena and Dominie Pokue was taken in August 1993 in Labrador, Canada. They are enjoying the Sheshatshiu Festival.

▶ Mary Ann Coffee

Mary Ann Coffee was photographed at the Montauk Shinnecock Reservation in 1902, when she was eighty-one years old. At the left is a stone pestle inside a wooden mortar. These traditional implements are used for grinding corn and other grains.

Conch Shell

This conch shell (right), found miles from the ocean at Spiro, Oklahoma, is evidence of the vast distances over which the Mound Builders traded. It is intricately engraved and was used as a drinking cup. Archaeologists and historians have been unable to determine the significance of the figure in the design (shown above). It is either a birdman god, or a dancing human dressed as an eagle.

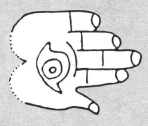

Hand and Skull

These hand and skull designs were found engraved on a burial vessel in Moundville, Alabama. Such designs appear frequently on Mississippi Mound Builder vessels. Sometimes the eye is missing from the center of the hand, but it is usually included.

MOUND BUILDERS

The Mound Builders—not a tribe but a succession of similar cultures—flourished in what is now the eastern United States from about 1400 B.C. to A.D. 1450. They got their name from the large systems of mounds and earthworks they built around their cities.

The earliest evidence of Mound Builders is found at Poverty Point, Mississippi. The site consists of six ridges with four avenues linking them. On the ridges were wooden structures, including houses and temples. Some archaeologists believe Olmecs built Poverty Point around 1400 B.C., perhaps as a trading center.

BURIAL MOUNDS

Beginning around 1000 B.C., another Mound Builder culture emerged near what is now Adena, Kentucky. The site includes sixty-foot-high mounds covering log buildings in which important people were buried. Researchers believe the Adena people fished and gathered wild plants.

A more elaborate Mound Builder civilization—known as the Hopewell culture after a mound site near Hopewell, Ohio—reached its peak between 400 B.C. and A.D. 400. The people of the Hopewell culture farmed and traded extensively all over eastern North America. The Ohio Valley is filled with Hopewell sites, many of which were built on terraces along river flood plains. The Hopewell people planted corn, beans, and squash. They fished and used the rivers for trade.

About 2,000 years ago, southern Ohio was covered with large Mound Builder sites, some of them more than two miles long. Many of them were shaped in geometric patterns or designed to look like birds or snakes from the air. Large cone-shaped burial mounds held the remains of great men, their wives, and servants. Some archaeologists suggest the mounds also served as observatories for studying the skies and maintaining a calendar for the planting schedule.

The Hopewell culture began to decline around A.D. 300. As the climate grew cooler, farming brought less food, and villages began to war with each other. Many of the Mound Builder cities became fortresses, and trade nearly disappeared.

Around A.D. 750, a new Mound Builder culture emerged near the confluence of the Mississippi and Missouri rivers. Its greatest city was Cahokia, which by A.D. 1000 covered nearly five square miles and housed over 30,000 inhabitants. At the center of the town was a huge pyramid-shaped mound over 100 feet high and covering an area larger than a football field. It was topped by a wooden temple.

Cahokia was mostly abandoned around A.D. 1450, though many of the nearby towns survived. Archaeologists are not certain why it was abandoned, but crop failure, disease, and war are possibilities. ◀

NAKOTA

- **LANGUAGE FAMILY: SIOUIAN**
- **LIFEWAYS: HUNTING & FARMING**
- **LOCATION: NORTH & SOUTH DAKOTA & MONTANA**
- **THEIR OWN NAME: NAKOTA**

PLAINS

Two Nakota Sioux tribes—the Yanktonai and Yankton—settled on four reservations. Yanktonai live in Crow Creek, South Dakota, and—with Lakota Sioux—on North Dakota's Standing Rock Reservation. At Fort Peck in Montana, the Yanktonai, Assiniboine, and Dakota lease farmland and mining land. The Yankton Reservation is in South Dakota.

Nakota culture is expressed in many ways, including in Ella C. Deloria's fiction, Clarence Rockboy's beadwork, and the paintings of Oscar Howe. ◀

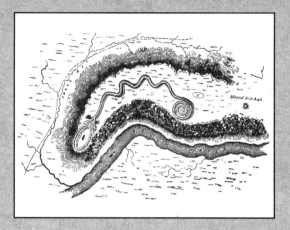

▶ Great Serpent Mound

This mound beside a creek near Chillicothe, Ohio, is nearly one-quarter of a mile long. It is in the shape of a giant, uncurling snake with an egg in its mouth. Although many mounds were burial sites, this serpent appears to have been a religious monument to the snake.

▶ Oscar Howe

This painting of a Nakota dancer is by Oscar Howe (1915–1983), a Nakota artist. He said, "It is my greatest hope that my paintings may serve to bring the best things of Indian culture into the modern way of life." Visual arts students can study at the Oscar Howe Summer Art Institute of the University of South Dakota.

Bow Hunting

Naskapi Indians made bows and arrows of dried juniper wood. In this 1928 photograph, Shushebish demonstrates the shooting of a blunt-headed arrow used to kill small animals and birds. Traditionally, a hunter had to prove his worthiness by passing tests, such as his ability to run faster than an animal before shooting it.

Sun Power

The Natchez invoked the power of the sun by smoking tobacco from a special pipe. The tobacco was smoked during ceremonies of dancing and chanting. In these ceremonies, the tribe could ask the sun god for rain, peace, good health, or the destruction of enemies. Here, a grand pipe is carried in a peacemaking procession.

Marche du Calumet de Paia

NASKAPI

- **LANGUAGE FAMILY: ALGONQUIAN**
- **LIFEWAYS: HUNTING**
- **LOCATION: NEWFOUNDLAND**
- **THEIR OWN NAME: INNU**

SUBARCTIC

The Naskapi and Montagnais consider themselves to be one people called the Innu. They were mistakenly renamed by the French in the 1600s. The Innu share a culture based on hunting animals such as caribou. They believe certain animals are their relatives and must be treated with respect (Subarctic). Much of their spiritual life is based on communicating with animal spirits through dreams and predicting the future by studying animal bones. Today, 10,000 Innu live in Canada. They are trying to maintain their traditions, though Canadian dams have flooded their land. ◄

NATCHEZ

- **LANGUAGE FAMILY: MUSKOGEAN**
- **LIFEWAYS: FARMING & TRADING**
- **LOCATION: NONE**
- **THEIR OWN NAME: NATCHEZ**

SOUTHEAST

The Natchez numbered 5,000 when the French met them in the 1600s (Southeast). Much about them is unknown. Like the Choctaw and Chickasaw, they spoke a Muskogean dialect. However, their dialect was unique, and experts long believed it was a different language. In fact, there were three related Natchez groups: the Taensa, the Avoyel, and the Natchez themselves, the largest.

The Natchez were descendants of the Mound Builders. They were advanced farmers who emphasized hierarchy. Their society was divided into two classes: nobles and commoners. The chief's family lived on top of a central pyramid in a large town. The Natchez worshipped the sun and believed their chief was a descendant of the sun god. He had absolute power. He maintained a large body of servants and a harem. When he died, many of these people were killed.

The Natchez were destroyed in a series of wars with the French. Many of the survivors went to live among the Cherokee and the Creek. When those tribes were moved to Oklahoma, the Natchez moved with them. They soon intermarried and began to lose their separate identity.

The last Natchez speaker, Watt Sam, died in 1965, and the last Natchez ceremony was performed in 1976. Some Natchez customs and ceremonies have been adopted by the Cherokee and Choctaw. The Cherokee still do the Natchez Mosquito Dance: When the men doze during long ceremonies, the women poke them with pins. ◄

NAVAJO

- **LANGUAGE FAMILY: ATHAPASKAN**
- **LIFEWAYS: HUNTING & FARMING**
- **LOCATION: ARIZONA, NEW MEXICO, & UTAH**
- **THEIR OWN NAME: DINEH**

SOUTHWEST

The Navajo tribe is the largest in the western United States. Most of the 200,000 Navajo live on America's largest reservation, a 28,000-square-mile spread in Arizona, New Mexico, and Utah.

The Navajo's origins are different from those of their neighbors in the Southwest. That's because they are an Athapaskan-speaking people who migrated southward from the Subarctic about 900 years ago. The name Navajo comes from the Pueblo language and means Newcomers. The

STUNG SERPENT, A NATCHEZ, SPOKE THESE WORDS IN 1720:

"We know not what to think of the French. Why… did the French come into our country?… [B]ecause their country was too little for all the men that were in it. We told them they might take land where they pleased, there was enough for them and for us; that it was good the same sun should enlighten us both, and that we would…assist them to build and to labor in their fields. We have done so; is this not true? What occasion then did we have for Frenchmen? Before they came, did we not live better than we do, seeing we deprive ourselves of a part of our corn, our game, and fish to give a part to them?… [B]efore the arrival of the French, we lived like men who can be satisfied with what they have; whereas [now] we are like slaves who are not [allowed] to do as they please."

▶ Black God

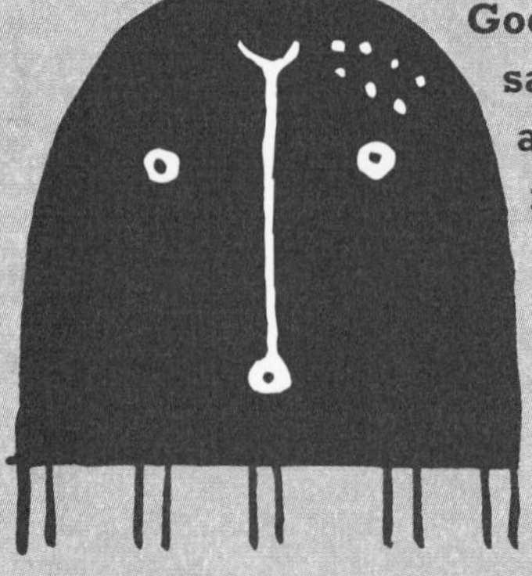

This is the face of Black God as he appears in a sand painting. He is always shown masked. On his forehead is the constellation of stars called the Pleiades. Black God is associated with the creation of fire and the light of the stars. Sand paintings are part of Navajo rituals to cure a sick person, cast out evil, or unite a person with nature. When the ceremony ends, the sand painting is always destroyed.

▶ Rug Weaver

This Navajo woman is weaving a rug using a loom based on a 300-year-old design. Some Navajo rugs, called chief's blankets because their patterns are those of Navajo chiefs, are woven so tightly that they are virtually waterproof.

▶ Silversmith

Besides rugs and baskets, the Navajo also make wonderful turquoise and silver jewelry. Men do the silverwork. This silversmith displays some of his work, including the silver belt he is holding in his hands.

Navajo call themselves Dineh, or People. More than 120,000 people speak the Navajo dialect as their first language. About 25,000 of them speak little or no English.

SAND PAINTINGS
▼▼▼

Navajo hold three different religious beliefs: traditional Navajo ceremonies, the Native American Church (Comanche), and Christianity. Some follow one of these beliefs, others mix them. Traditional Navajo spirituality is devoted to ceremonies of life and health. Each Navajo healer specializes in one kind of ceremony—the Blessing Way, for example. It is performed for good luck, and for two days the healer makes sand paintings and sings special chants. Sand paintings are made by arranging pollen and colored sand on the ground to illustrate legends and spirits. After the ceremony, the sand paintings are destroyed.

Navajo government has changed a lot in the past 100 years. Traditionally, Navajo were governed by clan leaders called *naat'aanii,* or "ones who make speeches." In this informal system, leaders were chosen by clan members and served for two to four years. They usually tried to persuade people to listen to them, rather than ordering them to obey.

In recent years the growth of the Navajo nation has required a more formal government, including an elected council and president. This is especially important when the Navajo are negotiating with outside businesses and governments. Navajo territory contains many resources, including coal, uranium, and oil. The Navajo government has earned millions of dollars by leasing land to corporations. However, Navajo President Peter MacDonald was sent to jail in 1989 for bribery and using tribal money for his own use. He has been replaced by Peterson Zah.

Because settlers did not want the Navajo's desert lands, the tribe kept most of its territory. The Navajo have raised sheep there ever since the Spanish brought sheep to the region in the 1600s.

Unfortunately, sheep raising has created new environmental problems in the 20th century. When sheep graze, they usually eat plants down to the very soil, which causes erosion when heavy desert thundershowers pour down.

During the past 100 years, sheep grazing has been a source of conflict between the Hopi and the Navajo. Hopi lands are surrounded by the larger Navajo reservation. The Hopi are very defensive about their lands and don't like intruders. Navajo sheep continually wander onto Hopi land, causing erosion there. After many court battles, a settlement between the two peoples was reached in 1992. The Navajo are leasing some of their land to the Hopi in exchange for the right to continue grazing their sheep around Hopi land.

The Navajo hold many festivals, powwows, and ceremonies, and the public is often invited. Their main festival occurs in early October. ◀

NEZ PERCE

- **LANGUAGE FAMILY: SAHAPTIAN**
- **LIFEWAYS: HUNTING, FISHING, & GATHERING**
- **LOCATION: IDAHO & BRITISH COLUMBIA**
- **THEIR OWN NAME: NUMIPU**

PLATEAU

The Nez Perce once lived on several million acres in present-day Idaho, Montana, and Washington. Members of the largest and most powerful Plateau tribe, they fished for salmon and trout in the Snake River and gathered roots and berries. They received their name—which means Pierced Nose in French—by accident. Many of the surrounding peoples pierced their noses with toothed shells. Although the Nez Perce did not, the name somehow stuck to them.

When Europeans brought horses to the region

ADAHOONIŁIGII
THE NAVAHO LANGUAGE MONTHLY

| VOL. 2 NO. 3 | WINDOW ROCK, ARIZONA | JANUARY 1, 1947 |

'AHKEAH HONEESNÁ 'ÁKO BÉÉSH BAAH DAH NAAZ NILIGÍÍ YÁ DAH NÁNIDAAHÍ SILĮĮ'!!

Niłch'its'ósí ndízídęę bighi' Naabeehá binont'a'í béésh bąąh dah naaxniłigíí yá dah nánidaahíí doolee? biniighé Sam 'Ahkeah dóó Chéé Dodge diné naaltsoos bá 'adayiiznił. Sam 'Ahkeah naaltsoos djidí miil dóó ba'aan naakidi neeznádiin bá 'aniidee'. Chee Dodge t'éiyá naaltsoos naakidi miil dóó ba'aan naakidi neeznádiin bá 'aniidee'.

TSASK'EH BA HOOGHAN DIILTŁA

Hayííłkąągo Atlanta Georgia hoolgheedi tsásk'eh bá hooghan nt'ęę' diiltła lá jiní. 'Éí Bilagáana t'áátáhádi neeznádiin dóó ba'aan dijts'áadah yilt'éego nabistseed dóó neeznádiin yilt'éego t'éiyá t'áá tidadiiłyaa lá jiní. T'áá

▶ **Language Monthly**

More than 120,000 Navajo speak the Navajo language as their first language. It was first written down in the 1930s, when specialists from the Smithsonian Institution devised an alphabet for it. This monthly newsletter in Navajo is used for teaching reading skills in Navajo. Its name, *Adahooniłigii,* means Current Events. The newsletter was first published in 1943.

▶ **Looking Glass**

Nez Perce chief Looking Glass was photographed in 1871 wearing traditional dress and carrying a bow and arrow. Looking Glass, who had befriended whites for years, sided with Chief Joseph when the Nez Perce fought removal to a reservation. The Nez Perce felt betrayed by the U. S. government and wanted to be free.

▶ Chief Joseph

American generals admired Chief Joseph (1840–1904) for his leadership during the Nez Perce's 1,700-mile flight and running battle during the winter of 1877. The chief, whose Nez Perce name means Thunder Rolling Over the Mountains, was called The Indian Napoleon by congressmen and diplomats who invited him to speak before them.

In 1879 he said, "The earth is the mother of all people and all people should have equal rights upon it. You might as well expect the rivers to run backward as that any man who was born free should be contented penned up and denied liberty to go where he pleases."

Despite his appeals, the Nez Perce were split up and moved several times before Chief Joseph's band finally settled on the Colville Reservation in 1885. There the chief continued his fight to protect tribal land. His legacy lives on in the Nez Perce revival of the Seven Drum ceremonies he originated.

▶ Woven Bag

The style of this bag was unique to the Nez Perce and shows their intricate weaving patterns. Nez Perce weaving was always done by women.

▶ Hattie Kauffman

Indians first worked in radio communications in the 1930s. Indian participation in television broadcasting began in the late 1960s. In 1990 Emmy Award–winning reporter Hattie Kauffman, a Nez Perce, became a national correspondent for *CBS This Morning.* She is a role model for Indians working in telecommunications.

in the early 1700s, the Nez Perce adopted a Plains way of life and roamed east to hunt buffalo. They bred their horses for speed in hunting and war. Their horse, the Appaloosa, is still bred in the Palouse River valley, for which it is named.

LEGENDS The Nez Perce have many legends. Their tale of the beaver and the pines explains how fire came to humankind: Long ago, the pines alone held the secret of fire. This might have been because lightning commonly starts forest fires in the summertime. One very cold winter, the beaver spied the pine trees in council around their fire. He snatched a burning coal, and the pines gave chase. Slowly they tired out, just as the forest thins from the mountains to the plains. The pines still hold fire, but humans can share it by rubbing two pine sticks together.

The Nez Perce have a reputation for being proud and stubborn, and those traits have served them well in their history with whites. Chief Joseph led them on a great escape trek in the 1870s.

In this century the tribe has fought long and successfully to regain fishing rights they were promised in treaties. In 1992 Nez Perce leader Horace Axtell won a fifteen-year legal struggle to get the Bear Paw Mountain Battleground declared an official historical site. It was there that Chief Joseph finally surrendered in 1877.

Today, about 3,000 Nez Perce live in Idaho on a 90,000-acre reservation. Others live in British Columbia, Canada. The tribe's fishing and forestry conservation programs are a great success. The Nez Perce have revived their arts and dances and Chief Joseph's Seven Drum ceremonies. Many annual ceremonies are held to celebrate the tribe's traditions. But most young people do not speak Sahaptian, the Nez Perce's language. To solve this problem, the tribe is investing in history and language projects. ◀

NIPMUC

- **LANGUAGE FAMILY: ALGONQUIAN**
- **LIFEWAYS: FISHING, HUNTING, & FARMING**
- **LOCATION: MASSACHUSETTS & WISCONSIN**
- **THEIR OWN NAME: NIPAMAUG**

NORTHEAST

Before 1617 the Nipmuc numbered about 5,000. That year, half of them died of smallpox. Their own name means Freshwater Fishing Place, after the many streams in their homeland, which comprised Massachusetts, Connecticut, and Rhode Island. By 1674 most Nipmuc had been moved to praying towns (Reservations and Northeast). They soon escaped to join the Wampanoag resistance. After their defeat by the English, the Nipmuc fled west with the Mahican. Today, about 1,400 Nipmuc live in Wisconsin and in Grafton, Massachusetts.◄

NOOTKA

- **LANGUAGE FAMILY: WAKASHAN**
- **LIFEWAYS: WHALING**
- **LOCATION: BRITISH COLUMBIA**
- **THEIR OWN NAME: NUU-CHAH NULTH**

NORTHWEST COAST

Nootka is an incorrect name given to the Nuu-Chah Nulth band by British sailors. Nut-ka means Circling About in Wakashan. The people were probably describing what the British ship was doing. Originally, the people on the west coast of Vancouver Island, British Columbia, lived in fifteen confederacies, each with local names.

The Nootka traded with the Makah and Kwakiutl and raided the Coast Salish for slaves. They shared whaling ceremonies with the Makah.

▶Metacom

After English settlers executed three of his people, Wampanoag chief Metacom (1639?–1676) led warriors from the Nipmuc and many other tribes in what whites called King Philip's War. He was shot and killed by a raiding party, then horribly mutilated. This painting is supposed to represent his death.

▶Hat

Among the Nootka, basketry hats were a sign of high social rank. They were woven of waterproof cedar bark to shed rain. Clan designs such as the whale crest were often woven into hats.

▶ Family Masks

David Neel photographed his wife, Sharon, and sons, Simon, Edwin, and Elvin, in 1991. They are dressed in traditional Nootka clothing with button blankets and dance masks. Edwin is holding a drum decorated with a raven fishing for salmon.

Nootka whalers washed themselves with special herbs before a hunt because they believed that whales didn't like human odor. Crews sang songs to ease the whale's spirit as they towed it home.

When the Spanish arrived in 1774, they forced Nootka women onto their ships and gave them syphilis. By 1824 the disease had reduced the 25,000-member confederacy to 7,000. The Nootka responded by attacking trade ships, but by 1835 the population had decreased still further, to 1,459.

In 1871 British Columbia joined Canada, and the Indians were forced onto reserves. The Nootka never signed a treaty giving up their land. In the 1970s a Nootka movement arose to restore self-government. The people officially named themselves the Nuu-Chah Nulth, which means All Along the Mountains. The 5,000-member tribe has revived its potlatch and winter ceremonials (Northwest Coast) and is pursuing land claims in the Canadian courts. ◀

CLANS

Algonquin and Iroquois societies were structured by membership in clans. Clan membership was based either on the mother's or father's family, and people lived with members of their clan. This flag (right) features the Iroquois Deer clan. Other clans were represented by the Eagle, Butterfly, or such vegetables as the Potato. Each clan had a legend of origin and special powers and responsibilities. Even when they did not live in the same place, clan members shared strong bonds and were obliged to help each other. Members of different tribes considered themselves related to people in another tribe who came from the same clan. Female leaders were called clan mothers.

NORTHEAST

- **TRIBES OF THE REGION: ABENAKI, HURON, IROQUOIS (CAYUGA, MOHAWK, ONEIDA, ONONDAGA, SENECA), KICKAPOO, LENAPE, MAHICAN, MALISEET, MASSACHUSETTS, MENOMINEE, MIAMI, MICMAC, MOHEGAN, NIPMUC, OJIBWA, OTTAWA, PASSAMAQUODDY, PENNACOOK, PENOBSCOT, PEORIA, PEQUOT, POTAWATOMI, SAC AND FOX, SHAWNEE, SUSQUEHANNOCK, WAMPANOAG, WAPPINGER, & WINNEBAGO**

NORTHEAST

The eastern woodlands spread from the Atlantic Ocean to the Mississippi River. The region blends into the Subarctic just north of the Great Lakes. The northern borders of Kentucky and North Carolina define its southern limit. The Appalachian Mountains run the length of the region, separating the lake country from the coast.

Broadleaf forests flash bright colors in the autumn and shelter many kinds of animal life. The native people hunted deer, bear, and birds. They gathered wild rice and berries by the lakes and collected shellfish on the coast. Plentiful spring rains watered their crops of corn, beans, and squash. People lived in villages and spoke at least sixty-eight different languages.

The main language families were Iroquoian and Algonquian. The Iroquois lived in bark-covered longhouses with barrel-shaped roofs. Algonquin Indians lived in smaller, oval-shaped bark cabins in winter and wigwams—domes of bent willow poles covered with bark or reed mats—in summer.

ANCESTORS The Northeast tribes are descended from the Mound Builders of the Mississippi Valley. The earliest signs of habitation there are at least 10,000 years old. The people of the Northeast share a common story of the continent's creation. A long time ago, they say, Sky Woman fell from her home in the sky. Below her was an endless sea. As she fell, Great Turtle rose to the surface to catch her. Birds spread their wings beneath Sky Woman to float her down to the turtle's shell.

When she landed she asked the animals to dive to the bottom of the sea and bring her what they found there. Many animals dove, but each came up for air before it reached the bottom. Finally, a muskrat succeeded. He brought clawfuls of mud from the ocean floor. When Sky Woman painted the cracks in the turtle's shell with the mud, plants sprouted there. The turtle grew until it became the size of North America, which the Northeast Indians call Turtle Island. All of the animals came to live on the turtle's back, and Sky Woman gave birth to the first Native Americans.

Although they shared similar origins, Algonquins and Iroquois did not always get along. They were in conflict over territory and trade long before Europeans arrived. To protect themselves,

WAMPUM

Wampum were beads carved from purple and white quahog (clam) shells collected from Atlantic beaches. The beads were polished, strung together, and used as jewelry and money. When they were woven into belts, their patterns could be read as messages. Each pattern had a special meaning, and entire stories could be woven into wampum belts. Long, elaborately designed wampum belts sometimes served as legal documents or records of tribal history. The wampum shown here is the Washington Covenant Belt.

▶ Stories in Stone

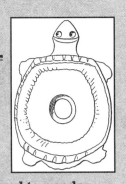

This early Algonquin slate pipe (right) was carved in the shape of a turtle, the hero of Northeast creation stories. Northeastern pipes had stone bowls affixed to wooden stems. Today, Northeast Indians still smoke tobacco during ceremonies (Plains).

This image of an Indian with a rifle (left) was carved on a cliff in the Hudson Valley near Esopus Landing. The rifle and the fact that a metal tool was used to make the pictograph interest historians because the picture combines ancient art techniques and new tools from Europe.

BLACK ROBES

French Jesuit missionaries were among the first Europeans to live in the Northeast. They differed from other missionaries in their tolerance for Indian traditions and their interest in Indian spirituality. In the 19th-century engraving shown below, a Jesuit missionary is preaching to Indians.

The French traders who accompanied the priests often married Indian women, learned their languages, and were sometimes adopted into their tribes (Métis). The Huron, Ojibwa, and Ottawa called the French priests Black Robes.

At first, Indians thought the priests had powerful magic that would cure smallpox and other new diseases. They grew angry at the Black Robes when this proved not to be true. Then, when the beaver started disappearing from overhunting, the Indians began to believe that Christian prayer had destroyed their ancient connection to the animals.

many tribes were allied in confederacies (Iroquois, Lenape, Ottawa, and Peoria). The competition between confederacies worsened in the 17th century, when the European fur trade began (Subarctic). Many tribes were forced west by these pressures (Huron, Ojibwa, and Shawnee).

And white colonists brought their European conflicts to America. The Dutch, French, and British competed for wealth and territory, allying with different tribes to achieve their goals. Beaver pelts quickly became the most popular fur in Europe, so when fur trade battles began, they were called the Beaver Wars. Although European trade goods enriched the tribes, the guns the colonists brought made it easier for old enemies to kill each other.

European alcohol was also new to Native Americans, and proved dangerous. At first, drunkenness seemed like having a vision, but the result was never spiritual wisdom. Instead, alcohol made people sick and needing more strong drink. Some Indian traders moved near the forts to drink with whites. A split developed between traditional Indians and the ones they called "hang-around-the-fort people," some of whom even sold their relatives' land and sacred objects without tribal consent (Sac and Fox).

DISEASES

Even worse than alcohol were European diseases, which wiped out entire tribes. Coast Indians such as the Wampanoag, who saved the Pilgrims and celebrated the first Thanksgiving with them, lost most of their population and land. As early as 1638, New England tribes were forced onto reservations. Resisters were killed, sent to Caribbean plantations as slaves, or forced to abandon their cultures in mission settlements of Christianized "praying Indians." Some tribespeople fled to Canada to avoid these fates.

During King George's War (1744–1745) and the larger French and Indian War (1754–1763), the English and French looked for Indian allies. The Iroquois fought alongside the British, while the Huron, Shawnee, Ojibwa, Ottawa, Peoria, Miami,

Abenaki, and Lenape fought for the French. When the French lost, their Indian friends found themselves without support or weapons. The former French allies began listening to the Lenape prophet Neolin, who preached sobriety, returning to ancestral ways, and driving off the Europeans. They rose up in Pontiac's War in 1763, but were finally defeated (Ottawa).

Most Indians sided with the British during the Revolutionary War. After the war, the British, who remained in forts in the west, encouraged the Indians to attack the American frontiers. The Shawnee chief Tecumseh and Sac chief Black Hawk, both allied with the British, were the last to attempt to drive the white Americans back over the Appalachian Mountains. Their forces were defeated in battle, Tecumseh's in 1811 and Black Hawk's in 1832 (Shawnee and Sac and Fox).

RESERVATIONS The new United States treated the Indians badly. They were attacked, their crops destroyed, and their hunting grounds reduced. Eventually, they were confined to reservations, where they suffered treatment unequal to their white neighbors. Indian spiritual practices were outlawed and their children were forced to go to distant boarding schools. Most of the rights and services promised to them by treaties were denied.

By the 20th century, many Indians could no longer live on their small, poor reservations, so they moved to cities. Beginning in the 1950s, members of the Iroquois, Ojibwa, and Menominee nations began to fight for their treaty rights (Red Power). Since then, eastern Indians have been able to reclaim some tribal lands, get the bones of their ancestors back from museums for reburial, attain fishing rights, and open up their reservations to new businesses. Indian centers are providing community housing in cities, and people are going back to the reservations to learn their traditions. They are daily gaining unity and pride.◄

Akwe: kon

Akwe: kon, Mohawk words meaning All of Us, is the name of the new American Indian Program House at Cornell University in Ithaca, New York. It was designed to reflect community spirit. Seen from above, the building appears to be an eagle with its protecting wings outstretched to the north and south. The ceremonial walkway surrounding Akwe: kon symbolizes the importance and equality of all beings.

Tribal Schools

Pauline Decontie was photographed teaching Algonquian language classes to children at the Kitigan Zibi School in Maniwaki, Quebec, in Canada in 1994. Algonquian is the basis of the Cree, Ojibwa, Montagnais, Naskapi, and Micmac languages traditionally spoken by tribes in the Quebec area. To encourage children to use the Algonquian words they have learned, no English is spoken during class.

▶ Grandfather's House

Northwest Coast Indians called the cedar the Grandfather Tree. For this 1900 photograph, a wedding party gathers in front of a cedar longhouse. The doorway is framed by totem houseposts, also carved of cedar. Northwest Coast longhouses were shared by several families and were the center of all social and ceremonial gatherings.

▶ The Raven

Raven is both the creator and the trickster of the Northwest Coast Indians. He is represented in many forms by various tribes. The **Kwakiutl** Hamatsa raven mask (right) symbolizes the man-eating spirit of the Raven Monster. During the Hamatsa ceremony the wearer of the mask is transformed into a wild creature who must be

ceremonially tamed. At important times during ceremonies, its beak can open and shut with a loud, clapping noise. A Kwakiutl boy holds a modern Raven mask.

NORTHWEST COAST

• **TRIBES OF THE REGION: CHINOOK, COAST SALISH, HAIDA, KWAKIUTL, MAKAH, NOOTKA, TLINGIT, & TSIMSHIAN**

NORTHWEST COAST

Northwest Coast Indians thrived along 2,000 miles of the Pacific Coast from southern Alaska to northern California. More than 500,000 people lived in the region prior to 1800. They spoke forty-five different languages. Ancestors of the twenty-seven main tribes settled some time after Ice Age glaciers melted 15,000 years ago. Most legends about tribal origins say that Raven found the first people in a clam shell. When he let the tiny people out, they grew to their present size and spread out over the area.

The Cascade Range to the east creates a unique environment. The mountains trap the wet ocean air, producing mild temperatures and frequent light rainfall. Forests were so thick that people traveled by canoe. Most villages were built on beaches and riverbanks. Towering cedars furnished wood for plank houses, canoes, and waterproof woven clothing. Rainy winters were spent in multifamily longhouses, where artists carved cedar totem poles and masks.

SEA LIFE The ocean and streams offered large amounts of salmon, shellfish, and great sea mammals. Whales and seals were hunted for their useful bones and skins, as well as for meat. Eulachon, or candlefish, oil was so rich it supplied long-lasting fuel to light torches at night.

Northwest people loved drama and expressed it in canoes carved and painted to look like giant animals. Some canoes were fifty-six feet long and six feet wide. Whole villages rowed to seaside feasts wearing their traditional clothing and masks.

People visited each other during the winter, after the fishing and berrying seasons were over. During winter ceremonials, children learned family stories from singers who belonged to secret societies. Hosts gave presents to hundreds of guests at Northwest Coast potlatch ceremonies. Potlatch means "to give away" in the Chinook language, and giving was a celebration of wealth and family pride. Friends and relatives feasted, sang, and danced for as many as twenty days at potlatches.

CLAN LIFE

Northwest Indians lived in clans, groups of families related to legendary ancestors (Tsimshian). Families measured their status in honored titles or the amount of furs, shell money, carvings, and slaves they owned. Although tribes did not go to war, villages competed by kidnapping people as slaves. Slaves lived as well as their masters and were not harmed, though sometimes a chief would ask to have his slaves killed when he died.

Wealthy men could have several wives. Newborn babies were pressed and bundled to shape their body parts, and an elongated head was a particular sign of beauty. Children played many games, including canoeing contests and tug of war. They were taught about hard work, peacefulness, and family honor. At puberty girls learned household tasks, while boys assisted elders. Children were toughened by icy ocean swims and night runs through rainstorms.

In the late 1700s everything changed. At first the changes were positive. The coastal people were already great bargainers when Chinese, Hawaiian, Spanish, Russian, and British trading boats arrived. At the same time, Iroquois travelers came over the mountains. The appearance of new people and goods was exciting, and Northwest Coast tribes controlled the trade: They killed or captured anyone who landed, so visitors stayed on their

TOTEM POLES

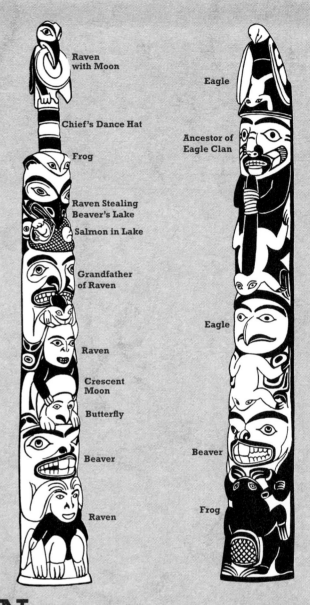

Raven with Moon

Chief's Dance Hat

Frog

Raven Stealing Beaver's Lake

Salmon in Lake

Grandfather of Raven

Raven

Crescent Moon

Butterfly

Beaver

Raven

Eagle

Ancestor of Eagle Clan

Eagle

Beaver

Frog

Northwest Coast totem poles feature a variety of designs, according to tribal and artistic styles. Traditional Haida totem poles use interlocking characters such as Beaver, Raven, Eagle, and Frog. The left pole tells the story of Raven, keeper of the sun, moon, and stars. The pole on the right symbolizes the history of the Eagle clan. Totem poles are carved from cedar logs and then painted. When a pole is completed, it is raised in a prominent place, depending on the type of pole. Housepoles and posts show the family's social rank, while memorial poles mark the graves of chiefs.

SALMON PEOPLE

Northwest Coast Indians caught vast numbers of salmon as the fish swam upstream to hatch their eggs. Salmon fishing is still an important part of the Northwest tribes' economic, social, and spiritual life. Each spring the bones of the first salmon caught that year are returned to the river. This salmon, called the Chief Salmon, is honored in prayer and song so that the fish will return to the river the following year.

▶ Paddle to Seattle

Northwest tribes participated in the Washington State centennial in 1989 by carving traditional canoes. A ten-year-old Klallam girl, Mandi Jones, stands in the honored skipper's position as her canoe docks in Seattle.

boats. The Indians decided how many otter skins to exchange for iron, blankets, guns, and windowpanes.

But the newcomers slowly established themselves. Armed conflicts arose when the Tlingit resisted Russian slave catchers. They burned Russian forts, killing the traders and their Aleut slaves. Once British trading posts were built, European diseases spread quickly. By 1825, 80 percent of the Northwest Coast Indians were dead.

Russia sold Alaska to the U. S. in 1867, and Washington became a state in 1889. United States treaties called the Northwest people the "uncivilized tribes." When they were confined to reservations, it was said to be temporary, but the real goal was to remove the Indians completely. Still, in exchange for their land, an 1854 treaty gave Indians the right to fish anywhere they liked.

There was an uprising by the Coast Salish in 1855. With the Yakima they attacked the city of Seattle, but were defeated. Missions were created to convert Indian children and absorb them into American society. Many Northwest children either ran away or died in mission boarding schools.

COMMERCIAL FISHING Canadian and United States policies were hard on Northwest people. Canada banned the potlatch in 1871, and by the Indian Act, women lost their tribal status when they married outside the tribe. In the States, Indians faced arrest if they competed with commercial fishers. Alaskan tribes lost 70 percent of their catch to outside companies that overfished the waters.

The tribes responded by organizing. Since 1953 they have successfully restored many land, fishing, and civil rights. Leaders meet to plan museums and schools. The tribes work with environmentalists to conserve salmon and protect forests. There has been major population growth since the 1970s, and most of today's tribe members are young people. Children are learning native arts and languages and participating in ceremonies. ◀

OJIBWA

- **LANGUAGE FAMILY:** ALGONQUIAN
- **LIFEWAYS:** HUNTING, FISHING, & GATHERING
- **LOCATION:** SASKATCHEWAN, MANITOBA, ONTARIO, & QUEBEC
- **THEIR OWN NAME:** ANISHINABE

NORTHEAST

The Ojibwa are the largest tribe north of Mexico. Diverse bands are spread across the United States from Michigan to Montana and in central Canada from Quebec to Saskatchewan. About 200,000 Ojibwa live in twenty-five bands in the United States. More than fifty bands of Ojibwa are located in Canada.

The Ojibwa and Cree consider themselves to be one people called the Anishinabe, or Human Beings. Ojibwa means Puckered Up, referring to the stitching on their moccasins. The tribe is also known as the Chippewa.

Kitche Manitou is the Ojibwa creator. Nanapush, his messenger, is half man and half rabbit. The Rabbit is the trickster of Ojibwa legend.

TOTEMS The totem, a sort of clan, was the most important Ojibwa group. Five main totem groups were shared by all Ojibwa-speaking tribes, including the Ottawa, Potawatomi, Sac and Fox, and Menominee. The Crane was a special leaders' totem because cranes have unusual voices: They rarely call, but when they do, all other birds stop to listen.

Children were born into their mothers' totems. They were named by elders who chose girls' names from flowers, times of day, or bodies of water and boys' names from animals, the weather, or stars. In their twelfth year, children went on vision quests. A girl became a woman when she reached puberty. A boy had to do something brave before he was called a man. Normally, childbirth was thought to be a woman's bravest act, but the Ojibwa were also the

The Ojibwa Understanding of Life

Ojibwa artist Del Ashkewe created this design to represent the Ojibwa understanding of life. At the top is Kitche Manitou, the creator. The semicircle below the creator is the sky and the universe, with the sun inside. The figure inside the circle is human life. The curved lines sweeping upward and outward from the circle represent the Tree of Life, the plant upon which all life depends. The tipis and figures of people and animals stand for the multitude of living creatures.

Gerald Vizenor

Of Ojibwa and French ancestry, Gerald Vizenor has had poems published in numerous anthologies and journals. He has also written several books about the Ojibwa-Chippewa and the Anishinabe cultures. He teaches American Indian Studies at the University of Minnesota and is working on his second novel.

► Louise Erdrich

Writer Louise Erdrich (born 1951) is the daughter of a German-American father and an Ojibwa mother. Among her many books are the novels *Love Medicine*, *The Beet Queen*, and *Tracks*, all of which deal in part with the Ojibwa experience. She has co-authored novels and other works with her late husband, Michael Dorris, who was Modoc. Her latest novel is *The Bingo Palace*.

► Quillwork

This buckskin bag was embroidered with porcupine quills. After they came into contact with Europeans, the Ojibwa used glass beads instead of quills. The Ojibwa are credited with some of the most extensive, elaborate, and beautiful beadwork ever made. Over the years, they remained faithful to the patterns and designs of their ancestors.

only tribe to have female war chiefs who fought in battle.

MIGRATION The Ojibwa originated in the Delaware area (Lenape). By 1600, conflicts with the Iroquois had forced them northwest. Ojibwa bands drove the Minnesota Sioux onto the Plains, where warfare between the tribes continued for two centuries.

When they first met the French in southern Ontario, the Ojibwa, Ottawa, and Potawatomi were already united in a confederacy called the Three Fires. By 1700 they were deeply involved in the fur trade (Subarctic). French missionaries converted many Ojibwa to Catholicism (Northeast). However, to protect traditions, a secret society—the Midewiwin—was born (Missions). The Midewiwin Society has healing lodges whose main goal is to prolong life. Healers learn about moral conduct as well as herbal medicine and ceremonies.

In the early 19th century, the Ojibwa avoided being moved to Oklahoma because settlers did not want their swampy, rocky land. Ojibwa bands have been self-governing since 1934. In the Great Lakes region, they have struggled to keep treaty fishing rights (Red Power). In 1984 the Wisconsin Ojibwa formed a central commission to defend their rights and protect endangered streams and lakes. The Ojibwa sell maple syrup, wild rice, and floral beadwork. Casinos also bring income to the tribe.

Crafts and culture have been preserved in tribal museums and live on in the works of Ojibwa artists. Midewiwin lodges and Potawatomi Big Drum ceremonies are among the most popular Ojibwa activities. The Ojibwa language is taught at tribal schools and colleges. Several Ojibwa are leaders of national Indian organizations.◄

OLMECS

- **LANGUAGE FAMILY: UNKNOWN**
- **LIFEWAYS: FARMING & TRADING**
- **LOCATION: NONE**
- **THEIR OWN NAME: OLMEC**

MESOAMERICA

From about 1000 to 300 B.C., Olmecs inhabited the first known Mesoamerican city, La Venta. The name Olmec, Rubber Land Dwellers, comes from the rubber trees that grew in swampy Veracruz-Tabasco on the Gulf of Mexico. The Olmecs made rubber balls for games they played in stone courts and used colored rubber to decorate clothing.

As developers of agriculture, writing, pyramids, calendars, and cities, the Olmecs are thought to have influenced the Maya. Among the items that remain from the Olmec civilization are carved stone tablets, altars and burial chambers, mounds full of jade figurines, and giant heads carved of basalt. The heads are about nine feet high and weigh up to forty tons. They are thought to be portraits of Olmec rulers, but they look more like Africans than Mesoamericans (Paleo-Indians).

SNAKES Olmec craftsmen also made concave magnetite (black stone) mirrors so highly polished that they can still be used to start fires. The Aztecs later used mirrors like these to read the future. The Olmecs carved the earliest portraits of Tlaloc, the Mesoamerican rain god, whose face was composed from the body of two snakes. Snakes are sacred to the native peoples of Mesoamerica because they are believed to know ancient secrets. Rain god ceremonies were performed by spiritual leaders in open plazas. The Olmec city of Teotihuacán was built around 200 B.C., near the site of modern Mexico City. Teotihuacán had 600 pyramids and was a cultural center for people from all of Mexico. Teotihuacán's influence spread as far as present-day Costa Rica and the American Southwest.◄

Faces of Tlaloc

These different masks of Tlaloc, the Olmec rain god, depict the many ways he was perceived over the centuries. The mask on the left (below) is believed to be the oldest of those shown here. Later versions follow counterclockwise, with the mask on the left (above) being the most recent.

Basalt Head

This huge and ancient sculpture of the head of an Olmec ruler or deity comes from the great Olmec center of La Venta in Mexico. It was carved from giant blocks of basalt, a volcanic rock. It took hundreds of men to transport the nearly twenty-ton stone through jungles and rivers to the site where it was carved.

▶ Earth Lodge

Traditionally, the Omaha lived on the Plains in present-day Nebraska. Their homes were lodges made of logs, branches, grass, and earth. The logs and branches came from cottonwood trees that grow near river banks in the Plains. Under an opening in the roof is the hearth, or fireplace. Around the hearth are sleeping benches. Up to forty people could live in a lodge like this one.

▶ Omaha Warriors

Above is a 1917 painting of Omaha warriors on the Plains. The man on horseback is wearing his hair plaited and has a band of silver disks hanging down from his hair.

OMAHA

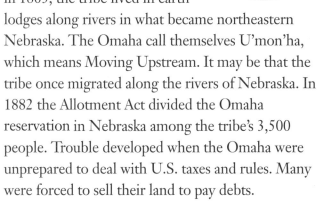

- **LANGUAGE FAMILY: SIOUIAN**
- **LIFEWAYS: FARMING & HUNTING**
- **LOCATION: NEBRASKA**
- **THEIR OWN NAME: U'MON'HA**

PLAINS

When explorers Lewis and Clark first met the Omaha in 1803, the tribe lived in earth lodges along rivers in what became northeastern Nebraska. The Omaha call themselves U'mon'ha, which means Moving Upstream. It may be that the tribe once migrated along the rivers of Nebraska. In 1882 the Allotment Act divided the Omaha reservation in Nebraska among the tribe's 3,500 people. Trouble developed when the Omaha were unprepared to deal with U.S. taxes and rules. Many were forced to sell their land to pay debts.

The LaFlesche family gained reforms for their tribe. Suzette and Susan LaFlesche lobbied Congress to uphold treaties and traveled around the country on behalf of the Omaha. In 1915 Susan became the first Native American woman physician. Her brother Francis LaFlesche was one of the first Indian anthropologists. His writings were dedicated to preserving Omaha culture.

FIRST POWWOW

Today, half of the 6,000 Omaha govern themselves on 52,000 acres of reservation land. Most work for tribal services, farms, and businesses.

The Omaha are credited with creating the modern powwow. Their yearly celebration of Whe'wahchee, or Dance of Thanksgiving, is the oldest gathering of its kind. At powwows, the Omaha give gifts and perform warrior songs and the Gourd Dance. Since 1989 they have celebrated the return of the Sacred Pole Umon'hon'ti, which means the Real Omaha. Years ago, Francis LaFlesche gave the pole to Harvard University for safekeeping, but now it stands again as a symbol of tribal unity.◄

ONEIDA

- **LANGUAGE FAMILY:** IROQUOIAN
- **LIFEWAYS:** HUNTING, GATHERING, & FARMING
- **LOCATION:** NEW YORK, WISCONSIN, ONTARIO, & QUEBEC
- **THEIR OWN NAME:** TIIONEN IOTE

NORTHEAST

The Oneida are in the Iroquois Confederacy. Their own name means People of the Standing Stone. In longhouse meetings they sit with the Younger Brothers—the Cayuga and Tuscarora. Their land is south of Oneida Lake in New York, west of the Mohawk territory, and east of the Onondaga. Their Gustoweh headgear has two upright plumes (Seneca).

HOSPITALITY The Oneida clan symbols—Turtle, Bear, and Wolf—are displayed above the doors of their longhouses, where the Oneida traditionally feed visitors as soon as they arrive. A favorite dish is cornbread with chestnuts, dried blueberries, and sunflower seeds.

Many Oneida were killed during the fur trade wars of the 1600s (Subarctic). They adopted Métis, Huron, and Ojibwa people to replace their dead relatives. They also adopted Tuscarora refugees in 1711 and Mahican refugees in 1785.

During the Revolutionary War, some Oneida allied with the British, while others fought for the Americans. Attacks from both sides devastated the tribe. After the war, Oneida land was confiscated.

In 1839 about 250 Oneida bought land in Ontario, Canada, and rebuilt their traditional government. Others moved to Green Bay, Wisconsin, where the Menominee provided them with land. In 1920 the Oneida who remained in New York had to fight in court to keep the thirty-two acres they had left. Today, the combined 21,000 Oneida are using money from Wisconsin tribal businesses to preserve their culture and sue for their New York homeland. ◀

Oneida Girls and Boys

These four Oneida girls (above) were photographed in 1924 in Oneida, Wisconsin. They are wearing traditional costumes of headbands, necklaces, fringed tunics, and moccasins. In contrast, the four boys below are dressed in European clothing. Many of the Oneida living in Wisconsin today are members of Christian churches, and these boys are altar boys in their church. They are dressed for church service, and two of the boys are carrying incensories—vessels in which incense is burned during a Mass.

Wampum Belt

Wampum belts were made of beads cut from colored shells. The beads were arranged in patterns to record or commemorate important events. According to legend, the first wampum belt was made by Hiawatha, an Onondaga who was a follower of the famous Peacemaker, Deganawida, founder of the Iroquois Confederacy (Huron).

The Bowl Game

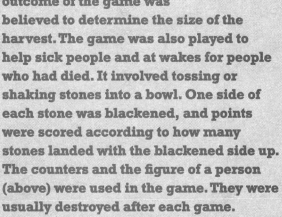

The Bowl Game was part of a sacred ritual performed at different times of the year by the Onondaga and other Iroquois tribes. The outcome of the game was believed to determine the size of the harvest. The game was also played to help sick people and at wakes for people who had died. It involved tossing or shaking stones into a bowl. One side of each stone was blackened, and points were scored according to how many stones landed with the blackened side up. The counters and the figure of a person (above) were used in the game. They were usually destroyed after each game.

ONONDAGA

- **LANGUAGE FAMILY: IROQUOIAN**
- **LIFEWAYS: HUNTING, GATHERING, & FARMING**
- **LOCATIONS: NEW YORK & ONTARIO & QUEBEC, CANADA**
- **THEIR OWN NAME: ONQTA KE'KA**

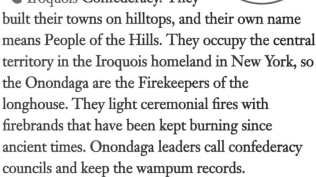

NORTHEAST

The Onondaga are part of the Iroquois Confederacy. They built their towns on hilltops, and their own name means People of the Hills. They occupy the central territory in the Iroquois homeland in New York, so the Onondaga are the Firekeepers of the longhouse. They light ceremonial fires with firebrands that have been kept burning since ancient times. Onondaga leaders call confederacy councils and keep the wampum records.

The Onondaga clans are Bear, Beaver, Snipe, Hawk, Turtle, Wolf, Deer, and Eel. Leaders wear one feather upright and one to the right side of their traditional headgear, the Gustoweh (Seneca).

JOSEPH BRANT During the European fur trade wars (Subarctic), the Onondaga were split into pro-British and pro-French parties. The Onondaga who were allied with the French became Christians in the 1750s (Northeast). After the Revolutionary War, about 250 Christian Onondaga followed Mohawk leader Joseph Brant to Canada, where they settled.

The Onondaga land is called a territory because the tribe is a sovereign nation. However, by 1822 all but 6,100 acres of Onondaga land had been taken by New York State. Today, the 2,000 Onondaga are governed by hereditary chiefs chosen by clan mothers. They continue to host longhouse councils and recitals of the Great Law of Peace. Their Tadodaho, or spiritual leader, is the spokesman for the Iroquois Confederacy. Tadodaho Leon Shenandoah has succeeded in convincing museums to return sacred wampum belts.◀

OSAGE

- **LANGUAGE FAMILY: SIOUIAN**
- **LIFEWAYS: HUNTING**
- **LOCATIONS: OKLAHOMA**
- **THEIR OWN NAME: WAZHAZHE**

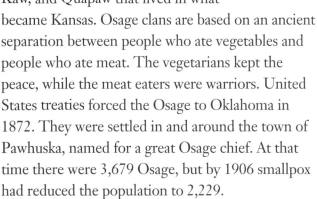

PLAINS

The Osage were once part of a group comprising the Ponca, Kaw, and Quapaw that lived in what became Kansas. Osage clans are based on an ancient separation between people who ate vegetables and people who ate meat. The vegetarians kept the peace, while the meat eaters were warriors. United States treaties forced the Osage to Oklahoma in 1872. They were settled in and around the town of Pawhuska, named for a great Osage chief. At that time there were 3,679 Osage, but by 1906 smallpox had reduced the population to 2,229.

OSAGE OIL

The discovery of oil on their reservation in 1896 brought large amounts of money to the Osage. By 1920 the tribe was called "the wealthiest nation in the world." Still, the U.S. government refused to grant the tribe its legal rights. Osage women were not allowed to vote for fear they would marry outsiders who would gain control of their tribal vote.

Oil prices fell during the Great Depression of the 1930s, and oil income dropped after World War II. Interest in Osage oil reawakened after Arab nations raised the price of their oil during the 1970s. In the 1990s the Osage economy and government still centers on the tribe's natural resources.

Most Osage live in Osage County, Oklahoma. Many work for the tribal government in Pawhuska, home of the oldest tribal museum in the United States. Others farm or ranch. The tribe continues its traditions through the Osage language, ceremonial dances, such crafts as finger-woven sashes, and the Native American Church (Comanche).◄

▶ Osage Girl

This Osage girl, photographed in 1904, is wearing a dress beautifully decorated with ribbon appliqué. The hand design was characteristic of Osage dress and comes from the traditional Friendship Blanket. The photograph was taken at the St. Louis Exposition celebrating the 100th anniversary of the Louisiana Purchase.

▶ Charlotte DeClue

Charlotte DeClue (born 1948) is a graduate of Oklahoma State University. She has been writing poetry since 1990 and has recently had some of her poems published in a collection of contemporary American Indian poetry called *Songs From This Earth on Turtle's Back* (**Northeast**). She currently lives in Lawrence, Kansas, with her husband and teenage son.

In a Canoe

This 1925 photograph of Ottawa Indians in a canoe was taken in Michigan during a tourist pageant. At that time, the Ottawa often performed traditional dances and sold arts and crafts to tourists. The clothes they are wearing here are not specifically Ottawa. Rather, they are general "Indian" costumes worn for the tourists.

Ottawa Fishermen

These Ottawa men, photographed in the early 20th century, earned their living by fishing on Lake Michigan. Ottawa have lived near the lake for more than 300 years. In 1855 a treaty guaranteed their rights to hunt and fish there, but the treaty has often been violated. In 1948 the Michigan Ottawa formed the Northern Michigan Ottawa Association to assert their rights.

OTTAWA

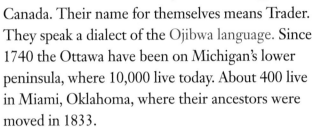

- **LANGUAGE FAMILY:** ALGONQUIAN
- **LIFEWAYS:** HUNTING, FISHING, & TRADING
- **LOCATION:** MICHIGAN, OKLAHOMA, & ONTARIO
- **THEIR OWN NAME:** ODAWA

NORTHEAST

The Ottawa homeland is on Lake Huron in Ontario, Canada. Their name for themselves means Trader. They speak a dialect of the Ojibwa language. Since 1740 the Ottawa have been on Michigan's lower peninsula, where 10,000 live today. About 400 live in Miami, Oklahoma, where their ancestors were moved in 1833.

GHOST SUPPERS In the past, Ottawa men hunted and fished, while women grew and gathered plants for food. The Ottawa believed in ghosts but were not afraid of them. They thought ghosts could be guardians if the right offerings were made. During Ghost Suppers a family prepared food and set the table. A spiritual leader spoke to the ghosts, put out the fires, and closed the door. It is said that when the family returned, the food had often been eaten.

With the Ojibwa and Potawatomi, the Ottawa were part of the Three Fires trade confederacy. After 1615 they were allies of the French and participated in the European fur trade (Subarctic). From 1763 to 1769, Ottawa chief Pontiac led an alliance of tribes that captured many British forts in the Ohio Valley. They were tricked at Fort Pitt (present-day Pittsburgh) when General Jeffrey Amherst gave them smallpox-infested blankets. The resulting epidemic wiped out Pontiac's army.

It was not until 1980 that the Ottawa received federal status as a tribe separate from the Ojibwa. Today, elders speak Odawa and young people are learning to make birchbark containers and beaded clothing. Ghost Suppers and baby-naming ceremonies were revived in the 1960s.◀

PAIUTE

- **LANGUAGE FAMILY: UTO-AZTECAN NUMIC**
- **LIFEWAYS: HUNTING, GATHERING, & FARMING**
- **LOCATION: NEVADA, CALIFORNIA, OREGON, UTAH, & ARIZONA**
- **THEIR OWN NAME: LOCAL NAMES**

GREAT BASIN

The Paiute once ranged from Oregon to Utah. Related to the Ute, their name means Water-Ute, an odd name, because their lands were very dry. Like others in the Great Basin, the Paiute were a hunting and gathering people. Small bands also farmed around Pyramid Lake in Nevada. There are two great branches of the Paiute: the Northern Paiute, who lived along the eastern slope of the Sierra Nevada Mountains in California, and the Southern Paiute, who lived in southern Nevada and Utah. They call themselves by local band names such as Mono and Winnemucca.

Paiute bands had far-reaching family networks. Since marriage among cousins was taboo, and since most young people in one band were related to each other, mates had to be found in other communities. A Paiute proverb says, "Your friend is your enemy," which means that you can truly count on no one but your relatives.

The Northern Paiute had the misfortune to live on land desired by whites. The Comstock Lode, among the world's richest silver deposits, was discovered in western Nevada in 1859. Miners forced Paiute around Virginia City to migrate and settle on reservations at Pyramid Lake and Walker River in western Nevada. Some formed small groups and migrated to California and Oregon.

WOVOKA The Paiute have a rich spiritual history. The prophet Wovoka was a Paiute (Great Basin). During a solar eclipse in 1889, Wovoka had a revelation and received five songs from the Creator. The songs spoke of morals,

Wickiups

The Paiute were nomads who followed the seasonal food supply. Their wickiups, made from brush reeds and willow poles, served as temporary shelters.

Kill the Bone

These Paiute Indians were photographed playing the game of Ni-aung-pi-kai, or Kill the Bone, in the Kaibab Plateau in northern Arizona around 1873. One member of the team on the left has a marked bone, and the team on the right must guess who is holding it. Chief Chuarumpeak stands in the center in a beaded shirt.

Sarah Winnemucca Hopkins

Sarah Winnemucca Hopkins (1844–1891) tried to regain land the Paiute had lost when they were moved to a reservation. She wrote *Life Among the Paiutes* to bring her crusade for justice to an English-speaking audience. She is wearing a lecture costume here, not traditional Paiute ornamentation.

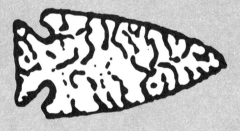

Spearpoint

Spearpoints like this one have been found throughout North America. They were a fundamental weapon used by many paleo-Indians to hunt for food.

rituals, and life after death. Wovoka is known among the Paiute as Tamme Naa'a, or Messiah.

In the 20th century, Los Angeles purchased the Owens River Valley watershed on the eastern slopes of the Sierra Nevadas. Sending water to the thirsty city turned the once-green valley into a desert.

Southern Paiute land was included in the Navajo reservation in the 1930s. The tribe lost its status in 1954. However, in 1965 the Southern Paiute won a large cash settlement from the federal government, and they have used the money for education and for business projects such as ranches and handicrafts.

Today, there are about 10,000 Paiute—about the same number as in the 1840s, when they came into contact with Europeans. Although many Paiute are Christians, most continue to sing, pray, and tell traditional stories. Plains spiritual practices such as sweat lodges and Sun Dances are popular among the Paiute.◄

PALEO-INDIANS

Paleo-Indians lived in the Western Hemisphere many thousands of years ago. They lived in small hunter-gatherer bands and used stone tools.

Archaeologists and Native American historians are still debating where the paleo-Indians came from and how they got here. Most archaeological evidence points to a date about 12,000 years ago, but America's first peoples may have lived here as early as 35,000 B.C. or as "recently" as 8000 B.C. Almost all archaeologists agree that people first came to North America from Asia by crossing the frozen Bering Strait during one of the ice ages of the Paleolithic Era, which is sometimes called the Stone Age (Arctic).

A few archaeologists and many historians

among the Native American community maintain that people lived in the Americas as far back as 100,000 B.C. They say that 100,000-year-old tools have been found at Calico Mountain in California. Others say it's impossible for humans to have come here that long ago. They point out that human bones were slightly different 100,000 years ago, and those kinds of bones have not been found in the Americas.

There's some debate, too, about where Native Americans came from. Some scientists suggest they may have come from Africa or across the Pacific Ocean. They point to 1,500-year-old Olmec statues in Mexico that resemble Africans. On the other hand, many Native Americans say that their people have always lived in the Americas.

ANCIENT ANCESTORS

There is no question that some human remains in North America go back about 12,000 years. These remains include distinctive bone tools and spearpoints carved from obsidian (black glass) and other hard rocks. The spearpoints were inserted into a slot in the wooden shaft of the spear and secured with twine.

A more finely carved spearpoint found near Folsom, California, dates from about 9,000 B.C. Archaeologists believe that both types of spearpoints were first made in what is now Mexico (Mesoamerica) and the Southwest United States. Travelers then carried them east and north over the course of many years.

At Debert, Nova Scotia, in Canada, a rich archaeological site gives a picture of paleo-Indian life more than 10,000 years ago. Remains include the markings of a semicircular camp of tents around a central hearth fire. Apparently, the inhabitants dug up quartz (a hard stone), then heated it over the fire to make it easier to carve. The bones of bison, deer, and other large mammals suggest what paleo-Indians ate. ◀

▶ Spearpoints

Before the horse was brought to the Americas, paleo-Indians hunted on foot. They often cornered their prey by a lake, surrounded it, and pierced its sides with hard spearpoints like the ones shown here.

▶ Olmec Head

This is a drawing of a giant head that was carved from stone by the Olmecs about 1,500 years ago. Its African features have convinced some archaeologists that Africans came to Central and South America in prehistoric times.

Palouse Falls

This drawing of Palouse Falls in eastern Washington was done by John M. Stanley in 1853. The Palouse Indians believed that the creator had made the falls so salmon could not swim upstream beyond the Palouse fishing grounds.

PALOUSE

- **LANGUAGE FAMILY: SAHAPTIAN**
- **LIFEWAYS: HUNTING, GATHERING, FISHING, & HORSE TRADING**
- **LOCATION: WASHINGTON**
- **THEIR OWN NAME: PALOUSE**

PLATEAU

The Palouse are closely related to the Nez Perce. They were active traders who often spoke two or three languages, perhaps Penutian and Salish as well as their own Sahaptian. The Palouse adopted Christianity, but they also maintained the Seven Drum ceremony (Nez Perce). Today, most Palouse share the 1-million-acre Colville Reservation in eastern Washington with the Nez Perce, Coeur d'Alene, Spokan, and Kalispel. A confederated tribal council manages timber and other resources, and is purchasing more land.◀

PASSAMAQUODDY

- **LANGUAGE FAMILY: ALGONQUIAN**
- **LIFEWAYS: HUNTING, FISHING, & SEA HUNTING**
- **LOCATION: MAINE**
- **THEIR OWN NAME: PESTEMOHKATIYEK**

NORTHEAST

The Passamaquoddy were in the Abenaki Confederacy. Their language is close to that of the Maliseet. In 1726, 150 Passamaquoddy lived on the Maine–New Brunswick coast. They divided after a quarrel between land- and ocean-hunting groups in 1852.

Today, tribe members from the two groups number 2,500. They bought land with money won in a 1979 court settlement shared with the Penobscot. The tribe runs a blueberry farm and a wildlife center, and holds a festival in August that includes Blueberry ceremonies.◀

Denny Sockabasin

This watercolor portrait of Denny Sockabasin was done in 1817. Denny was the daughter of Passamaquoddy chief Francis Joseph Neptune. Beside her is a doll swaddled and laced on a miniature cradleboard. The two armed soldiers seen through the window behind her are perhaps the artist's symbols of the whites' conquest of Native Americans.

PAWNEE

- **LANGUAGE FAMILY:** CADDOAN
- **LIFEWAYS:** FARMING & HUNTING
- **LOCATION:** OKLAHOMA
- **THEIR OWN NAME:** CHAHIKSICHAHIKS

PLAINS

Four central Plains bands belonged to the Pawnee tribe: the Chaui, the Pitahawirata, the Skidi, and the Kitkahahki. The Pawnee once lived in large earth lodges in what is today western Nebraska and eastern Wyoming. There they grew corn, hunted, and looted Comanche villages for horses. The Pawnee call themselves Men of Men. The name Pawnee comes from *pariki*, or "horn." It describes the Pawnee hairstyle: The men shaved their heads on the sides, leaving a central scalp-lock that they stiffened with grease until it curved like a horn.

STAR PEOPLE

Pawnee men and women joined Hedushka—societies devoted to dances and ceremonies. They regarded the stars as spirits, basing planting activities on star patterns. Pawnee earth lodges were built to line up with constellations on certain nights of the year. Star legends were passed down through the generations and acted out in ritual dramas.

The Pawnee fought the Sioux and Cheyenne but were friendly to whites. Pawnee served as scouts for U.S. soldiers. By the mid-1800s, many white settlers were crossing Pawnee land, killing the buffalo, and bringing smallpox and cholera. The Pawnee were moved to Oklahoma in 1876, where the diseases spread quickly. By 1906 their population had decreased from 10,000 to 600.

Today, there are about 2,500 Pawnee. They do the Ghost Dance in their roundhouses in Oklahoma (Great Basin). Unfortunately, their language is fading. Many children sing Pawnee songs without knowing what the words mean. ◀

▶ A Pawnee Woman

This woman is dressed for a ceremony. She is wearing a necklace of bone beads, each of them several inches long, and holding a fan of eagle feathers used in ceremonial dances. Her hair is arranged in two braids in the traditional Pawnee style. The insignia on her clothing and headband—including the sun and the four cardinal points of direction—have spiritual meaning for the Pawnee.

▶ Larry EchoHawk

In 1994 Pawnee Larry EchoHawk became attorney general of Idaho, the first Native American to hold that office. He led the Idaho delegation to the Democratic National Convention in 1992—again, the first Native American to do so—and gave a speech there. George Washington University awarded him its Martin Luther King medal for his contributions to human rights. *USA Weekend* has called EchoHawk one of the twenty "most promising people in politics."

Basket

This Pennacook basket is made of partially dyed ash splints woven in a checked pattern. It is lined with a *Boston Daily Courier* newspaper from 1835, though the basket is probably much older than the newspaper.

Andrew Sockalexis

Andrew Sockalexis, a Penobscot, was a champion long-distance runner in the early years of the 20th century. This photograph was taken in 1912, the year he took second place in the Boston Marathon.

PENNACOOK

- **LANGUAGE FAMILY:** ALGONQUIAN
- **LIFEWAYS:** HUNTING, FARMING, & GATHERING
- **LOCATION:** NEW HAMPSHIRE & QUEBEC
- **THEIR OWN NAME:** PENQKOK

NORTHEAST

The Pennacook were part of the Abenaki Confederacy. They hunted moose but also grew corn near their wigwam villages. Although the tribe's doctors were famous for their healing powers, by 1674 European diseases had reduced the 6,000 Pennacook to 1,000. Most of the Pennacook fled to Canada when the English attacked their Wampanoag allies in 1675. In 1865 they began to return to New Hampshire, when their baskets became popular among whites. Today, the tribe counts 700 members in New Hampshire and 300 in Quebec. ◄

PENOBSCOT

- **LANGUAGE FAMILY:** ALGONQUIAN
- **LIFEWAYS:** HUNTING & GATHERING
- **LOCATION:** MAINE
- **THEIR OWN NAME:** PANAWAHPSKEK

NORTHEAST

The Penobscot are related to the Micmac, Passamaquoddy, and Abenaki. Their name means Rock Land. Since their land is too rocky for farming, they gathered clams and wild potatoes and hunted animals on land and at sea. Penobscot canoes could hold a family of six and their dogs and belongings.

In 1775 Massachusetts took most of the Penobscot land. Two centuries later, in 1979, the 1,984 Penobscot received money for their land in a court settlement. The tribal museum in Old Town, Maine, displays and sells traditional crafts. ◄

PEORIA

- **LANGUAGE FAMILY: ALGONQUIAN**
- **LIFEWAYS: HUNTING, FISHING, GATHERING, & FARMING**
- **LOCATION: OKLAHOMA**
- **THEIR OWN NAME: PIWAREA**

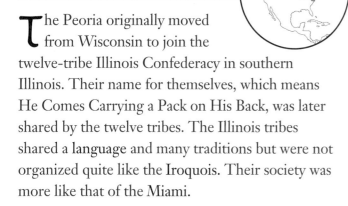

NORTHEAST

The Peoria originally moved from Wisconsin to join the twelve-tribe Illinois Confederacy in southern Illinois. Their name for themselves, which means He Comes Carrying a Pack on His Back, was later shared by the twelve tribes. The Illinois tribes shared a language and many traditions but were not organized quite like the Iroquois. Their society was more like that of the Miami.

BIRD CRIES The Peoria believed that birds gave people supernatural powers during war. Warriors kept bird skins, and before battle they honored those skins in all-night ceremonies. The leader carried the skins into battle. While attacking, the warriors gave bird cries, and victorious warriors were honored by the Eagle Dance.

As allies of the French in the 1700s, the Peoria were attacked by British allies, including the Iroquois, Sac and Fox, Shawnee, and Chickasaw. In the Revolutionary War, the Peoria sided with the colonists and lost many people to the British-allied Kickapoo and Potawatomi. Because of these conflicts, the Peoria lost their land. By 1800 they had been driven west to Kansas.

Following the Civil War, the Peoria were pushed into Oklahoma, where they became members of the United Peoria and Miami Tribe. The state of Oklahoma took the tribe's land in 1907. The tribe lost its status in 1950 but won it back in federal court in 1978. The 2,000-member tribe has purchased land and is recording its history. Although few people speak the language, many perform Peoria songs and dances at Quapaw ceremonies.◀

▶ Chief Shabonee

Chief Shabonee was one of the few Indian leaders in present-day Illinois who were friendly toward American settlers after the War of 1812. His village in De Kalb County, Illinois, was later named after him: Shabbona.

LES ILLINOIS

▶ Peacekeeping

This engraving by a French artist depicts a Peoria man offering a *calumet,* or peace pipe, to a European settler. At first, the Peoria and whites lived in peace. They established trade relations and lived alongside each other without incident. But European settlers in Illinois eventually forced the Peoria out.

Pequot Symbols

The logo of the Mashantucket Pequot shows important aspects of their culture. The Pequot were known as the Fox People, and a fox is at the center of the logo. Behind the fox is a tree that stands for "the many wooded lands" (which is what the word *mashantucket* means) where the tribe originally lived. The insignia on the ground is the sign of Chief Robin Cassasinamon. He held the tribe together after the 1637 massacre at Mystic in Connecticut.

Foxwood Casino

The Pequot's Foxwood casino in Connecticut opened in 1992 and quickly became the most profitable casino in the Western Hemisphere. Much of the profit goes toward educating Pequot children and other Native Americans and helping preserve Indian culture.

PEQUOT

- **LANGUAGE FAMILY:** ALGONQUIAN
- **LIFEWAYS:** HUNTING, GATHERING, & FARMING
- **LOCATION:** CONNECTICUT
- **THEIR OWN NAME:** MASHANTUCKET

NORTHEAST

The Pequot, also known as the Fox People, hunted, fished, and traded in what became eastern Connecticut. Their own name means Many-Wooded Lands. The name Pequot comes from the Mohegan word Paquatauog, meaning Destroyers. That's because the Mohegan and Pequot quarreled over territory and trade. Competing European traders only deepened the existing hostility between the Pequot and Mohegan.

MYSTIC The Pequot Massacre of 1637 started as a family quarrel. Mohegan chief Uncas aided the English settlers in an attack on Pequot chief Sassacus's Mystic Village. Sassacus was Uncas's father-in law. Half of the 600 Pequot men, women, and children were killed. About 200 people were sold as slaves in the Caribbean.

Although their art forms and language declined after the removal, the Pequot have made a remarkable recovery. In 1975, when Richard Hayward was elected chairman of the tribe, there were only fifty-four Pequot on 214 acres of land. In a famous 1983 court case, the tribe won federal status and 1,800 acres of land. Since then hundreds of Caribbean Pequots have come home.

The tribe's Foxwood casino brings in about $600 million a year. These funds are used to provide housing, jobs, and services to tribe members. The Pequot have also contributed $10 million to the National Museum of the American Indian and are building their own museum. Today, the 846 Pequot have a strong economic base in eastern Connecticut.◄

PIMA

- LANGUAGE FAMILY: UTO-AZTECAN PIMAN
- LIFEWAYS: FARMING
- LOCATION: ARIZONA
- THEIR OWN NAME: AKIMEL AU-AUTHM

SOUTHWEST

The Pima are related to the Tohono O'odham, who are descended from the Hohokam cliff dwellers. The tribe has traditionally lived in the hot, dry desert lands from the Gila River in Arizona to Mexico's Sea of Cortés. The Pima call themselves Akimel Au-Authm, meaning River People. Pima is a name given to the tribe by Spanish missionaries. It is the Piman word for "no."

To irrigate their corn fields, the Pima built extensive canals along the Gila and Salt rivers. But Apache raids made it difficult to maintain the canals. In the 1600s the Spanish brought disease and war—as well as Christianity and livestock, which changed the Pima way of life (Missions).

STORIES The Pima survived partly because of their sense of history. Pima historians were selected for their ability to tell stories of origins and events. One story tells of Elder Brother, an ancestor who learned from the Vulture how to channel river waters. Another tells of the coming of fire, stolen from the lightning god and brought to the Pima by the Roadrunner.

Today, about 9,000 Pima live on two reservations in central Arizona. Another 2,000 live in nearby towns and cities. People on the reservation farm with irrigation waters from the Salt and Gila rivers. The farms grow cotton, fruit, grains, and vegetables. The Pima have recently banned dumping of radioactive waste on their lands. The Gila River Arts and Craft Center includes a tribal museum featuring 2,000 years of Pima history. On the Salt River Reservation, the Hoo-hoogam Ki Museum displays Pima baskets. ◄

Desert Eagle School

The Pima were famous for their basketry. The Desert Eagle School's 1994 logo incorporates the spiritual Pima basketry symbol Man in the Maze. The ancient design symbolizes the Pima search for truth and self-knowledge. Students at the school chose the logo to reflect pride in their heritage.

Woman

This unidentified Pima woman was photographed in 1883. Her face tatoos are unique to the tribe.

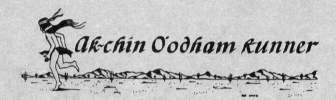

Newspaper

The *Ak-chin O'odham Runner* is the newspaper of the Ak-Chin Pima and Tohono O'odham community and is published in Maricopa, Arizona. The newspaper prints not only news but stories, birthday wishes, and trivia contests. An article in February 1995 issue told how local students were preparing to compete in a national spelling bee in Washington, D.C.

Buffalo Nation

The buffalo gave Plains Indians everything they needed to live. A good hunt provided not only enough meat to last for months but also hide for robes, tipis, clothing, and pouches. Bones were made into tools and weapons, and their marrow into paint. Buffalo hair was used for rope, and dung for fuel.

To Indians, buffalo were more than just game animals. They were members of a great nation, related to human tribes but closely connected to the creator. Painted buffalo skulls remain the centerpieces of Plains altars today, and people continue to lift skulls in prayer, as this Mandan hunter did in 1908 (left).

Plains Lodges

Plains dwellings reflected regional materials and lifeways. Southern wickiups (right) were made of grasses. In the north, nomadic hunters carried hide tipis (left), while earthlodges (below) were built by northern farmers.

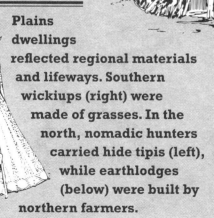

PLAINS

• TRIBES OF THE REGION: ARAPAHO, ARIKARA, ASSINIBOINE, BLACKFEET, CADDO, CHEYENNE, COMANCHE, CROW, GROS VENTRE, HIDATSA, IOWA, KAW, KIOWA, MANDAN, MISSOURIA, OMAHA, OSAGE, OTOE, PAWNEE, PONCA, QUAPAW, SARCEE, SIOUX (DAKOTA, LAKOTA, NAKOTA), TONKAWA, & WICHITA

Native Americans have inhabited the Great Plains since A.D. 300, when they invented the bow and arrow. They roamed nearly one million square miles of land west of the Mississippi River and east of the Rocky Mountains. Indian settlements stretched from present-day Canada to the southern tip of Texas. Although the area contains the Platte, Mississippi, and Missouri rivers, and rugged plateaus and cliffs, most of the Plains was endless grassy prairie, home to the buffalo.

Most Plains Indians were hunters who followed the buffalo herds. They packed their hide tipis and moved with the seasons, from forests in winter to prairies in summer. To hunt buffalo, one man in a wolf-skin costume acted as scout. He reported back to the other hunters, who surrounded the buffalo and either shot them with arrows or scared them into running off a cliff.

FARMING Some tribes relied on farming. These people occupied the fertile riverbanks of the Plains. Northern farmers, such as the Mandan, Hidatsa, and Pawnee, lived in villages of round earth lodges. Southern farmers, including the Caddo, Tonkawa, and Wichita, built grass tipis called wickiups.

Although they had different languages and homes, all Plains tribes observed similar customs. Everyday life blended with religion. Ceremonies signaled major events, such as a buffalo hunt or important phases of life. Stories told how people, animals, and plants came from the earth and sky and must be respected. Men smoked sacred pipes with friends and guests to honor the spirits. Medicine people, or spiritual leaders, had varied roles in different tribes.

Experienced spiritual leaders trained children to be healers. Children learned of their callings during vision quests, which were part of puberty ceremonies. At that time a child was sent to a solitary, sacred place, usually for four days. During a vision quest, the child did not eat or drink but prayed for a vision. A vision, or a waking dream, usually involved a spirit guide that appeared to the child in animal or other form. This spirit would be the child's protector for life. Only certain kinds of spirits were guides for healers.

Every family member had a special job in the community. Women and men formed societies to carry out their tasks. The women guarded tribal skills and beliefs and taught them to their children. They harvested sage, cedar, and sweetgrass for ceremonies, and roots and corn for food. Men protected the family. They hunted for meat and led war parties to defend the village or strike back at other tribes after an attack. Elders raised tobacco for Pipe ceremonies and passed on their wisdom in stories. Most important was a spirit of caring for each other and for Mother Earth and Father Sky.

SKY DOG

Fossils show that horses once lived on the Plains. But they mysteriously vanished for thousands of years. Early Indians traveled by foot, helped by trained dogs. The dogs dragged travois—sleds of tipi poles and skins that held belongings (Blackfeet).

Then Spanish explorer Francisco Vásquez de Coronado brought horses back to the southern Plains in 1541. With stronger, swifter animals, the Indians traveled farther and faster. Horses pulled greater loads than dogs, allowing families to move more goods and build larger tipis. Indians believed the horses were sent by the spirits. The Lakota

GOOD MEDICINE

Plains people call spiritual power "medicine." Good medicine is more than a cure, it is a way of living close to the higher powers.

SACRED PIPE

Today, as long ago, Plains Indians smoke tobacco to connect with all of life. Pipes usually have wooden stems and bowls of red pipestone (Dakota). They are often decorated with eagle feathers, as it is believed that eagles carry prayers to the creator in pipe smoke.

THE RED ROAD

Lakota Indians call their spiritual path the Red Road. Being on the Red Road means living in harmony with the creator. Plains tribes share similar beliefs about spiritual leadership. Plains spiritual leaders are usually men, though some have been women. Leaders guide ceremonies and interpret spiritual information for the people (below). While they have special gifts as seers and healers, Indian spiritual leaders are expected to act just like ordinary people. They make jokes, marry, and hold jobs. They do not charge for their services, though they often receive gifts in payment.

SUN DANCE

The Sun Dance has been performed since ancient times to pray for the well-being of the land and its people. The Sun Dance is a serious responsibility, and dancers endure hunger and pain during the four-day ceremony. Today, as in the past, young men pledge to dance only if they have had a strong vision requiring them to do so. These Cheyenne Sun Dance pledges (right) painted their bodies in 1911 to show their intention.

SWEAT LODGE

Plains Indians have always purified themselves in sweat lodges before participating in ceremonies. The sweat lodge symbolizes the womb of Mother Earth. Inside the darkened lodge, a leader pours water on rocks that have been heated in a fire. Special songs and prayers help people endure the steamy heat.

FEATHERS

Fans of powerful eagle feathers are used during Plains ceremonies. Feathers are sacred to all Indians because they represent messages from the creator.

called them *sunka wakan*, meaning "sky dogs."

The first contacts with Spaniards resulted in peaceful trade. The Indians swapped buffalo and deer hides for European guns and metals. By the mid-1800s, however, many more Europeans had arrived, bringing diseases the Indians were unable to resist. In 1837 the Mandan tribe was nearly wiped out by smallpox. By 1870 smallpox and cholera had spread to all Plains people.

Wagon trains of settlers pushed across the Plains seeking buffalo hides and land. They were followed by trainloads of pioneers wanting gold, coal, and more land. In 1835 war began on the southern Plains, when Texas settlers invaded Comanche hunting grounds. In 1848 the United States defeated Mexico, expanding its boundaries in the Southwest and attracting more settlers to the Plains. The Kiowa joined the Comanche resistance, while on the northern Plains, tribes such as the Sioux, Cheyenne, and Arapaho banded together to fight white soldiers.

MASSACRES One of the worst disasters for Plains Indians was the Sand Creek Massacre of 1864. Colonel John Chivington ordered 700 soldiers to attack a peaceful southern Cheyenne and Arapaho camp in eastern Colorado. About Indians, Chivington had said: "Kill them all, large and small. Nits make lice." Cheyenne chief Black Kettle had an American flag and a white flag of peace on his tipi. Unmoved, Chivington signaled the bayonets and cannons to press forward, killing 200 Cheyenne men, women, and children. Black Kettle and his wife fled to the Lakota, and the tribes won several victories between 1866 and 1867, including the famous Battle of Little Bighorn (Sioux). The 1890 massacre of 300 unarmed Sioux at Wounded Knee officially ended the wars on the Plains.

The United States military also exterminated buffalo herds in order to weaken the power of Plains Indians. Before Europeans arrived about 60 million buffalo roamed the Plains. By the 1890s, the buffalo were almost gone. Without buffalo the Plains way of life was destroyed. The United States and Canada pressed tribes to give up their land in exchange for food and supplies. Each time the Indians signed treaties, they were broken.

Tribes such as the Crow, Caddo, and Blackfeet kept peace with whites, but the results were the same. Plains Indians were removed from their lands and confined to reservations, where corrupt government agents stole most of their food and supplies. In the early 20th century, more land was lost to allotment.

Once, Native Americans roamed the Plains freely. Today, many tribes are developing businesses such as tourism, casinos, and buffalo ranches. But they still gather at powwows, pray in the sweat lodge, and perform sacred dances to honor the earth, their spirits, and their people.◀

PLATEAU

• **TRIBES OF THE REGION:** COEUR D'ALENE, FLATHEAD, KALISPEL, KLAMATH, KUTENAI, MODOC, NEZ PERCE, PALOUSE, SHOSHONE, SPOKAN, UMATILLA, WARM SPRINGS, & YAKIMA

The Plateau region is a land of great diversity and beauty. The Cascades—a chain of volcanic peaks in central Oregon and Washington—form the western boundary, and the Bitterroot Mountains of Idaho bound the territory on the east and north. To the south stretch the barren highlands of the Great Basin. The rest of the Plateau is dry prairie and green river valleys. The Snake River cuts a deep canyon in the eastern Plateau. The once-mighty Columbia River, now dammed, forms a wide valley through the Plateau heartland.

▶ Miracle Calf

In August 1994 a female albino (white) buffalo calf was born on a Wisconsin ranch. Named Miracle, she is the first calf of her kind born in the last 100 years. Female white buffalo are sacred to Plains Indians. Lakota prophesy holds that the birth of such a calf heralds the healing of the earth and of the Indian nations. Miracle has had hundreds of visitors from many tribes.

▶ Chief David Young

Cayuse chiefs wore grand headdresses with horns and fringed ermine robes. The chief known as David Young (above) was photographed in front of his band's tipi encampment in about 1900. His horse is adorned with a matching mask and martingale (decorated halter).

THE GREAT COUNCILS

As Europeans arrived on Indian lands in great numbers, tribes of all regions met in councils to decide how best to deal with the newcomers. Tribal leaders signed many peace treaties with whites that were later disregarded by the federal government.

WALLA WALLA In 1855 the Nez Perce rode to Walla Walla, Washington, to meet with the Walla Walla, Cayuse, and Umatilla in a peace conference with United States representatives. The tribes wished to restrict gold miners from trespassing on their lands. Despite their efforts, members of all four tribes were soon moved to the Umatilla Reservation in Oregon.

DIVIDE AND CONQUER Many tribes that had formerly been mortal enemies made peace with each other to defend their lands against the white invasion. Others were hired by the United States Army to fight each other. During the Modoc War of 1872–1873, Warm Springs Indians such as Loa-Kum-Artnuk (below) were armed with Spencer rifles to attack the Modoc along the Oregon-California border.

The climate is generally mild compared with the freezing cold of the Subarctic region to the north and the hot and arid Great Basin to the south. However, winters are long and cold, and summers are gentle. Rainfall varies greatly. The mountains get much snow in winter, but the lowlands—in the rain-shadow of the Cascades—receive less than twelve inches of rain each year. Dense evergreen forests cover the mountains, though much of the territory is grassland.

Plateau peoples fall into two general language and cultural categories: the Sahaptian-speaking peoples, such as the Nez Perce, Palouse, Yakima, and Umatilla; and the Salish speakers, including the Flathead, Coeur d'Alene, Spokan, Kalispel, and others. There are also differences in diet and social organization that cut across language and tribal groups. Some tribes built villages of wooden houses along the rivers where they fished for trout and salmon. Some communities used slaves from other tribes to build salmon traps and set nets (Northwest Coast).

Away from the rivers, the Plateau peoples were more nomadic, as they searched far and wide for wild onions, potatoes, and other sources of food. They returned to the rivers during the spring salmon runs and hunted game such as elk and antelope. They even went after buffalo on the Plains. This required temporary hunting groups that often included members of different tribes. This was to provide protection from Plains peoples who defended their territory, such as the Blackfeet.

SALMON LEGEND Salmon were not only for eating but were believed to be powerful spirits (Northwest Coast). Traditional salmon legends were told during long winter nights in the Plateau. In one story the Salmon Chief defeats the North Wind brothers, melting the ice to bring spring to the area and allowing the salmon to swim upriver to lay their eggs.

The human presence in the Plateau region is an

ancient one. Some archaeologists estimate that the first people arrived in the Plateau country from the north as early as 10,000 B.C. Others say humans arrived much earlier and that they could have come from any direction (Paleo-Indians).

The first whites came around 1800. From 1804 to 1806, a Shoshone woman named Sacajawea guided Meriwether Lewis and William Clark as they explored the region. Troubles followed in their wake. Traders and trappers brought smallpox and other diseases that killed the Indians. White settlers arrived a decade or two later. Although the settlers were mostly passing through to richer lands in Oregon's Willamette Valley, west of the Cascades, the Plateau peoples felt increasingly threatened.

WAR In the 1870s several Plateau peoples, including the Modoc and the Nez Perce, went to war to defend their lands. Both tribes followed new leaders who refused to accept the humiliation and poverty of reservation life. Modoc chief Kintpuash (Captain Jack to white Americans) led his people back to their ancestral lands in northeastern California. They demanded payment from white ranchers, but they were defeated in a series of battles known as the Modoc War of 1872–1873. The Nez Perce were led by Chief Joseph (actually a medicine man, or healer) on a difficult, 1,500-mile journey to a Canadian refuge. The tribe fought a series of losing rearguard battles during the trek, then surrendered just fifteen miles from the border. When Chief Joseph surrendered, he said these famous words:

> I am tired of fighting. Our chiefs are killed. Looking Glass is dead. Toohoolhoolzote is dead....It is cold and we have no blankets. The little children are freezing to death.... I want to have time to look for my children and see how many I can find....Hear me my chiefs! I am tired; my heart is sick and sad. From where the sun now stands, I will fight no more forever.

Cayuse Cradle

Plateau women carried their babies in traditional hide cradles lined with soft deerskin and decorated with quill- or beadwork designs. A wooden hoop at the top of the cradle could be pulled forward to protect the baby's head. Kupt, a Cayuse woman photographed around 1900, is wearing a basketry hat and beaded shoulder band.

Jaune Quick-To-See Smith

Jaune Quick-To-See Smith is a Cree-Flathead-Shoshone artist who works with paint and collage. Her colorful paintings contrast historical and modern Indian imagery in a contemporary style. Smith's work expresses the energy, determination, and vision she sees reawakening in Indian people after so many difficult years. She hopes her work will teach people about Indian spirituality and experiences.

Living in Harmony

The Salish (Flathead) and Kutenai tribes publish a coloring book titled *Living in Harmony* to teach children about the importance of preserving natural resources. The tribes are working with conservation groups to protect their land.

Today, the land on our reservation is much like it was long ago.
Sakił sukni na ka-amak'ni's mayaqaqaki nis pikak. / Y
es č?eymi?i

Susan Billy

Pomo basketmaker Susan Billy sees her baskets as a way to connect to "all the grandmothers who have gone before me." She uses traditional Pomo techniques such as weaving bright feathers into her designs. Many Pomo basketmakers are internationally known for their work.

European diseases sharply reduced the Plateau population. White ways and English-language education damaged their culture in the late 19th and early 20th centuries (Boarding Schools and Reservations).

The years since the end of World War II, however, have been more promising for the Plateau peoples. Several major court decisions—based on treaty violations by the United States government—have awarded Plateau tribes large cash settlements. This money has been invested in education and job-producing industries such as timber, ranching, and tourism. There has also been a strong revival of native cultures. Many families sponsor Sun Dances—inherited from Plains tribes—as well as other, more traditional, Plateau ceremonies such as the Umatilla Spring Root Feast. ◀

POMO

- **LANGUAGE FAMILY:** HOKAN
- **LIFEWAYS:** HUNTING, FISHING, & GATHERING
- **LOCATIONS:** CALIFORNIA
- **THEIR OWN NAME:** POMO

CALIFORNIA

There are 4,800 Pomo living in Mendocino and Sonoma counties in California. Spirituality helped the Pomo recover from the widespread slaughter and mission imprisonment of the 1800s. The Ghost Dance movement of 1890 helped them regroup and return to their homes (Great Basin). Families pooled their money to buy land. The Pomo take traditional summer trips to the coast, eat acorns, speak Hokan, dance, sing, and play games. They have founded many ecological projects. Their Ya-Ka-Ama Indian Center's native plant nursery is a model for the state. ◀

151

PONCA

- **LANGUAGE FAMILY: SIOUIAN**
- **LIFEWAYS: FARMING**
- **LOCATION: NEBRASKA & OKLAHOMA**
- **THEIR OWN NAME: PONCA**

PLAINS

The Ponca divided in two after the U.S. government gave their Nebraska reservation to the Dakota in 1876. Ponca Standing Bear talked to the press—the first Indian to do so. As a result, the Ponca tribe was the first to have some of its land returned. But the division among the Ponca remained: The Northern Ponca returned to Nebraska, the Southern Ponca remained in Oklahoma. Today, annual Ponca powwows feature drumming, singing, and dancing. ◀

POTAWATOMI

- **LANGUAGE FAMILY: ALGONQUIAN**
- **LIFEWAYS: HUNTING, GATHERING, FISHING, & FARMING**
- **LOCATION: OKLAHOMA, WISCONSIN, & MICHIGAN**
- **THEIR OWN NAME: POTAWATAMINK**

NORTHEAST

The Potawatomi, Ojibwa, and Ottawa were joined in a confederacy called the Three Fires. The Potawatomi called themselves People of the Fire. Their villages were organized by clans similar to those of the Ojibwa. Several animals represented each of the five social groups. Leaders' clans were birds. Warriors belonged to the Bear, Wolf, or Lynx clans. Turtle and Otter were healers' clans. Hunters were represented by the patient Beaver and Moose. Teachers were members of the Fish clan because, although fish humbly hide

NEBRASKA INDIAN
NICC
COMMUNITY COLLEGE

▶ **College Logos**

These are the logos of Nebraska Indian Community College, which held its eighteenth annual graduation ceremony in 1995. The logos feature important aspects of the culture of the Ponca and other **Plains** tribes: the buffalo, the eagle and feathers, and the sacred pipe.

▶ **A Family Portrait**

This photograph of Potawatomi women and their children was taken in a photographer's studio in the early 20th century. Their costumes are characteristic of the Potawatomi: metal jewelry and clothing decorated with ribbon appliqué that employs geometric designs made from porcupine quills.

Wabaunsee

Potawatomi war chief Wabaunsee (c. 1780–1840) sided with the United States in the War of 1812. After the war he signed the Treaty of Wabash, selling tribal lands to the U.S. government. This angered many Indians, one of whom tried to kill Wabaunsee. He survived the assassination attempt, and in 1835 he signed a treaty that gave away the rest of the Potawatomi ancestral lands in exchange for land farther west.

Medicine Men

The Potawatomi were firm believers in the power of the medicine man. They believed he made contact with spirits through dreams and visions, thus learning how to drive away evil and heal the sick. In this etching, a medicine man mixes curative ingredients while chanting.

themselves in river depths, they remain steady in strong currents.

In 1616, French explorers met about 9,000 Potawatomi on the western shores of Lake Huron. Soon the Potawatomi were incorporating French ribbons and beads into their clothing designs. During the colonial wars (Northeast), the Potawatomi allied first with the French, then with the English. Despite signing 19th-century treaties with the United States, most Potawatomi were moved to the southern Plains in 1838. The Potawatomi call their forced march to Oklahoma the Trail of Death.

TRIBAL TRADITIONS

Today, the 3,000 Oklahoma Potawatomi have invested in tribal businesses that bring in several million dollars each year. There are another 3,200 Potawatomi living in small groups in Kansas, Wisconsin, and Michigan. Many are fluent in the Potawatomi language, and elders tell children star legends in Potawatomi.

The Potawatomi Drum Dance Society represents peace between the Sioux and the Three Fires Confederacy. The dance is also called the Dream Dance because it originated in a vision that came to a Dakota woman. After U.S. soldiers killed most of her band in 1878, a spirit showed her how the dance could unite Indian people and save their cultures. A large decorated drum is central to Drum Dance ceremonies. Potawatomi are also members of Ojibwa Midewiwin lodges and the Native American Church (Comanche).

The Potawatomi often gather to celebrate their traditions. A yearly powwow in Michigan is called Kee-Boon-Mein-Ka, meaning We Have Finished Picking Blueberries. A Michigan Potawatomi tribesman says, "The most meaningful aspect of life as a Potawatomi today is the culture. We are learning the language and dancing the powwows. Underlying it all is the practice of spiritual ways. The sacred sweat lodge and longhouse ceremonies have returned."◄

POWHATAN

- **LANGUAGE FAMILY: ALGONQUIAN**
- **LIFEWAYS: HUNTING, GATHERING, & FARMING**
- **LOCATION: VIRGINIA & NEW JERSEY**
- **THEIR OWN NAME: RENÁPE**

SOUTHEAST

The Powhatan is a branch of the Lenape Confederacy. There were about 20,000 Powhatan living along the middle Atlantic coast in the early 1600s. Their temples were spread throughout the woods. Sacred fires burned in the temples, which were surrounded by tall wooden poles. Each pole was carved with a fierce face to frighten away intruders. Inside the temples were treasures, carved wooden oracles, and the mummified bodies of ancestors.

TOBACCO

When the English founded Jamestown, their first American settlement, in 1607, they did not know how to survive on the swampy land they had chosen. The Powhatan fed the colonists and taught them how to grow corn. They gave them tobacco, which became a major cash crop.

By 1622 the colonists' demands for food and land had become too much for the Powhatan, who began killing settlers. The Indians stuffed the dead colonists' mouths with bread to symbolize their greed and with dirt as a warning not to "eat up all the land." However, by 1700 the Powhatan population had been reduced by European diseases, and the Powhatan had been pushed out of their home by the growing number of settlers.

The Virginia Renápe tribes of today are the Chickahominy, Mattaponi, and Pamunkey. The 4,000-member Powhatan-Renápe nation has a reservation in Rancocas, New Jersey. The tribe manages wildlife areas and has built a museum, a ceremonial mound, and a traditional village. ◄

POWHATAN
Held this state & fashion when Capt. Smith was delivered to him prisoner. 1607

► Wahunsonacook

Wahunsonacook (1550?–1618)—or Chief Powhatan, as English colonists called him—organized a federation of Algonquin tribes in Virginia and represented them in their dealings with Captain John Smith and the settlers of Jamestown. The colonists frequently demanded that Wahunsonacook supply them with food, so the angry chief ordered his warriors to capture John Smith. He is pictured here in 1607, awaiting the arrival of the prisoner.

► Pocahontas

Pocahontas (c. 1595–1617), Chief Powhatan's favorite daughter, converted to the Anglican religion and eventually married John Rolfe, developer of the Virginia tobacco industry. She is best known, however, for her association with John Smith, whom she supposedly saved from execution by her tearful pleas. She died in England of smallpox when she was only twenty-one.

Acoma and Taos Pueblos

These two pueblos are still lived in today. Acoma Pueblo (above), west of Santa Fe, New Mexico, is the oldest continuously occupied town in the United States. About sixty people live there today. Pueblo (below) is north of Santa Fe. There, visitors can see pueblo residents weaving, making jewelry, and cooking traditional food.

Baking Bread

Pueblo Indians bake bread in ovens called *hornos* that are made of the same materials as their pueblos—dried earth and straw. This woman is placing a loaf of bread in the oven. Bread baking is one of the many traditional aspects of life that the people in the pueblos still practice.

PUEBLO

- **LANGUAGE FAMILY: UTO-AZTECAN PIMAN**
- **LIFEWAYS: FARMING & HUNTING**
- **LOCATION: ARIZONA, NEW MEXICO, & TEXAS**
- **THEIR OWN NAME: LOCAL NAMES**

SOUTHWEST

The name Pueblo is not an Indian word. It is used for a number of Indian communities located mostly in New Mexico. Pueblo means "town" in Spanish, and is used both for the Pueblo people and for the towns they built.

The original Pueblo territory spread from what is now eastern Arizona to the Texas Panhandle and from central Utah and Colorado into present-day Mexico. In Mexico the Pueblo homes resembled those of the northern Aztecs. Today, there are twenty-one Pueblo communities in the United States, where a total of about 40,000 Pueblo people live.

Most Pueblo people are descended from the Anasazi (Cliff Dwellers). Around A.D. 800, a distinctive Pueblo culture began to form in New Mexico. Some of the Pueblo towns that emerged from that culture now comprise thousands of houses. They are built of adobe, or clay brick, and some of them rise to four or more stories.

CULTURAL DIFFERENCES

While most of the Pueblo people share a common history, they differ in their culture and society. For example, most have blended their traditional beliefs with Catholicism, which was introduced by the Spanish. Different communities emphasize more of one religion or the other—some emphasizing traditional beliefs, some Catholicism.

The Santa Ana and the Taos Pueblo are more traditional. Others, such as the San Felipe and San Ildefonso Pueblo, are more devoted to the Catholic

Church. In fact, their names come from patron saints of the Catholic Church.

The Pueblo communities are the Acoma, Cochiti, Isleta, Jemez, Laguna, Nambe, Picuris, Pojoaque, Sandia, San Felipe, San Ildefonso, San Juan, Santa Ana, Santa Clara, Santo Domingo, Taos, Tesuque, Tigua, Ysleta, Zia, and Zuni. Three of the largest—and one ruin—are discussed here.

FOUR PUEBLOS
▼▼▼

Bonito Pueblo is one of the largest prehistoric Pueblo ruins in New Mexico. In 1907 it was declared a national park—the Chaco Culture National Historical Park, which covers 34,000 acres in northwest New Mexico. Many of the artifacts archaeologists found at Bonito Pueblo are now in the American Museum of Natural History in New York City. Unlike many pueblos, Bonito Pueblo is no longer inhabited.

The Acoma Pueblo people live on the Acoma Mesa west of Albuquerque, New Mexico. Acoma means Eternal Place. In fact, Acoma Pueblo is the oldest continually inhabited town in the United States. There were about 8,000 people living there when the Spanish arrived in 1540. Because it is located high on a mesa, or plateau, Acoma Pueblo is often called Sky City.

Today, most of the 3,000 Acoma Pueblo live on a nearby reservation. Only about sixty live in the old pueblo. To preserve Sky City, the Acoma Pueblo do not allow electricity or running water within the pueblo. Many Acoma Pueblo attend festivals and ceremonies, including an annual feast day in September.

The 7,000 Laguna Pueblo have the largest population of any Pueblo community. Their six villages are located west of Albuquerque, New Mexico, and are stretched out over more than 500,000 acres.

From 1953 to 1983, the Anaconda Mineral Company operated the largest uranium mine in the world on lands leased from the Laguna Pueblo,

Young Photographers

The Oo-oonah Art Center at the Taos Pueblo displays work by Native American artists. These two photographs were taken by young photographers in 1992. The girl is Cindy Stout, and her picture is a self-portrait taken when she was eleven years old. The man sticking his tongue out was photographed by Janell Lujan when she was fifteen. These photographs were made as part of a program called Shooting Back from the Reservation, which taught young Native Americans to take and develop photographs.

▶ Pueblo Author

Leslie Marmon Silko, author of *Ceremony* **and** *Storyteller,* **is probably best known for her novel** *Almanac of the Dead.* **It is the story of tribe members caught between two cultures and two times, struggling to reconcile modern-day life with Native American tradition.**

▶ Family Portrait

William J. Connor took this early-20th-century photograph of Chief Peter Clapper and his family in Wyandotte, Oklahoma. They are standing with Frank Valliere (right), an interpreter for the Quapaw.

many of whom worked there. Today, the Laguna Pueblo are restoring land that has been damaged by the mines.

The pueblo of Taos is one of the most popular tourist spots in the Southwest, with nearly one million visitors each year. The multistoried town is located northeast of Santa Fe, New Mexico, and is set against a backdrop of the spectacular Sangre de Cristo Mountains. As in Acoma, electricity and running water are not permitted in the old pueblo.

The 3,000 Taos Pueblo create traditional art and jewelry for tourists and for the galleries in the nearby artist's colony, also called Taos—where D.H. Lawrence, Georgia O'Keeffe, and Frank Lloyd Wright lived and worked.

The Taos Pueblo hold an annual feast-day celebration and powwow in September.◀

QUAPAW

- **LANGUAGE FAMILY:** SIOUIAN
- **LIFEWAYS:** FARMING
- **LOCATION:** OKLAHOMA
- **THEIR OWN NAME:** UGAKHPA

SOUTHEAST

Before 1700 the Quapaw migrated up the Mississippi River to what became Arkansas. They farmed near earth-lodge settlements and became expert potters. By 1833 the tribe had been forced onto a reservation in Oklahoma. But the Quapaw resisted dividing their land until the U.S. agreed to a settlement in 1893. The discovery of lead and zinc further benefited the tribe. Today, the 2,000 Quapaw are members of the Miami Intertribal Council. They attend an annual powwow, where couples pretend to "steal" each other's partners during the Rabbit Dance.◀

RED POWER

Red Power is the name of a Native American political movement that started in the 1960s. Its followers believed that Native Americans should return to Indian values of cooperation and communal living. But they also believed that they had to fight for their land and their civil rights. Many decided that peaceful protest and legal battles were not enough. They thought they would have to confront the government directly, with arms if necessary.

The Red Power movement—and the many organizations that grew out of it—came from urban ghettos, not Indian reservations. It was started by young Native Americans influenced by the African-American civil rights movement. Because the Red Power movement encouraged Indian self-rule, non-Indians were usually excluded from positions of power.

ORIGINS The Red Power movement began in the Pacific Northwest. Government agencies and non-Indian fishermen had been trying to prevent Native Americans there from using nets to catch fish in Puget Sound and on the Columbia River. Beginning with the arrest in 1961 of two Muggleshoot Indians, the struggle over fishing rights led to battles with police and, finally, to a Supreme Court ruling in the Indians' favor. Equally important, the struggle triggered the Red Power movement.

The most important organization to come out of the Red Power movement was the American Indian Movement (AIM). AIM was founded in 1968 by Native Americans in Minneapolis who were trying to stop police brutality against Indians. AIM formed patrols, confronting the police with cameras when they used excessive force.

Soon AIM members made contacts with reservation Indians, and the organization quickly

▶ Protest!

This 1971 photograph shows Indians protesting the U.S. government's violations of their tribal fishing rights along the Columbia River in Washington State. Such treaty violations have been frequent since the beginning of Indian-white relations. However, it was not until the 1960s that Indians began militantly protesting the violations.

▶ Commemorative Poster

This 1970s poster is a powerful reminder of the massacre at Wounded Knee: It depicts a woman and child facing men who have rifles and bayonets. In 1890, hundreds of Lakota Sioux were surrounded by U.S. soldiers at Wounded Knee Creek. As the unarmed Indians stood by, a shot was fired. In the panic that followed, 100 Sioux were killed.

▶ Wounded Knee

In 1973, members of the American Indian Movement (AIM) and many Oglala Sioux seized the village of Wounded Knee—site of the massacre—in an attempt to have their grievances heard by the U.S. government. This resulted in a seventy-day siege between Indians and federal agents, during which two Indians were killed. Dennis Banks, one of the leaders of AIM, is pictured here during the siege. He is in the center with binoculars.

▶ Leonard Peltier

Leonard Peltier, part Ojibwa and part Lakota, was convicted in 1976 of killing two FBI agents. Peltier has always maintained his innocence. He has won international attention because of the circumstances of the murders, which occurred on tribal land at Pine Ridge Reservation in South Dakota, and because of questions about the U.S. government's evidence against him.

spread across the country. AIM protested the government's refusal to accept Native American claims to sacred land and water.

AIM members came up with a way to attract attention to their cause when Alcatraz prison in San Francisco Bay was closed. Under an old treaty, abandoned federal property was supposed to be returned to the Indians. AIM members occupied Alcatraz, symbolically claiming the abandoned island on which the prison stood. This act won publicity and support for the Indian cause.

DIVISIONS However, some Native Americans did not like AIM. When AIM organizers arrived on the Ojibwa reservation in Minnesota, they were called publicity-seekers who didn't understand local concerns. The most violent struggle between AIM and a reservation government occurred on the Oglala Sioux Reservation at Pine Ridge, South Dakota. The reservation was controlled by Dick Wilson, who used gangs to keep the people in fear. When AIM members arrived on the reservation in 1972, they were attacked by the gangs. AIM members then seized the village of Wounded Knee—site of a 19th-century massacre of Indians (Sioux). For over two months they held the village against the FBI and police. Then the federal agents attacked and reoccupied the village.

In 1974 AIM and other Native American groups organized the International Indian Treaties Council. Four years later the council planned the Longest Walk, a cross-country march on Washington to protest the treatment of Indians.

At this time the government considered AIM a dangerous organization. The FBI infiltrated AIM in the 1970s, and many of the infiltrators tried to get AIM members to do illegal things so they would be arrested. The police efforts hurt AIM, though many of its members continue to organize on reservations today.◀

RESERVATIONS

A reservation (reserve in Canada) is an area of land set aside by the government for a particular Native American nation or group of nations. In most cases Native Americans were forced to live on the reservation, sometimes by warfare and sometimes because their food sources had been destroyed.

ORIGINS Although most of today's reservations were created in the 1800s, the beginnings of the reservation system date back to the earliest days of colonization. After losing a war with the English in 1646, the Powhatan ruler Opechancanough agreed to maintain his people in a section of York County, Virginia. In New England, Indians who accepted Christianity were permitted to live on small reservations—praying towns—under the spiritual and civil control of the colonial government. Those who didn't accept Christianity were forced out of the colony.

In the years leading up to the Revolutionary War, colonial governments established boundaries between white colonists and large Indian confederacies such as the Iroquois and the Creek. These were not truly reservations since the two sides negotiated as equals and the Indian nations maintained self-rule. Still, the treaties set the pattern by which Indians would later be confined to specific tracts of land.

In the 19th century, the U.S. government began using its stronger position to dictate terms to the Indians. Native Americans were not only confined to reservations but were often forbidden to pursue traditional activities such as hunting, trapping, and trading. Virtually every decision over their lives was placed in the hands of agents of the Bureau of Indian Affairs.

Many of the agents were political appointees.

Native American Boys

These Indian boys were photographed in Pennsylvania in about 1900. Their clothing and short haircuts—which reflect white fashions of the period— show the success of the U.S. government's policy of "civilizing" the Indians by making them adopt white ways.

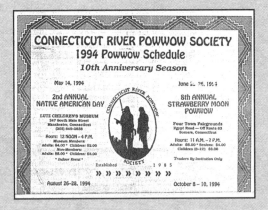

Powwow Schedule

This ad, featured in a spring 1994 issue of the *Connecticut Eagle,* outlines upcoming events sponsored by the Connecticut River Powwow Society, including the Strawberry Moon Powwow and Native American Day. Both events celebrate Native American traditions and ceremonies.

Sioux Powwow

This modern-day Sioux powwow in South Dakota draws many spectators. Some of the Sioux dancers are dressed in traditional furs, feathers, fancy bustles, hair pieces, shawls, and moccasins. Others are wearing bright costumes decorated with ribbons, fringes, and bells.

New Income

This 1993 advertisement from *Indian Country Today* encourages people to come to the Dakota Sioux Casino. Except on the reservation, gambling is illegal in South Dakota, so this casino attracts people from miles around and provides the Sioux with a source of income.

That is, they were given their jobs as a reward for helping politicians get elected. Few of them knew anything about Indian ways of life. Many were corrupt and stole money that had been set aside for the Indians.

The poverty and powerlessness of reservation life often demoralized Native Americans, many of whom turned to alcoholism and crime. Beginning in the 1880s, a religious movement known as the Ghost Dance spread among western reservation Indians (Great Basin). It promised a new world in which the whites would be defeated. The dance was outlawed by the U.S. government, but not before soldiers had massacred hundreds of Sioux who practiced the Ghost Dance on the Wounded Knee Reservation in 1890.

SELF-RULE In the 20th century, power has gradually returned to Native Americans on reservations. In 1934 Congress passed the Indian Reorganization Act. This law permitted tribes to organize and write constitutions for themselves. In the 1970s these rights were extended to include control of education, health, and jobs programs funded by the federal government.

In the 1980s and 1990s, Native Americans have continued to gain self-rule on their reservations. A Supreme Court decision said that state laws against gambling do not apply to reservations. This allowed reservation Indians to open casinos, which bring in needed money for education, housing, and health care. But the casinos are not popular among all reservation Indians, many of whom argue that they encourage crime and corrupt the young.

Most Indians do not live on reservations today. Still, reservations are at the center of Indian traditions, customs, and festivals. Many reservations welcome the public to visit and learn about the Native American way of life.◄

SAC & FOX

- **LANGUAGE FAMILY: ALGONQUIAN**
- **LIFEWAYS: HUNTING, FARMING, & MINING**
- **LOCATION: OKLAHOMA & IOWA**
- **THEIR OWN NAME: OSA KIWUG AND MESQUAKI**

PLAINS

The Sac (People of the Yellow Earth) and Fox (People of the Red Earth) were once separate tribes. They lived in neighboring wigwam villages in what is now Illinois, Wisconsin, and Missouri. The Kickapoo were their close relatives and main allies.

Sac and Fox ceremonies center on drumming and the Crane Dance. The Otter is the hero of Sac and Fox legends, which also speak of the sun and moon. There are eleven Sac and Fox clans, including Fish, Peace, Bear, Thunder, and Potato.

Participating in the fur trade in the 1700s, the Fox did not get fair exchanges from the French (Subarctic). War between the Fox and the French began in 1712. Indians allied with the French—the Dakota, Huron, and Ottawa—killed many Fox. So the Fox joined the Sac, who defended them from the French. The tribes officially united in 1804.

That year, a Sac named Kwaskwami drank alcohol with the governor of the Indiana Territory. While drunk, he signed a treaty selling all of the Sac and Fox lands for a tiny annual payment. He had no authority to sell land, and the tribal councils still refuse to accept the treaty.

BLACK HAWK Sac chief Black Hawk joined Tecumseh and the British to fight the U.S. in the War of 1812 (Shawnee). After the war, Illinois settlers attacked the Sac and Fox, who retreated to Iowa. In 1832 Black Hawk led 1,000 warriors back to Illinois, where they fought the militia and U.S. soldiers.

But Black Hawk was tricked by the whites' Indian allies. Potawatomi, Winnebago, Omaha, and

▶ Black Hawk

When a treaty between the Sac and Fox and the U.S. government gave all the Sac and Fox land to the United States, Black Hawk (1767–1838) claimed the treaty was invalid. In 1832 he led a war against the United States. After being captured, he was taken to Washington, D.C., where he met President Andrew Jackson. His *Autobiography of Black Hawk* is a classic. This portrait of him was done by George Catlin, who painted many Indian portraits.

▶ Kiyo'kaga

Kiyo'kaga (1780?–1848), also known as Keokuk, disagreed with Black Hawk about the treaty, advising that the Sac and Fox turn over their land. Kiyo'kaga himself was given land in Iowa, where a town, Keokuk, was named after him. This early photograph, called a daguerreotype, was taken of him in Washington, D.C., in 1847.

Jim Thorpe

The Sac and Fox athlete Jim Thorpe (1888–1953) was born in Oklahoma. After starring in the 1912 Olympic Games—where he won the decathlon and pentathlon—he went on to an outstanding career in professional football and baseball. He was the first president of the American Professional Football Association. A 1950 newspaper poll named him the "greatest athlete of the first half of the twentieth century."

Painted Jacket

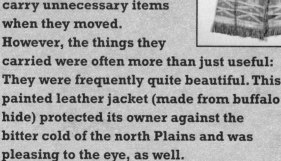

The nomadic lifestyle of the Sarcee made it impossible for them to carry unnecessary items when they moved. However, the things they carried were often more than just useful: They were frequently quite beautiful. This painted leather jacket (made from buffalo hide) protected its owner against the bitter cold of the north Plains and was pleasing to the eye, as well.

Sioux warriors had offered to help Black Hawk defeat the Americans. However, when the two sides approached Bad Axe River (now in Wisconsin), the other tribes turned on the Sac and Fox and the Kickapoo, who remained with Black Hawk. The Sac and Fox lost the battle. They were chased down, and four months later more than 200 of the tribes' men, women, and children were killed. Jailed at first, Black Hawk later returned to his people. He wrote his autobiography in 1833.

Three Sac and Fox groups have lived in Iowa and Oklahoma since 1857. Today, their combined 3,330 members are preserving their history in the Sac and Fox National Public Library in Stroud, Oklahoma. Clan customs such as baby namings, dances, and feasts continue in Oklahoma. The Sac and Fox Drum Society is important in Iowa. Both the Oklahoma and Iowa groups teach the Sac and Fox language and make fine ribbonwork clothing. ◀

SARCEE

- **LANGUAGE FAMILY: ATHAPASKAN**
- **LIFEWAYS: HUNTING & FARMING**
- **LOCATION: ALBERTA**
- **THEIR OWN NAME: TSUT'INA KOSA**

PLAINS

The Sarcee was a Subarctic tribe that migrated down the Saskatchewan River to hunt buffalo on the Plains. Some of the Sarcee continued on to the Southwest, where they are now called the Apache. In 1670 the 700 northern Sarcee joined the powerful Blackfeet Confederacy to defend themselves against the Assiniboine and Cree. But by the mid-1800s the Sarcee were limited to a small reservation in what is now the Canadian province of Alberta. Sarcee Jeanette Starlight says the tribe is "fierce and stubborn" about its privacy. ◀

SEMINOLE

- LANGUAGE FAMILY: MUSKOGEAN
- LIFEWAYS: FISHING & HUNTING
- LOCATION: FLORIDA & OKLAHOMA
- THEIR OWN NAME: SIM A NO LE

SOUTHEAST

The Seminole tribe was formed in the early 19th century when some of the Creek fled white settlers and soldiers. They settled in the swamps and jungles of Florida and took the name Seminole, which means Runaway in the Creek language.

Like the Cherokee, the Seminole nation has a long of history of resistance to the U.S. government. But whereas the Cherokee fought in court, the Seminole relied on warfare. When that did not work, they retreated to the swamps.

In the early 1800s the Seminole lived in northern and central Florida. Their villages became havens for runaway slaves from Florida and Georgia plantations. In fact, most Seminole are of mixed Native American and African-American ancestry (Southeast).

OSCEOLA

In the 1820s a great leader arose among the Seminole. His name was Osceola. For several years Osceola and his army of Seminole and African-Americans both eluded the American army and defeated it in battle. U.S. soldiers finally defeated him, but they had to use trickery. When he came to negotiate with them in 1837, they captured him. He died in prison the next year.

Some Seminole continued to fight until the late 1850s, but most surrendered in 1842 and were sent to Oklahoma. There are 12,000 Seminole in Oklahoma today—and 2,000 in Florida who proudly claim they have never surrendered to the U.S. They wear traditional patchwork clothing, make baskets and carvings, and hold tribal ceremonies. ◀

Hunting Alligators

The Seminole used to hunt alligators in the Florida swamps. They would push a log down the animal's throat, turn it over, then kill it with clubs. Alligators can be very large, but they are not as big as in this fanciful engraving. Modern Seminole wrestle alligators for entertainment.

Two Seminole Leaders

Osceola (left) and Billy Bowlegs (below) were leaders in the Seminole resistance to the U.S. government in the 1800s. The United States wanted the Seminole to move west of the Mississippi River, but the tribe refused. Osceola led the resistance in the Second Seminole War, which lasted two years, until his capture in 1837. He died in prison in 1838. Billy Bowlegs continued to resist and led the Third Seminole War. He finally agreed to go west to Kansas in 1842, where he died of smallpox sometime between 1859 and 1864. It is estimated that 1,500 U.S. soldiers died in the Seminole Wars.

A Seminole Family

This Florida Seminole family was photographed in the late 1800s. Their clothing is made of strips of cotton cloth in contrasting colors, and each of the women is wearing several bead necklaces.

Red Jacket

Red Jacket (1758–1830), or Sagoyewatha, was a great Seneca chief and orator. He spoke for the Seneca tribe within the Iroquois Confederacy and also in negotiations with the U.S. government. Red Jacket supported friendship with whites but opposed the Seneca's conversion to Christianity. This painting shows him wearing the medal President George Washington gave him in 1792.

Ely S. Parker

Seneca Ely S. Parker (1828–1895) was a friend of Ulysses S. Grant. He served in the U.S. Army as an aide to Grant during the Civil War and was present at Appomattox when Robert E. Lee surrendered to Grant. When Grant became president in 1869, he appointed Parker commissioner of Indian Affairs. Parker was the first Native American to hold that post.

SENECA

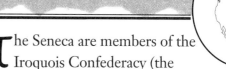

- **LANGUAGE FAMILY: IROQUOIAN**
- **LIFEWAYS: HUNTING, GATHERING, & FARMING**
- **LOCATION: NEW YORK, OKLAHOMA, ONTARIO, & QUEBEC**
- **THEIR OWN NAME: ONENIUTE A KA**

NORTHEAST

The Seneca are members of the Iroquois Confederacy (the Haudenosaunee). Their own name means People of the Great Mountain. Because their homeland is in what is now western New York State, the Seneca are called Keepers of the Western Gate. In the longhouse, they sit with the Mohawk in the Elder Brother position. The Seneca clans are Turtle, Bear, Wolf, Snipe, Hawk, Heron, Beaver, and Deer.

The Seneca and other Iroquois tribes did not wear Plains-style eagle-feather headdresses. Instead, each Iroquois nation had its own Gustoweh, or ceremonial cap. Seneca anthropologist Arthur Parker says the Seneca Gustoweh is "a flurry of feathers … [with] one splendid plume whirling from a spindle at the top."

SCORCHED EARTH

In the late 1700s the U.S. Army attacked the Seneca. The burning of Seneca land was called the "scorched earth campaign." Many Seneca fled to Canada. Those who stayed in New York lost most of their land. The Quakers gave the Seneca some land in Pennsylvania, but it was flooded by a dam in the 1960s.

Today, 10,000 Seneca live in New York, Oklahoma, and Ontario and Quebec, Canada. They are diverse groups, some with a traditional government and some with a constitutional government. Some attend longhouse and clan ceremonies, while others follow the Law of Handsome Lake (Iroquois) or are Christians. ◀

SHAWNEE

The Shawnee name means Southerners. The tribe is originally from around South Carolina's Savannah River. The Shawnee follow the laws and ceremonies given to them by Our Grandmother, the Creator. They believe the world began when she started weaving a basket. When she finishes the basket, the world will end.

After Europeans arrived in 1670, the Shawnee began having trouble with the Cherokee and Catawba. One group of Shawnee joined the Lenape in what became Pennsylvania, while others moved into Iroquois territory. The Iroquois drove them out, and in the late 1700s they moved to the Ohio Valley and allied with the Creek.

TECUMSEH The Shawnee fought for the British in the Revolutionary War. After the Americans won, the Ohio tribes united to hold on to their land. The Shawnee and Lenape were allied with the Miami from 1790 to 1793. Then, in the early 1800s, the Ottawa and Creek joined Shawnee warrior Tecumseh. But Tecumseh and his brother lost two battles to the Americans in the War of 1812, and in 1813 the Shawnee were forced west.

In Oklahoma today the Shawnee do the Buffalo Dance. They also continue to dedicate ceremonies to Our Grandmother. In the spring Ritual Football Game, girls and women play against boys and men. The men can only kick the ball, while the women can carry it. The 11,600 Shawnee of Oklahoma and Missouri are represented by the Miami Intertribal Council. ◄

▶ Tecumseh

Tecumseh (1768–1813) was a Shawnee leader who, with his brother Tenskwatawa (known as the Prophet), led the Native American resistance to U.S. expansion in the region between the Ohio and Mississippi rivers. When a treaty was proposed by which the tribes would sell their land to the United States, Tecumseh opposed it, saying, "Sell the land? Why not sell the air, the clouds, the great sea?" Fighting on the British side during the War of 1812, Tecumseh was killed in 1813.

▶ A Shawnee Couple

Ely and Eliza Ellis, a Shawnee couple, were photographed at their Sperry, Oklahoma, home in 1936. Eliza is grinding corn with a mortar and pestle.

Sacajawea

In 1804 President Thomas Jefferson sent his secretary, Meriwether Lewis, and a soldier, William Clark, to explore the region from the Rocky Mountains to the Pacific Ocean. The expedition would not have survived without the help of many Indian guides. Sacajawea, a Shoshone woman, is the best known. She had been captured by the Hidatsa in 1800 and sold to a trader, Toussaint Charbonneau, around 1804. Sacajawea was sixteen years old when she and Charbonneau joined Lewis and Clark. She bore a baby on the journey, and it was no accident that she left the expedition, and her husband, once they reached her father's band in Montana.

Video

In 1977, Shoshone tribe members made a videotape called "Living with Indian Ways" at the Northern Sho-Ban Alternate School, an Indian-run school. This photograph was taken during the shooting.

Schoolchildren

Western Shoshone students from the Duckwater Elementary School—an Indian-run school in Nevada—pose at a graduation party in a 1983 photograph.

SHOSHONE

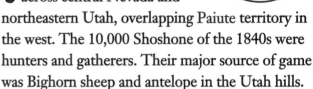

- **LANGUAGE FAMILY: UTO-AZTECAN**
- **LIFEWAYS: HUNTING & GATHERING**
- **LOCATION: UTAH, IDAHO, NEVADA, & CALIFORNIA**
- **THEIR OWN NAME: SHOSHONE**

SOUTHWEST

Shoshone lands once stretched across central Nevada and northeastern Utah, overlapping Paiute territory in the west. The 10,000 Shoshone of the 1840s were hunters and gatherers. Their major source of game was Bighorn sheep and antelope in the Utah hills.

HEALERS Shoshone healers, or "users of power," cured illnesses by prayer, bleeding, and herbal cures. One famous healer was John Trehero, known as Rainbow. He brought the Plains Sun Dance to the Shoshone in the 1940s. Another Plains dance adopted by the Shoshone was the Grass Dance, during which men and women hold hands and dance in a circle. For several days, they pray for the grass to grow and for a good supply of roots, berries, and fish.

In the 1860s the Shoshone fought a brief war to defend their homeland against silver miners. They were defeated but never actually surrendered. Not until 1979 did the Indian Claims Commission grant the Western Shoshone $26 million in exchange for their 24 million acres in Nevada.

Today, about 4,000 Shoshone live on reservations in several western states with the Arapaho, Bannock, and Paiute. Many speak the Shoshone dialect. Tribal historians have recorded the poetic songs of the Grass Dance and written several histories. After World War II, the Shoshone included veterans' songs in their Sun Dance. Traditional War dances are performed during powwows. In 1957 women did the War Dance for the first time, and added their own fancy steps. Women have also broken new ground by forming their own drumming groups.◀

167

Sioux

- **LANGUAGE FAMILY: SIOUIAN**
- **LIFEWAYS: HUNTING, FISHING, & PLANTING**
- **LOCATION: NORTH & SOUTH DAKOTA, MINNESOTA, & MONTANA**
- **THEIR OWN NAME: ICKE WICASA**

PLAINS

The name Sioux refers to fourteen bands that roamed across about 100 million acres in present-day Wisconsin, Minnesota, and southern Manitoba, Canada. The Sioux nation includes three main tribes, the Lakota, Nakota, and Dakota. These people do not like the name Sioux because it comes from an Ojibwa insult meaning Snake People. The nation's own name means The Common People, but because there is no one name for all three divisions, historians call the tribe the Sioux.

MIGRATION

Because there are Siouian-speaking people in the Southeast (Catawba), historians believe the Sioux may have come from there. Between 1300 and 1830, the Sioux farmed and hunted along the forested banks of the Mississippi River. Warfare with the Ojibwa pushed them onto the Plains of present-day North and South Dakota and Montana.

The eastern Sioux—the Dakota (or Santee)—included four tribes: the Sisseton, Wahpeton, Wahpekute, and Mdewkanton. Dakota means Friend. These were the Indians represented on the Indian-head nickel and in Buffalo Bill's Wild West Show. They were expert horsemen who wore eagle-feather headdresses, fringed shirts, and buffalo robes painted with sun symbols. The Nakota lived in the central Plains. The group was made up of four tribes: the Yankton, Yanktonai, Hunkpatina, and Assiniboine. The Lakota (or Teton) tribes were the Oglala, Brule, Hunkpapa, Miniconjou, Sans Arcs, Oohenunpa, and Sihasapa. They occupied the western Plains.

Red Cloud

Red Cloud (1822–1909) was a leader of the Oglala Lakota Sioux. He led a successful war against the U.S. government in the 1860s that led to the closing of the Bozeman Trail through Lakota land. He said, "When the Great Father in Washington sent us his chief soldier to ask for a path through our hunting grounds...we were told that they wished merely to pass through our country....Yet before the ashes of the council fire are cold, the Great Father is building his forts among us."

Sitting Bull

Sitting Bull (1834–1890) was a Hunkpapa Lakota Sioux and spiritual leader. He became head of the Sioux war council in 1875, and was one of the Sioux leaders who defeated George Armstrong Custer at the Battle of the Little Bighorn in 1876. Later, faced with starvation, Sitting Bull and his followers surrendered to U.S. soldiers. Taking part in Buffalo Bill Cody's traveling rodeo, he gave away all his money to poor street children. At the time of the Ghost Dance spiritual movement, U.S. officials saw him as a threat. He was arrested and assassinated in 1890.

Crazy Horse

USA 13c Crazy Horse

Crazy Horse (1849?–1877) was an Oglala Lakota Sioux who joined Red Cloud in the war against the Bozeman Trail and Sitting Bull in the Battle of the Little Bighorn. He was mortally wounded during his arrest in 1877. His final words were, "All we wanted was peace and to be left alone. Soldiers ... destroyed our villages....They tried to confine me, I tried to escape, and a soldier ran a bayonet into me. I have spoken." Crazy Horse never allowed himself to be photographed, but this likeness was issued by the U. S. Postal Service in 1982.

▶ Wounded Knee

In December 1890 the U.S. Army massacred hundreds of Sioux—most of them unarmed and many of them women and children—near Wounded Knee Creek in South Dakota. The injured were left to die on the ground during a three-day blizzard, then were buried in an open grave as soldiers posed for photographers (above).

▶ Vine Deloria

Vine Deloria, Jr., (born 1933) is a scholar and the author of many books on the Native American experience. He is the son of an Episcopalian priest and the grandson of a Yankton Nakota Sioux chief. Deloria, who was executive director of the National Congress of American Indians in the 1960s, teaches at the University of Colorado at Boulder. His many books include *Custer Died for Your Sins* and *Behind the Trail of Broken Treaties*.

The Plains Sioux quickly adapted to hunting buffalo and riding horses. Camps of skin-covered tipis could break up in minutes and move to follow the buffalo. The Sioux believed the buffalo and sun were associated with sacred powers. Following the buffalo meant following the sun and keeping the world in order, which was partly achieved by the Sun Dance, a two-week celebration of life (Plains). The ceremony included the Buffalo Dance in honor of the buffalo. After settlers destroyed the buffalo in the 1880s, the Sioux joined the Ghost Dance (Great Basin) movement. They danced and sang to restore their dead loved ones and fading way of life.

WARRIOR CHIEFS

Some of America's most famous warrior chiefs were Sioux. From the mid-1800s until 1890, Red Cloud, Sitting Bull, Crazy Horse, and others joined the Cheyenne and Arapaho in defending their land and people from intruding soldiers, miners, and settlers (Lakota).

In the 20th century, Sioux have been leaders in the American Indian Movement (AIM) to gain Indian rights and revive traditions. In 1964 some members of AIM temporarily occupied Alcatraz prison in San Francisco Bay, which was no longer being used. The symbolic takeover was based on an old Sioux treaty that gave unused U.S. land to Indians. In 1973 AIM occupied Wounded Knee, South Dakota, the site where Oglala Sioux were massacred in 1890 (Red Power).

Today, the Sioux are part of the Inter-Tribal Bison Cooperative that includes the Navajo, Cheyenne, and Crow. The twenty-seven-nation group raises money to buy and breed buffalo on Plains Indian tribal lands. They believe that buffalo can reverse the environmental imbalance created by years of cattle ranching. Many Sioux believe that White Buffalo Calf Woman, who gave her people the Pipe and Truth, will return to restore the buffalo.◀

169

SOUTHEAST

- **TRIBES OF THE REGION: ALABAMA-COUSHATTA, APALACHEE, CALUSA, CATAWBA, CHEROKEE, CHICKASAW, CHITIMACHA, CHOCTAW, CREEK, LUMBEE, NATCHEZ, SEMINOLE, TIMUCUA, TUNICA-BILOXI, YAMASEE, YAZOO, & YUCHI**

SOUTHEAST

The Southeast region of the United States has many different kinds of geography. The southern Appalachian Mountains form the region's spine. The Appalachians are about 100 miles wide and include peaks up to 6,700 feet high. Wide plains stretch away from the mountains to the shores of the Atlantic Ocean and the Gulf of Mexico. Many rivers cross these plains. Along the coast, the land is often quite swampy. On the inland side of the Appalachians are the great valleys of the Ohio and Mississippi rivers. The region was almost uniformly covered with thick woods.

CLIMATE

The climate also varies, but not as much as the landscape. Most of the Southeast gets lots of rainfall. Winters are short and mild, summers are long and steamy. Along the southern coast, the climate is subtropical and practically free of frost.

The mild, wet climate supported a large population. The main nations of the region were the Cherokee, Chickasaw, Choctaw, Creek, and Seminole. Because they were farmers and lived in settled villages, white Americans called them the Five Civilized Tribes. Rough estimates put the region's native population at about 120,000 in the 1600s. By then, however, many of the Indians had died from European diseases and war.

Evidence of the earliest people in the region is lost, probably forever. Over the centuries, thick layers of mud have buried river valleys. The Atlantic Ocean slowly rose to cover the ancient coast. Paleo-Indian stone spearpoints from 10,000

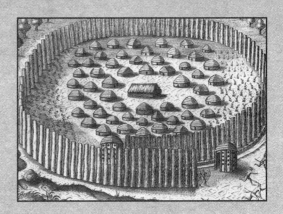

▶ A Southeast Village

This depiction of a Native American village in Florida is based on a description by a French explorer. In the middle of the village was the ceremonial center. Gardens were maintained just outside the stockade, or fence. The stockade provided needed protection, since Southeast tribes were sometimes at war with one another.

▶ Acolapissa

This sketch by a white Louisiana man depicts a temple in the village of Acolapissa in spring 1732. This temple is one of many in the region that served as burial places for chiefs.

RED & BLACK

The term Black Indian describes the offspring of African-American and Native American people. Black Indians have been part of Indian life since the earliest days of slavery. Many Black Indians are descendants of runaway slaves and Native Americans of the Southeast and Texas, where tribes bordered on slave plantations districts.

While colonies of maroons (runaway slaves) and Indians had been common in the Caribbean since the 1500s, the first large community of Black Indians in the United States was in Florida in the early 1800s. About half the Seminole—Seminole means runaway in Creek—had black ancestry. Slave hunters and the U. S. Army frequently attacked the Seminole because they harbored runaways.

Out West, James Beckwourth, a black fur trapper, married the daughter of a Crow ruler and became chief of the Crow in the 1850s. Famed outlaw Cherokee Bill was a Black Indian who both robbed banks and conned white ranchers out of their money until the 1890s. And Nat Love (above)—nicknamed Deadwood Dick—was a Black Indian well known for his marksmanship and range riding.

B.C., and America's earliest pottery—from about 2500 B.C.—have been found in Georgia. Archaeologists believe that settled villages began around 5000 B.C., especially around coastal shellfish beds. Three-thousand-year-old remains of farms and large planned towns have been discovered along the lower Mississippi River. Some archaeologists believe these towns traded with the Olmecs across the Gulf of Mexico.

From 200 B.C. until A.D. 1539, Southeastern people shared a trade and ceremonial network with Indians as far away as Ontario and the Rocky Mountains. Southeastern tribes exchanged tortoise shells, shark's teeth, and freshwater pearls for silver, copper, and obsidian (black glass). These materials were made into the beautiful objects found in local burial mounds (Mound Builders). Most of the mounds of Georgia, Mississippi, and Alabama are flat-topped earth pyramids. Many, however, are shaped like bears, birds, or snakes and can only be seen as designs from above. Some of the mounds line up with constellations in the sky. Inside the mounds, Indians buried ritual objects such as carved hawks and snakes. Hawks were admired because they are far-seeing. Snakes were believed to be powerful spirits because they can move quickly without legs and change themselves by shedding their skin.

CORN DANCERS

The greatest ceremony in the Southeast was the Green Corn Dance, celebrated in the early summer when the corn was green. It was a time of renewal and thanksgiving. Women put out their hearth fires, cleaned house, and broke all of their cooking pots. Men painted buildings and mended old quarrels. Everyone gathered in the town square to fast and pray. They wore white clothing and painted their faces and bodies red. Drums accompanied the Green Corn Dance until a new sacred fire was lit. Women took coals from the central fire to light their home fires. Then everyone

171

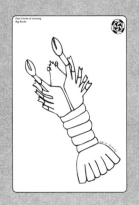

bathed in a stream and feasted in celebration.

The first Europeans to come to the region were the Spanish (in the 1500s) and the French and English (in the 1600s). By the end of the century, the English had settled colonies from Maryland to South Carolina.

Warfare began almost immediately between the English and the Indians. The first war was fought between the colonists of Jamestown, Virginia, and the Powhatan, members of the Lenape Confederacy. That war went well for the Indians, but by the late 1700s, the coastal plain had been cleared of Indians. This was mainly the result of European diseases that killed the Indians—and of settlers who wanted their land. After 1800, whites pushed into the interior and encountered the great Indian nations they called the Five Civilized Tribes.

MIGRATION

White settlers wanted the land for cotton plantations. Then, when gold was discovered in northeastern Georgia in 1829, the United States ordered all of the tribes to move to Oklahoma. Most tribes refused and were forced to leave in the 1830s (Cherokee).

Today most of the descendants of the five tribes live on reservations in Oklahoma—except those of the Cherokee and others who escaped to hideaways in the Appalachian Mountains. Also, some Seminole hid in the swamps of Florida, where they fought the U.S. Army for thirty years.

In that time, many escaped slaves sought refuge with Indian tribes. Today many African-Americans are discovering their Native American roots and some have formed mixed Indian and black communities in southern states. Since the 1970s, many Native American community groups have been formed in cities, as well. They provide cultural and business resources, and are social centers for Southeast Indians.◄

▶ T-Shirts

These T-shirts designs were made by children of Southeast tribes in an Oklahoma tribal school. The students were asked to choose an animal or other object in nature and use it as the design for a T-shirt. Louise Jennings chose a crayfish, and Sally Whitecrow picked an oak tree on a turtle's back.

▶ Healthy Living

The Indian Health Service ran a camp in Nashville, Tennessee, in 1985. The camp received recognition among Southeast tribes when an article about it was published in *The Uset Calumet,* an Indian publication named after the sacred decorated pipe that is a frequent symbol of peace and friendship among Indians.

▶ Petroglyphs

The ancient petroglyph, or rock drawing, above was done by Pueblo in present-day Oakley Springs, Arizona. It represents the sunrise. The petroglyph below, found in Segy Canyon, Arizona, depicts Baho-li-kong-ya, a serpent god worshipped by Southwest Indians. He was believed to be the source of both water and animal blood.

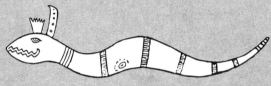

▶ Cliff Dwellings

Cliff dwellings in Canyon de Chelly, Arizona, were home to the Anasazi Indians. They lived high in the cliffs to protect themselves from enemies. The typical adobe (clay-brick) village included a circular spiritual house with a deep hole in the floor to remind the Anasazi that their ancestors had come from within the earth. Anasazi means Basket Maker.

SOUTHWEST

• **TRIBES OF THE REGION: APACHE, HAVASUPAI, HOPI, MOJAVE, PIMA, PUEBLO, TOHONO O'ODHAM, YAQUI, YAVAPAI, YUMA, & ZUNI**

Indian legends say that the creator spared nothing when he made the beautiful deserts and mountains of the southwestern United States and northwestern Mexico. The multicolored Painted Desert, the vast Grand Canyon, the rugged, pine-covered Sangre de Cristo Mountains, and the sculpted pinnacles and flat mesas (plateaus) of Monument Valley are just some of the exquisite natural settings of the region.

But the Southwest is a harsh land as well. Much of it is bone-dry. Rainfall in Arizona and New Mexico averages less than ten inches a year. During droughts, rainfall disappears for several years—though the Rocky Mountains, the eastern boundary of the Southwest, receive deep snowfall in winter. Temperatures average over 100°F in summer, especially in the low-lying deserts of southern Arizona, New Mexico, and northwestern Mexico. The lack of heat-retaining moisture means nights get very cold year-round. In winter, temperatures plunge to well below freezing.

POPULATION The major Indian nations of the region include the Pueblo, Hopi, Apache, Navajo, and Zuni, as well as other, less numerous peoples. Estimates of the total population of the Southwest when the Spanish came in the 1500s range from 100,000 to 200,000 people. They were surrounded by the Plains and Great Basin peoples to the north and east, the California peoples to the west, and the great civilizations of Mesoamerica to the south.

The region's environment and geography have deeply shaped the lives and beliefs of Southwest peoples. In the arid climate and barren landscape of their desert home, they have developed a special appreciation of nature's gifts. Their myths often focus on how people were taught which wild foods to eat and how to plant crops such as corn, beans, and squash. The vast empty spaces and clean air make southwestern peoples especially aware of their surroundings. The Navajo, for example, measure their lands by four sacred mountains—Colorado's Blanca Peak and La Plata Mountains and New Mexico's Mount Taylor and San Francisco Mountains.

ARCHAEOLOGY The human presence in the Southwest is a long and eventful one. Archaeologists have identified 10,000-year-old human remains and tools at Ventana Cave in Arizona and Dead Horse Gulch in New Mexico. Agriculture began here about 1000 B.C., with maize (corn). Archaeologists believe the people learned to farm from the Olmecs of central Mexico. Around A.D. 300, towns appeared, pottery was made, and irrigated farming began.

Two of the greatest civilizations of the Southwest, the Hohokam and the Anasazi, appeared 400 years later. The Hohokam dug irrigation systems for their corn fields. Their descendants, the Tohono O'odham and Pima, appreciated their ingenuity. The Anasazi—Navajo for Ancient Strangers—were the ancestors of the modern Hopi and Pueblo. Some built their homes on the tops of great mesas. To protect themselves in time of war, they also built homes on cliffs in what is now Colorado and Arizona (Cliff Dwellers). Drought in the 1300s ended their society. Not long afterward, descendants of the Anasazi built large, multistoried villages in New Mexico. The last native peoples to arrive were the Navajo and Apache (Sarcee). Archaeologists say they came from the north in the 1400s (Subarctic). Navajo and Apache legends say the same thing.

The Spanish came to the Southwest in the 1500s from their base in the Valley of Mexico.

▶ Pottery Designs

The bear-paw design above was found on the exterior of a food bowl at Four Mile Ruin. Bears had special significance for many Native American tribes (Maidu). The pottery bowl below dates from between the 9th and 12th centuries. Many Southwest tribes are famous for their pottery, and both of these bowls are very delicately made. Their fine, thin construction complements the beautifully balanced black-and-white designs. Interestingly, these bowls were buried with the dead—but first the bowls themselves were "killed" by being punctured.

COYOTE TALES

Coyote is a trickster celebrated in Indian songs and stories from the Gulf of Mexico to the northern Plains and from the Pacific Ocean to the Mississippi River. But nowhere is he more infamous than in the Southwest, where he appears in many forms. Coyote is a wise fool who teaches tribal rules by breaking them. No matter how tricky he is, the joke is always on Coyote in the end. The most important thing he teaches is that people shouldn't take themselves too seriously.

He's Appointed to Study the Stars
(A Pima Tale)

This guy, Coyote, was always appointing himself over people, wanting to show them he could do anything, however hard it was. So the medicine men, wanting to find out if it was true, said, "Maybe he's just a fraud." They said to him, "Uncle! Uncle! You're so fast and wise about everything that you should go and find out for us what those things are doing shining up there every night." As they said this, they pointed to the stars. Coyote took them seriously.

So Coyote went off and didn't return for a long time. Then suddenly, he came back, singing:

> *Beneath the heavens above us*
> *There are round pools of water.*
> *Each time Coyote drinks from one,*
> *He sees his reflection and says,*
> *"I'toi" (all drunk up).*
> *But when he catches on,*
> *He laughs quietly at himself.*

Francisco Vásquez de Coronado, with over 700 Spanish soldiers and Mexican servants, was the first to arrive, in 1540. On a quest to find the legendary Seven Cities of Cíbola—which he believed were made of gold and which probably were Pueblo towns—Coronado quickly made himself very unwelcome. When the Pueblo refused to give up their food supplies, Coronado massacred hundreds of them. Of course, Pueblo towns were not made of gold, and the Spanish did not return until the end of the century. In 1598 they established the first southwestern mission and fort at Santa Fe, New Mexico.

For the next several hundred years, Spanish missionaries forced Christianity on the Pueblo and others. The Indians fought back, and for a twelve-year period in the late 1600s, the Spanish were driven from Santa Fe. To the Spanish the Southwest was little more than an outpost of their great empire to the south. Mexican independence in 1821 did not change things much, though the United States conquest of the region in the Mexican-American War of 1846–1848 did.

From the beginning, relations were tense between the United States and the native peoples of the Southwest. The government accused the Navajo of raiding settlements along the Rio Grande during the Civil War and ordered them onto a reservation. Their refusal led to the Navajo War.

APACHE WARS

Generally, however, peace reigned between the Navajo and the United States. This was not so with the nomadic and warlike Apache. Beginning with an uprising in the early 1860s, the Apache successfully fought off the armies of two nations—the United States and Mexico—for over twenty years.

One of the most famous Apache leaders of that time was Chiricahua Apache chief Cochise. Fifteen years earlier, in 1846, a Mexican "trading party"—led by American James Kirker—had rested and eaten dinner with a group of Apache, then killed 130 of them with a cannon. Cochise's father was probably one of the dead, and Cochise came to hate Mexicans after that. In 1861, white Americans gave him reason to hate them, too. A little white boy was kidnapped by a group of Apache, but Cochise knew nothing about it. Lieutenant George Bascom of the U.S. Army didn't believe Cochise, so he arrested him, his brother, and two nephews. Cochise daringly slashed his way through Bascom's tent with a knife and escaped by dodging bullets. It made him famous among the Chiricahua, but Bascom killed Cochise's brother.

SURRENDER

After fighting the whites for many years—often in near-starvation in their mountain hideaways—Cochise and the Chiricahua Apache surrendered in 1872. Cochise died in 1874 on the Chiricahua Reservation in Arizona, believing his people had been promised the reservation land forever. Two years later the Chiricahua Reservation was closed and the Apache were moved. Geronimo, another Apache chief, renewed the war and fought until 1886. When he surrendered, he was sent first to Florida, then to Oklahoma. He never saw his homeland again.

The defeat of the Apache made room for large numbers of U.S. settlers looking for ranch lands in the 1880s and afterward. However, another southwestern people, the Pueblo, won the right to keep their land by a Supreme Court decision in 1913.

Since World War II, there have been new struggles. Navajo and Hopi lands contain large deposits of uranium, coal, and minerals. While some tribal leaders have leased mineral rights to large corporations, many Navajo and Hopi oppose this practice. The growth of western cities and irrigated corporate farms are also using up the limited amounts of water on tribal land. Ongoing lawsuits will decide many of these questions.◄

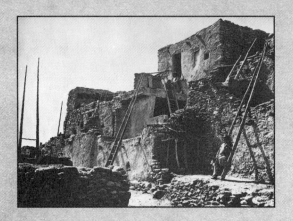

▶ Pueblo

This modern-day pueblo village, equipped with glass windows and electricity, was built on the site of an older pueblo village dating from 1250. Pueblos are constructed by covering stones with plaster. Sometimes, food is dried beneath overhanging beams that support the roofs. Ladders lead to second-story rooms. Hopi religious ceremonies still take place in underground ceremonial chambers called *kivas.*

▶ Debbie Tewa

Debbie Tewa is the solar electrician for the Hopi Foundation. Hopi culture is based on respect for the sun. Some Southwest Indians reject electricity, but solar energy, which converts the sun's energy into electricity, is an accepted way of life. It also allows Hopi to feel independent from government services.

Traditional Dress

Bird Rattle, photographed in 1910, was a member of the Spokan tribe. He is pictured here in traditional dress with a beaded top and heavy jewelry.

Threes

The Naskapi medicine pouch design (right) illustrates three layers of relationships in its central star: humans, society, and the earth. The three outer curved patterns symbolize nature, spirits, and stars. The three members of the Beaver family (below)—Samson, Leah, and baby Frances Louise—are shown in Alberta, Canada, around 1907.

SPOKAN

- **LANGUAGE FAMILY:** SALISHAN
- **LIFEWAYS:** FISHING & GATHERING
- **LOCATION:** WASHINGTON
- **THEIR OWN NAME:** SPOKAN

PLATEAU

The Spokan lived along Washington's Spokane and Columbia rivers, where they invented special nets and reed sluices to catch salmon. After smallpox killed half the tribe in the 1840s, many Spokan joined Protestant missions. The tribe lost a battle against the United States Army in 1858 and was sent to a reservation. In 1955 the Grand Coulee Dam reduced salmon runs on the Columbia River, but now about 2,100 Spokan run a hatchery in Wellpinit, Washington. Young tribe members are reviving traditional Spokan spirituality, but many elders dislike their inclusion of Plains practices.◄

SUBARCTIC

- **TRIBES OF THE REGION:** BEAVER, CARRIER, CHIPEWYAN, CREE, KUTCHIN, MÉTIS, MONTAGNAIS, & NASKAPI

SUBARCTIC

The Subarctic region stretches from the Atlantic Ocean in the east, across the Arctic, and into central Alaska. Most of the region is covered by great forests called the *taiga*. But the greenery can be misleading. Winters are long and cold, but not very snowy. Summers are short and cool.

Two main languages are spoken in the Subarctic region. The 25,000 to 30,000 Athapaskan speakers, who call themselves the Dene, or People, are related to the Navajo of the Southwest. The 150,000 Algonquian speakers call themselves the

SUBARCTIC

Anishinabe, which means Human Beings.

Until recently, it was believed that the Subarctic peoples had migrated to the region from Asia about 10,000 years ago. But new findings have convinced some scholars that people traveled north from Mesoamerica (Paleo-Indians). They may have settled in the Subarctic about 6,000 years ago, when the climate began to warm up. There, coastal peoples hunted sea mammals, while river peoples fished for salmon. Northern hunters went after musk ox and caribou, and the peoples of the southern forests followed buffalo onto the Plains.

The first Europeans to arrive were the Vikings, about 1,000 years ago. A Beothuk legend says that the Indians destroyed the Vikings' settlement in Newfoundland. In the 17th century the French began trading goods for beaver pelts (Northeast). During the next 200 years, French and English people settled in Canada and divided the land into provinces. The Europeans signed land treaties with Indian tribes—called First Nations in Canada—but the Indians meant to share the land, not give it up.

FIRST NATIONS

In 20th-century Canada there is a new energy among Subarctic people. National health care has helped the population grow. Satellite communications and snowmobiles have shrunk the great distances of the region and brought the fifty-three Canadian First Nations together with Northwest Coast, Arctic, and Northeast people for cultural, business, and political activities.

Almost every First Nation government has filed land and treaty rights lawsuits in the Canadian courts. First Nations are also concerned about the environment. The largest threat they face today began in 1989, when a company called Hydro-Quebec built dams in James Bay in order to sell electricity to New England. The dams flooded 7,500 square miles of the Cree and Inuit homelands. Although New York and Vermont have

FUR TRADE

Subarctic Indians brought their furs to French and British trading posts in Canada. By 1600, fur-bearing animals were scarce in Europe. American fox, mink, otter, and muskrat skins brought high prices, but beaver pelts were the most valued. By the late 19th century, Indians had come to depend on the guns, knives, cloth, kettles, and rum they received at trading posts such as that of the Hudson's Bay Company in Saskatchewan (above).

HUNTING MAGIC Animals such as beaver and caribou commanded deep respect from Subarctic Indians. Since ancient times, hunters had developed personal rituals for effective hunting. This beaver symbol (right) was carved on the wooden handle of a Naskapi knife to attract the animal. Indian hunters' dreams of caribou (below) told them where herds were located and how many animals to take. After the hunt, the bones and other remains of the animal were used in rituals.

First Nations

First Nations leaders gather in Canadian cities for conferences, protests, and legal negotiations with Canadian leaders. A Constitutional Conference (shown above) took place in Toronto in 1988.

Antler Combs

The Susquehannock made these finely carved combs from deer antlers. The combs were found at various sites in Pennsylvania where the tribe lived.

rejected the plan, Hydro-Quebec is building more dams, which will destroy six rivers and flood an area the size of France.

When wilderness land is flooded, birds and animals are driven away. When trees are suddenly covered in water, they die. Not only have people lost their homes, food sources, and sacred sites, they have lost their way of life. This causes poverty and breaks up families. Many environmental groups are actively defending tribes threatened by dams. And the First Nations are working to heal their communities and continue the ways of their ancestors.

Ovide Mercredi, Grand Chief of the Assembly of First Nations, spoke at the United Nations in 1993: "We call upon the governments of the world to begin to meet with us as equals…to create a new world where all people can live in harmony."◀

SUSQUEHANNOCK

- **LANGUAGE FAMILY: IROQUOIAN**
- **LIFEWAYS: TRADING, HUNTING, & FARMING**
- **LOCATION: OKLAHOMA**
- **THEIR OWN NAME: SUSQUESAHANOUGH**

NORTHEAST

The Susquehannock were traders who controlled the Susquehanna River valley, which served as an intertribal trade route. Their name comes from an Iroquois word for Great Field. The tribe's clan ceremonies and dances combined Iroquois and Lenape beliefs. The Susquehannock was a large tribe, though by 1700 most of the tribe had died from war and disease. Today, a few Susquehannock live among the Seneca and Cayuga in Oklahoma.◀

179

TIMUCUA

- **LANGUAGE FAMILY: MUSKOGEAN**
- **LIFEWAYS: FISHING & GATHERING**
- **LOCATION: NONE**
- **THEIR OWN NAME: TIMUCUA**

SOUTHEAST

The Timucua were one of the largest Indian groups to live on the Gulf Coast. The tribe was also one of the earliest groups to live in the region, having been there since at least 500 B.C. By the year 1500, they numbered about 13,000 and were scattered across much of central and eastern Florida.

In 1521 the Spanish conquistador Juan Ponce de León came to Timucua land looking for the legendary fountain of youth. The explorer believed that there was a spring whose waters guaranteed everlasting youth. Carib Indians had sent him north to the land the Spanish called La Florida, the Flowers.

The Timucua were used to raids by the Carib and other Florida Indians. They attacked Ponce de León's landing party and severely wounded him. He went to Cuba and died shortly afterward.

FORTRESSES Timucua palm-trunk houses surrounded a ceremonial building and a central plaza. Their villages were always protected by strong stockades. The Timucua fished for most of their food. They also gathered the root of the coontie plant, which is an evergreen. They pounded the root into a flour to bake bread.

Unfortunately for the Timucua, the Spanish did not give up their quest to conquer Florida. They built St. Augustine—the first European city in North America—in Timucua territory in 1545. By 1700 the Timucua had completely died off from war, enslavement, and European diseases. ◄

Saturiova

Timucua chief Saturiova is shown here ready for war. He is said to have assembled his men before battle and, flinging water into the air, to have cried, "As I have done with this water so I pray that you do with the blood of your enemies!" The cup he is holding is probably filled with Black Drink, a ritual beverage often drunk before war.

Burial Ceremony

This drawing, dated 1591, depicts the burial of a Timucua chief. The deceased was buried beneath a mound of earth that was encircled by arrows stuck into the ground. Mourning lasted for three days and included fasting. At the end of three days, all of the chief's possessions were put inside his house and burned.

POTLATCH

Potlatches were hosted by prominent Northwest Coast Indian families who gave valuable gifts to their guests. Northwest Coast Indians made elaborate clothing and masks to wear during potlatch ceremonies. The Kak-Von-Ton brothers (above) are holding ceremonial rattles and have chilkat blankets woven of dyed cedar bark and embellished with clan crests. The middle brother has a clan totem mask.

DANCING DAY

Tlingit Indians in Klukwan, Alaska, prepare to dance at an outdoor potlatch held around 1901 (right). The man on the left is wearing a hide tunic painted with clan symbols. Some men wear metal nose rings, while others carry ceremonial poles carved for the potlatch dance.

A RICH MAN IS COMING A

Tlingit chief and his son in ceremonial

dress watch potlatch dancers from a carved and painted platform displaying their clan's history (left). A Tlingit song goes, "A rich man is coming. Keep your thoughts to yourself."

TLINGIT

- **LANGUAGE FAMILY: TLINGIT**
- **LIFEWAYS: HUNTING & FISHING**
- **LOCATION: ALASKA**
- **THEIR OWN NAME: TLINGIT**

NORTHWEST COAST

About 20,000 Tlingit villages once occupied southeastern Alaska, northern British Columbia, and Canada's Yukon Territory. Smallpox epidemics reduced the tribe in the 19th century.

The Tlingit created dramatic painted carvings and woven blankets. These treasures were traded for Haida canoes and candlefish oil. Women led trading voyages and were mothers of either the Raven or Eagle clans. The most dazzling clan ceremonies were potlatches honoring the dead. The entire clan took part in preparing the ceremony. Guests feasted on seal, oiled berries, candlefish grease, and dried fish. They ate and danced until they grew sick, an honor for the host. The guests received clothes, food, and blankets according to their places in their clans.

The Russian Orthodox clergy discouraged Tlingit spiritual practices. Tlingit publicly accepted Christianity but held their own beliefs in private. In 1867 Russia sold Alaska, including Tlingit land, to the United States. The new owners came in larger numbers than the Russians, threatening the Tlingit way of life.

GROWTH Today, most of the 20,000 Tlingit live in Washington and Oregon. A few hundred speak Tlingit. Alaskan Tlingit are members of native equal-rights movements (Red Power). They are also shareholders in Sealaska Corporation, which awards scholarships and provides money for Tlingit theater groups and language courses at the University of Alaska. Most rural Tlingit are traditional. They hold potlatches and produce world-famous art.◄

TOHONO O'ODHAM

- **LANGUAGE FAMILY: UTO-AZTECAN PIMAN**
- **LIFEWAYS: FARMING & TRADING**
- **LOCATION: ARIZONA**
- **THEIR OWN NAME: TOHONO O'ODHAM**

SOUTHWEST

The Tohono O'odham is a nation of 17,500 people who live on three reservations in southern Arizona. Tohono O'odham means People of the Desert. The tribe was formerly known as the Papago, a name anthropologists gave it from its language dialect. The Tohono O'odham were the first Native American people to legally change back to their original name.

The Tohono O'odham is one of few tribes to occupy its original homeland, though on a much smaller scale. One reason may be that the tribe lives on some of the hottest and driest land in the United States, land that white settlers did not want. The Tohono O'odham have always lived in close association with their Pima relatives. They speak similar dialects of the Uto-Aztecan language family and share the heritage of their Hohokam ancestors (Southwest). The Pima and Tohono O'odham were among the last tribes to meet outside people.

SACRED SALT

The Tohono O'odham grew corn and beans and gathered such desert plants as mesquite beans and saguaro cactus fruit. They collected salt from the Gulf of California and traded it for the goods of other tribes. The annual four-day journey in search of salt symbolized seeking life by bringing the ocean to the desert. Children as young as sixteen years old went on the trip as a rite of passage into adulthood. The ceremony included

Tohono O'odham Girl

Tohono O'odham girls traditionally wore basketry hats and breastplates made of shells and beads. This little girl was photographed wearing such a costume in the early 20th century.

Toka

Toka is a ball game played by Tohono O'odham women. Each player holds a long stick with a crook at the end. The "ball" is actually two balls connected by a thong. The object of the game is to hook the thong with the stick and toss the balls into the opponent's goal area.

▶ The Path of Life

This man-in-the-maze design symbolizes the individual on the path of life. Each step through the maze is part of his search for truth and knowledge, a search that eventually ends in the center circle. The symbol is carried by the lead dancer in the Tohono O'odham's Chelkona Dance.

▶ Warriors

The Toltecs were warriors. They built menacing, fifteen-foot-tall statues to ward off invaders from their capital city, Tollan. The great figures were carved from basalt and held spears and bags of incense.

purification and vision quests. Salt pilgrims had to return to the desert without once looking back at the ocean. Each band had legends explaining the salt spirit.

The Tohono O'odham government remains traditional: Decisions are made by a tribal council and require the agreement of all members. The council protects tribal interests and helps preserve the Tohono O'odham culture, including ceremonies of gratitude to I'itoi, the creator.

The tribe has also preserved many of its traditional arts. Tohono O'odham artisans produce more baskets than any other tribe. One of their special baskets is based on the man-in-the-maze design.

In other ways, however, Tohono O'odham life has changed in recent years. Once among the most pure-blooded of Native American peoples, the Tohono O'odham now often marry members of other tribes. ◀

TOLTECS

- **LANGUAGE FAMILY: NAHUATLAN**
- **LIFEWAYS: WARRING & TRADING**
- **LOCATION: NONE**
- **THEIR OWN NAME: TOLTEC**

MESOAMERICA

The ancestors of the Toltecs were members of the Olmec elite who fled north after the downfall of Teotihuacán. Around A.D. 900 these people, joined by nomads from farther north, swept back into the Valley of Mexico. There they founded their capital, Tollan. From this base the Toltecs conquered much of central Mexico and even areas in the Yucatán and Guatemala.

Legends about the Toltec leader Ce Acatl Topilizin mixed with those of the god Quetzalcoatl (Aztec). This feathered serpent god represented light, learning, and all good things. The rulers who came after Ce Acatl Topilizin were believed to be incarnations of Quetzalcoatl. Like the Aztecs and Maya, the Toltecs believed that they lived in the fifth world. Legends said this world was created when Nanautzin, the lowliest of the gods, jumped into a fire to light up the sun.

During the 200 years their empire lasted, the Toltecs were known as warriors, traders, master builders, and painters. They introduced fine gold-, silver-, and copperworking to Mesoamerica and traded their products for turquoise from New Mexico and feathers from Central America. At the height of the Toltec civilization, the followers of Quetzalcoatl split from the followers of Tezcatlipoca, the god of war and death. Forced to leave, Quetzalcoatl's followers invaded Mayan lands. The followers of Tezcatlipoca ruled for another hundred years until Tollan was destroyed by feuds and invaded by Chichimecas from the north.◀

▶Human Sacrifice

Human sacrifice was practiced in homage to the god Nanautzin. Victims' hearts were removed with obsidian (black glass) knives and stored in temple altars.

TONKAWA

- • LANGUAGE FAMILY: CADDOAN
- • LIFEWAYS: HUNTING & FARMING
- • LOCATIONS: OKLAHOMA
- • THEIR OWN NAME: TONKAWEYA

PLAINS

The Tonkawa were part of the Caddo cultural group. Tonkaweya means They All Stay Together. In 1700 the Spanish confined the 5,000 Tonkawa to a mission, but abandoned it in 1728. During the Civil War, Tonkawa scouts aided the United States Army against the Comanche and Kiowa. War and smallpox had reduced the tribe to thirty-four people by 1921. By that time, they had been moved to Tonkawa, Oklahoma, where about 186 Tonkawa live today. Their language is extinct, but they have revived their ceremonies.◀

▶Dance

Although dancing and religious ceremonies have been a part of Tonkawa culture for hundreds of years, they were forbidden by the U.S. government for several years until the early 20th century. This dance, which is still performed by tribe members in Oklahoma, was photographed in 1901.

William Penn

Arrested in England for practicing Quakerism, William Penn came to America and founded Pennsylvania, where he hoped to establish religious freedom. He also wanted to develop friendly relations with the Indians. In this engraving, Penn and some Lenape Indians are signing a treaty that guaranteed the Lenape's land rights and freedom to worship. The treaty was signed in 1682.

Metacom

Chief Metacom of the Wamapanoag (known to whites as King Philip) was angered by repeated violations of the treaty his father had signed with the Pilgrims in the 1620s. Since then, Indians had been harassed, imprisoned, and severely punished for not following the Christian religion. In 1671 the Puritans forced Metacom to acknowledge the sovereignty of the king of England and to promise to pay annual tribute. Metacom is shown here signing the treaty—against his will.

TREATIES

In the 500 years since Columbus first landed in the Americas, at least 400 treaties have been signed between Native American nations and the governments of European colonizers (England, Holland, France, and Spain) and their successors (Mexico, Canada, and the United States). These treaties have dealt with a wide range of subjects, including land rights, labor, religion, cultural rights, education, economic development, citizenship, and political self-rule. Most of the treaties have been broken by whites.

Treaties between whites and Native Americans fall into three general historical periods: colonial, national, and 20th-century.

During the colonial period in North America, representatives of the English, Dutch, French, and Spanish governments negotiated in their countries' interests. Except for the Spanish, who made Indians subjects of the Spanish king, the European governments usually tried to balance the interests of the Native Americans and the white colonists. Indian nations were still powerful, and the Europeans did not want to fight them. Also, trade with the Indians was important to the colonial economies, so the European governments often wanted to keep good relations.

England's Proclamation of 1763 (issued after England won the French and Indian War) made it illegal for white colonists to settle on Indian lands west of the Appalachian Mountains. The colonists resented this restriction, which was one of the causes of the American Revolution.

NATIONAL PERIOD

During the national period—beginning with independence in the United States in 1776, in Mexico in 1821, and in Canada in 1867—the balance of power shifted, and trade with the Indians became less important. The North American governments generally negotiated harsh treaties with the Indians, usually after defeating them in battle. The pattern began with the Fort Stanwix treaty in 1784. The Iroquois, many of whom had supported the British in the Revolutionary War, were forced to give up much of their land in western New York and Pennsylvania.

For more than 100 years, Native Americans signed treaties only to find them broken when white settlers pushed west. In 1868, for instance, the Sioux signed the Fort Laramie Treaty, which confined them to a large reservation in the Dakota territory. When gold was discovered in the sacred Black Hills in the 1870s, the U.S. government waged war on the Sioux and forced them to give up the Black Hills. The story of the Oklahoma Indians—moved there from the Southeast in the 1830s—is similar. The Indians were originally promised much of Oklahoma in exchange for the lands they had been forced to give up. But Oklahoma was mostly taken away from them in 1890 and given to white settlers.

Many treaties concerning citizenship were also broken. When the United States seized half of Mexico in 1848, it signed a treaty promising all Mexicans full American citizenship. Indians had been Mexican citizens since Mexico became independent in 1821, but the U.S. government refused to grant the Indians of the Southwest full citizenship until 1924. In Canada most Native Americans were not granted citizenship until 1960.

20TH CENTURY In the 20th century Native Americans have won back some of the lands they lost in 19th-century treaties. In a series of court cases since World War II, Native Americans in all parts of the United States have received land, money, fishing rights, and other compensation for the broken treaties of the past. In Canada much of the vast Arctic—770,000 square miles in all—has been returned to the Inuit. ◀

▶ Ft. Laramie Treaty

Thomas Fitzpatrick (1779–1854) was an Irish-born American who became well known as a trapper and guide. Appointed Indian agent for the Upper Platte, he met with representatives of several Plains tribes and negotiated the Fort Laramie Treaty in 1851. The Indians were guaranteed certain territories in exchange for land, but the effect was to divide the tribes. Once they were separated on small parcels of land, it was easier for whites finally to take away all their land.

▶ Going to Court

In 1927, suing for land rights guaranteed them by an 1858 treaty, the Yankton Nakota Sioux sought the assistance of attorneys and witnesses (above). The legal actions begun by the tribe were at first decided against the Indians. However, in 1928, seventy years after the original treaty, the tribe received compensation for its land.

Tsimshian Artisans

As a wealthy trading tribe, the Tsimshian could supply artists with the best materials for creating dramatic and intricate totems and other art objects. Clans distinguished themselves by displaying items such as painted drums. This drum (left) was painted for the Eagle Clan. The eagle is surrounded by other creatures symbolic of the clan's legends. This wooden bowl carved in the form of a raven (below) was used by the Raven Clan during feasts.

Button Blankets

The Tsimshian began making button blankets after they traded for European buttons and cloth. Designs were appliquéd on red or blue cloth, and clan crests were sewn on using pearl buttons. This 20th-century button blanket (below) was made by Shona Hah of the Lelooska family to represent the wealthy and powerful Killer Whale clan.

TSIMSHIAN

- **LANGUAGE FAMILY: TSIMSHIAN**
- **LIFEWAYS: FISHING & TRADING**
- **LOCATION: BRITISH COLUMBIA**
- **THEIR OWN NAME: CMSYAN**

NORTHWEST COAST

Villages of large Tsimshian plank houses lined banks of the Skeena, Niska, and Nass rivers in British Columbia, Canada. The tribe's original name, Cmsyan, means Inside the Skeena River. The Tsimshian language is unique. It is spoken by 10,214 people today, but only one group is called Tsimshian. The others are the Carrier (Gitksan) and Nisga.

TRADING Plentiful candlefish from the Nass River gave the Tsimshian a near monopoly over local trade. The tribe traded fish oil for Haida canoes and carved wooden boxes. They got copper from the Tlingit to the north, and furs and hides from inland Subarctic tribes. By the end of the 1700s, the Tsimshian had developed major trade routes along the Northwest Coast.

Each village had separate laws and firm class divisions. The main clans were the Killer Whale, Wolf, Eagle, and Raven. Each clan was divided into *smkiket*, "real people," and *liqakiket*, "other people." Lower classes were *wahaayin*, "having no relatives," and *lu-nkit*, "slaves." The Tsimshian held potlatches, carved totem poles, and recited legends. A popular legend was the story of a girl who married a bear. The moral is that love knows no limits.

In 1857 an English lay minister, William Duncan, came to live among the Tsimshian. He learned their language and encouraged the blending of Christian and tribal beliefs. In 1862 Duncan and about fifty Tsimshian established a mission village called Metlakahtla on Annette Island in Alaska. Trade had led some Tsimshian chiefs to build villages close to Fort Simpson, a

British trading post. After a smallpox epidemic at Fort Simpson, many Tsimshian fled to Metlakahtla. In 1891 Duncan and 800 followers founded New Metlakahtla Reserve.

In 1961 the Tsimshian received exclusive fishing rights in waters up to 3,000 feet from the reserve. Because of this bounty, they were not involved in the Indian land-claims cases of the 1960s (Arctic). In 1990, the 2,432 Tsimshian were self-governing.

Although the Tsimshian on Annette Island are Christian, their Nisga relatives are traditional, following clan laws as well as seasonal fishing cycles. Among current issues important to the tribe are land claims and a dispute with a mining company. In the 1970s the Carrier revived their clans, potlatches, and winter ceremonies. They regularly raise totem poles and speak Gitksan at home. ◄

TUNICA-BILOXI

- **LANGUAGE FAMILY: MUSKOGEAN**
- **LIFEWAYS: FARMING**
- **LOCATION: LOUISIANA**
- **THEIR OWN NAME: TUNICA**

SOUTHEAST

Before 1700 about 2,000 Tunica lived along the Mississippi River in present-day Louisiana. Tunica women made cloth from mulberry plants, while the men grew corn. During the 1700s the Tunica supported the French, which caused problems with English-allied tribes such as the Chickasaw, Alibamu, and Natchez. Many Tunica were killed, and by 1908 there were only thirty left. They allied with the Biloxi, a southern Plains tribe of about fifty people. Today, 430 Tunica-Biloxi maintain joint tribal ceremonies in Louisiana. ◄

Tsimshian Nation

The Nisga Chief of the Tsimshian (below) wears a carved bear and ermine headdress and button blanket at a ceremony welcoming Prime Minister of Canada Brian Mulroney in 1989. The shape of his beaver staff indicates that the chief is a speaker. The symbol of the Tsimshian Nation (left) is a killer whale set against the sun.

Pottery Design

These six designs are typical of those found on Tunica pottery. Besides pottery, the Tunica made intricate dugout canoes and fine cloth woven from mulberry plants. Both the Tunica and Biloxi built permanent villages, where they farmed and created their crafts.

▶ Alfrus Hewitt

Alfrus Hewitt, a Tuscarora Indian, fought for the North in the Civil War and was wounded twice. This photograph was taken in 1913, almost fifty years after his military service.

▶ Beaded Satchel

This black velvet bag was made with glass beads. Before Europeans arrived, the Tuscarora made their satchels of leather and embroidered them with shells from nearby rivers. The level of intricacy evident here would have been difficult, if not impossible, to achieve without glass beads. The floral design also reflects European influences.

TUSCARORA

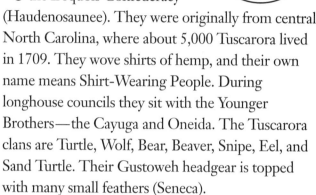

- **LANGUAGE FAMILY: IROQUOIAN**
- **LIFEWAYS: HUNTING, GATHERING, & FARMING**
- **LOCATION: NEW YORK, & ONTARIO, & QUEBEC**
- **THEIR OWN NAME: SKA-RU-REN**

NORTHEAST

The Tuscarora are members of the Iroquois Confederacy (Haudenosaunee). They were originally from central North Carolina, where about 5,000 Tuscarora lived in 1709. They wove shirts of hemp, and their own name means Shirt-Wearing People. During longhouse councils they sit with the Younger Brothers—the Cayuga and Oneida. The Tuscarora clans are Turtle, Wolf, Bear, Beaver, Snipe, Eel, and Sand Turtle. Their Gustoweh headgear is topped with many small feathers (Seneca).

BASKETS AND BOWLS

The Carolina Tuscarora were fruit growers who traded baskets and wooden bowls for furs and copper from western tribes.

In 1711, after a war with European colonists, 1,500 Tuscarora fled north, where the Oneida gave them land. The Five Nations of the Iroquois thus became the Six Nations.

Even though the Tuscarora and Oneida fought on the American side during the Revolutionary War, the United States forced the Tuscarora to sell all of their land. Fortunately, the tribe was paid for the land taken by the state of North Carolina. The Tuscarora used that money to buy land in New York.

By the early 1900s, the Tuscarora had become successful fruit growers. Today, the 1,200 New York Tuscarora are self-governing. They continue to use the chief's council and clan system. The Iroquois National Lacrosse Team is headquartered on Tuscarora land, and the sport is popular among Tuscarora high school students.◀

UMATILLA

- **LANGUAGE FAMILY: SAHAPTIAN**
- **LIFEWAYS: FISHING & HUNTING**
- **LOCATIONS: OREGON**
- **THEIR OWN NAME: UMATILLA**

PLATEAU

ntil the 20th century, the Umatilla lived in multifamily lodges built from pine and reeds. Like many of their Plateau neighbors, they relied on salmon fishing and trapping game for their food. They built a complicated system of walkways, nets, traps, and spears to take advantage of the annual salmon runs. They also caught trout and freshwater eels. The fish were smoked or dried, then eaten throughout the winter.

THE SALMON RUN

The Umatilla believed the salmon were beings who migrated from their deep-sea homes to their river homes each year. They respected the salmon they caught. This was so that the others might go back to the sea village and tell of the respect they received from the Umatilla people. This, they believed, assured the return of the salmon the following year (Northwest Coast).

After Europeans brought horses to the region in the late 1700s, the Umatilla joined other Plateau peoples in bison hunts on the nearby plains. This supplemented their traditional fish diet but did not replace it. Today, old ways continue in several ceremonies celebrated by the Umatilla and their cousins the Walla Walla. Each spring, they celebrate the salmon run by welcoming and honoring the first catch. At the Spring Root Feast, traditional foods are gathered and cooked. The people bless the roots and give thanks to the creator who provides them. After the feast, the people face the east—the direction of the rising sun—and pray.

Today, many Umatilla work for a company that

Hoo-sis-mox-mox

Leander Moorhouse photographed Hoo-sis-mox-mox, an Umatilla and probably a chief, around 1900. Hoo-sis-mox-mox is wrapped in a traditional blanket with a simple geometric design. Moorhouse died in 1926, leaving 10,000 glass-plate negatives documenting the Umatilla tribe and its region.

Ceremony

This group of Umatilla women dressed in colorful traditional clothing has formed a circle during a ceremony. Tribal leaders sit on horseback behind them.

▶ Umatilla Children

These Umatilla children were photographed in traditional dress in 1995. They are being led by elders in a ground-breaking ceremony to celebrate the construction of a cultural center, the Tamustalik Cultural Institute. The center is scheduled to be completed in summer 1997.

builds mobile homes on their reservation in northeast Oregon. The tribe belongs to the 2,300-member Confederated Tribes of the Umatilla Indian Reservation, which includes the Walla Walla and Cayuse. A joint council runs tribal schools, clinics, and centers, as well as campgrounds for tourists. It also manages the reservation's natural resources and organizes ceremonies.

Until the Snake River dams were built in Oregon in the 1930s, area tribes had plenty of fish. Now the salmon are nearly gone. In June 1995 Umatilla leaders presented the U.S. Congress with a plan to save the salmon. The plan calls for changes in the dams so that young salmon can get out to sea. Representative Elizabeth Furse of Oregon said, "I've been learning about salmon for twenty-five years, and the most valuable information that has come to me is from the Pacific Northwest tribes." ◀

UTE

- **LANGUAGE FAMILY: UTO-AZTECAN**
- **LIFEWAYS: HUNTING & GATHERING**
- **LOCATIONS: COLORADO & UTAH**
- **THEIR OWN NAME: UTE**

GREAT BASIN

The Ute people lent their name to the state of Utah. Traditionally, Ute territory stretched across the central Rocky Mountains from Colorado to western Utah. It is spectacular land that now includes six national parks. The abundant game in the mountains provided most of the Ute diet, though gathering wild plants and insects was also important.

The origin of hunting among the Ute has a curious legend attached to it. A story tells of a very old man who found a large clot of blood on the

▶ Ouray and Chipeta

Chief Ouray of the Ute is pictured here with his wife, Chipeta, in 1880, the year he died. Ouray spoke English, Spanish, and two Indian languages. His disillusionment with the U.S. government is summed up in a comment he made to newspaper reporters in 1868: "The agreement an Indian makes to a United States treaty is like the agreement a buffalo makes with his hunters when pierced with arrows. All he can do is lie down and give in." During a Ute uprising in 1879, three white women were kidnapped from the Ute Agency. Chipeta entered the all-male Ute tribal council to negotiate their release, which she achieved in six days. When her husband died, Chipeta became a famous Ute chief.

ground. He wiped up the blood with his shirt and brought it home. A baby appeared the next day, and the man and his wife called him Blood Clot. The boy matured in only a few days. He started killing mice and was soon hunting buffalo for his parents and nearby Ute villagers.

Animal ceremonies are an important part of Ute culture. The Bear Dance, performed in late May, originated in a shaman's dream of a dancing bear. The dreamer received spiritual instructions from the bear and gave them to his people (Maidu).

In 1868 the Ute signed a treaty in Washington that guaranteed them a 16-million-acre reservation in Colorado. Five years later an official of the Bureau of Indian Affairs convinced Ute chief Ouray to sell one-quarter of the Ute territory. Then, in September 1879, politicians in Washington and Denver—and greedy silver mining companies— led the U.S. Army to invade the Ute reservation. Twelve soldiers and thirty-seven Ute were killed. In 1881 the army moved the Ute off their land to a new and smaller reservation in Utah.

SHEEP RAISING

The land left to the Ute was land no one else wanted. Soon they were suffering from malnutrition and tuberculosis. A population close to 4,500 in the 1840s had shrunk to a quarter of that size by 1900. However, things began to change in the 1920s, when the government agreed to purchase sheep for the tribe and help it set up a wool business.

In the 1950s United States courts awarded the Ute a large cash settlement for land that had been taken from them. The Ute council has used this money to develop schools, housing, and businesses operated by the 6,000-member tribe. Few Ute have moved to cities in search of jobs. Living close to nature makes it easier to retain spiritual unity and perform ceremonies such as the Bear and Sun dances (Plains). Elders speak the Ute language during public ceremonies, but it is usually translated for the young people. ◄

Great Warrior

The Ute acquired horses in the 1600s. This enabled them to conduct regular raids on both Indians and the Spanish and to wage war on the Arapaho, who lived on the other side of the Rocky Mountains. They quickly gained a reputation as a warlike tribe. Arrow- and spearhead makers held a place of honor in Ute society, as did warriors like the one pictured here in 1915.

the Southern Ute DRUM   25¢

Newspapers

The *Southern Ute Drum*, published in Ignacio, Colorado, keeps Southern Ute informed about reservation news such as federal land allotments and the hunting season. The *Ute Bulletin* is the official newspaper of the Ute Indian tribe and features news relating to all of Ute country.

$1.00 UTE BULLETIN OFFICIAL NEWSPAPER OF THE UTE INDIAN TRIBE   NEWS FROM UTE COUNTRY   Vol. 29 No. 10   February 28, 1995

WAMPANOAG

- **LANGUAGE FAMILY: ALGONQUIAN**
- **LIFEWAYS: FISHING, GATHERING, & FARMING**
- **LOCATION: MASSACHUSETTS**
- **THEIR OWN NAME: WAMPANOAG**

NORTHEAST

The Wampanoag of Massachusetts are one of the main New England tribes. Their chiefs governed the coast and islands east of Narragansett Bay.

The Wampanoag are known for celebrating the first Thanksgiving with the Pilgrims. The Pilgrims' Puritan religious community was not tolerated in England, so they crossed the Atlantic to settle where they could worship as they chose. Although the Wampanoag saved the Pilgrims from starving, the tribe soon found that Pilgrims did not tolerate Indian beliefs. To convert Indians to Christianity, the Pilgrims built "praying towns" in the Northeast.

METACOM

In 1675 Wampanoag chief Metacom resisted Puritan land seizures and taxes. His 500 warriors were joined by 20,000 men from neighboring tribes (Nipmuc). But by then the English numbered 50,000 and, with the help of the Mohegan, almost exterminated the Wampanoag.

Today, about 2,700 Wampanoag live in five bands in eastern Massachusetts. The largest communities are Gay Head on Martha's Vineyard and Mashpee on Cape Cod. Grand Sachem Drifting Goose formed the Wampanoag council of chiefs in the 1970s. Only the Gay Head band has federal tribal status. The other bands are applying for status and land. In October Wampanoag children have a day off from school to celebrate Cranberry Day. The tribe meets in the cranberry bog to pray and harvest cranberries. Everyone carries baskets of cranberries to the town hall, where the public joins in a feast and dance. ◀

▶ Drifting Goose

Drifting Goose, also known as Ellsworth Oakley, is the leader, or grand sachem, of the Wampanoag. In the 1970s he appointed new chiefs for the tribe's five groups: Mashpee, Gay Head, Herring Pond, Assonet, and Nemasket.

▶ Mashpee Fisherman

The Mashpee Wampanoag live on Cape Cod, Massachusetts. Their population is around 1,600, and many of them earn their living as fishermen.

WAPPINGER

- **LANGUAGE FAMILY:** ALGONQUIAN
- **LIFEWAYS:** FARMING, FISHING, & HUNTING
- **LOCATION:** NONE
- **THEIR OWN NAME:** WAPPINCK

NORTHEAST

The Wappinger tribe was a branch of the Lenape. Wappinger territory included what became New York's Dutchess and Putnam counties. The Wappinger lived in longhouse villages and traded wampum shells. In 1600 they joined the Mahican Confederacy. Never a large tribe, the Wappinger had been reduced to just a few people by 1700. Although the Wappinger tribe no longer exists, its history is preserved by the Mahican on the Stockbridge-Munsee Reservation in Wisconsin. ◄

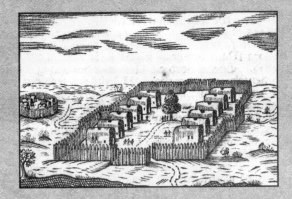

▶ Two Villages

These two Wappinger villages—shown on a 1635 engraving—are somewhat unrealistic. The houses would not have been equal in size, since the chief's house typically was much larger than the rest. Also, the woods around the village would have been burned to make room for gardens. The Wappinger moved their villages every eight to twelve years to find new fertile ground in the forest.

WARM SPRINGS

- **LANGUAGE FAMILY:** SAHAPTIAN
- **LIFEWAYS:** HUNTING & FISHING
- **LOCATION:** OREGON
- **THEIR OWN NAME:** TIKUNI

PLATEAU

The Warm Springs Confederacy gets its name from its Oregon home, where volcanoes have produced many natural warm springs. Six small tribes were moved to the Warm Springs Reservation in 1855. Among the many ceremonies taught by the 19th-century prophet Squsachtun are native healing methods and dances borrowed from the Shaker religion. The Root Festival is held in April (Umatilla). The 2,750-member tribe creates the fine bead- and featherwork sold at their successful Kah-Nee-Ta resort and campground. ◄

Spilyay Tymoo
(Coyote News)
March 17, 1995
Vol. 20 No. 6
35¢

▶ Newspaper

The *Spilyay Tymoo,* which translates as Coyote News, is published in Warm Springs, Oregon. The paper informs people on the reservation about local museum and school events. It also features personal reflections on Warm Springs history by village elders. The newspaper's logo is a howling coyote.

▶ Grass Houses

This engraving from the mid-1800s shows the beehive-shaped wickiups the Wichita lived in. The houses were made of grass applied to wooden frames. Each house had two doors and a hole for smoke at the top. The Wichita were systematic farmers, as the neat fields of corn in front of their houses show.

▶ War Dance

This 1820 engraving depicts a group of warriors performing the Dog Dance ceremony. With shields, spears, and raised tomahawks, they dance around the fire to the beat of a drum, preparing for war. The ceremonial lodge is similar to what conquistador Francisco Vásquez de Coronado saw in the 1540s, which demonstrates the stability and continuity of Wichita culture.

WICHITA

- **LANGUAGE FAMILY: CADDOAN**
- **LIFEWAYS: FARMING**
- **LOCATION: OKLAHOMA**
- **THEIR OWN NAME: KITIKITI'SH**

PLAINS

The Wichita were originally a confederation of small bands. They received the tribal name Wia Chitoh, meaning Big Arbor, from the Choctaw because of their beehive-shaped grass wickiups (Plains). The Wichita preferred the name Kitikiti'sh, meaning Raccoon-Eyed, which recalled their traditional face painting.

Before 1700, about 4,000 Wichita lived in the Arkansas River valley in what became Oklahoma. They grew corn, squash, melons, and tobacco near their villages. The tribe is related to the Arikara and Pawnee. In the early 1600s, when the Arikara moved north, the Wichita became the link between Arikara and Caddo horse traders.

ATTACKED During the 1700s European diseases weakened the farming tribes of the Plains. Hunting tribes invaded their territories. The Wichita battled the Comanche to the west and Osage to the east. In the 1760s the Comanche made peace so they could trade with the Wichita's French allies. But the Osage, who had better English guns, drove the Wichita from the valley.

Some Wichita fought for the Confederacy in the Civil War. They were disappointed by their postwar treaty and moved to what is now Wichita, Kansas. By 1867 the federal government had removed all the Wichita to a Caddo reservation in Oklahoma. There the Wichita suffered from diseases and poor reservation conditions. By 1894 the Wichita population had dropped to 153. Today, about 1,800 people living in Anadarko, Oklahoma, are counted as Wichita. They are trying to revive their culture. ◀

WINNEBAGO

- **LANGUAGE FAMILY: SIOUIAN**
- **LIFEWAYS: HUNTING, GATHERING, & FARMING**
- **LOCATION: WISCONSIN & NEBRASKA**
- **THEIR OWN NAME: HOCHUNGRA**

NORTHEAST

The Winnebago's own name means People of Real Voices. It was given to them by the Ioway because Winnebago leaders made great speeches. The name Winnebago came from a Sac and Fox insult—*winipig*, meaning "dirty water."

Winnebago legend tells of their creation on Red Banks Peninsula in Wisconsin. According to the story, Rabbit was the first of the Winnebago. The son of Earthmaker and a human mother, he was raised by his grandmother, the Earth. Because Rabbit made the world safe for humans by killing all of the evil spirits, he is honored in the Medicine Lodge ceremony.

EARTH AND SKY

The Winnebago was a farming tribe of about 7,000 people when the French arrived in 1634. They were organized in two main clans, Earth and Sky. Sky clans are comprised of birds, and Earth clans are made up of land and water animals. The tribe grew rich from selling muskrat and beaver pelts to fur traders (Subarctic). But European diseases reduced the Winnebago population to 1,500.

The Winnebago were forced to move to Iowa in 1840 and to Nebraska in 1865. Many returned to Wisconsin in the 1880s. Today, the tribe has 5,000 members in Wisconsin and about 1,600 in Nebraska. The language is spoken by only one person in ten. However, other traditions remain strong. Winnebago people respect warriors, and both young men and women are encouraged to join the military. Special clan ceremonies give soldiers courage before they leave home. ◄

Otter Skin

Found in streams and lakes, the playful otter was highly prized for its skin. This dance pouch, made of a whole otter skin, shows European influences. It is decorated with floral designs on cloth, which are like the needlework taught to the Winnebago by Roman Catholic nuns.

Chief Big Wave

This 1927 photograph of Winnebago chief Big Wave was taken in Wood County, Wisconsin. Although many Winnebago were forced to move to Nebraska in the 19th century, some remained in—or returned to—Wisconsin. The largest lake in the state is named for them, Lake Winnebago.

▶ Mount Shasta

Mount Shasta in northern California is sacred to the Wintun and other area tribes as the place where humans were created, spirits reveal themselves, and ancestors are buried. Environmentalists have joined the Wintun to stop development on the mountain.

▶ Wingdress

Frank LaRoche photographed this Yakima woman in 1899. She is wearing a traditional deerskin wingdress. Today, the dress is often made of canvas, though other Yakima customs remain as before. These include cradleboards for babies— which often display high levels of detail and craftsmanship—and long hair for men.

WINTUN

- **LANGUAGE FAMILY: PENUTIAN**
- **LIFEWAYS: HUNTING, FISHING, & GATHERING**
- **LOCATION: CALIFORNIA**
- **THEIR OWN NAME: WINTUN**

CALIFORNIA

Wintun refers to the original 12,000 Wintun, Nomlaki, and Patwin people of northern California. Between 1840 and 1900, 75 percent of these people were killed by miners and federal troops. Others died from drinking water polluted by copper mines. In 1990 there were 2,244 Wintun, 332 Nomlaki, and no Patwin left. Finding a safe home is an ongoing struggle for the tribe. In 1984 the federal government bulldozed a Wintun area and removed the people. Environmentalists have joined the Wintun to stop toxic-waste dumping on native lands.◀

YAKIMA

- **LANGUAGE FAMILY: SAHAPTIAN**
- **LIFEWAYS: FISHING**
- **LOCATION: WASHINGTON**
- **THEIR OWN NAME: WAPTAILMIN**

PLATEAU

Waptailmin means People of the Narrow River. Like other Plateau peoples, the Yakima once traveled to the rivers during salmon runs. They lived in Northwest Coast–style multifamily longhouses and viewed their mountainous home with wonder. According to legend, their region's rugged landscape comes from a time when the creator got angry with people for constantly fighting and caused landslides to bury them. The Yakima say they can hear the spirits of the dead in the winds whistling through the mountains.

In the 1850s Yakima chief Kamiakin led his

people in several battles against trespassing white settlers and the military. Eventually, he was defeated. Kamiakin escaped to British Columbia, Canada, but fourteen other Yakima leaders were executed. The rest of the tribe—starving from raids on its cattle and the burning of its crops—surrendered in September 1858. By 1910, the tribe's population had dropped from 7,000 to 1,360 members.

Today, about 8,000 Yakima live on a 250,000-acre reservation in eastern Washington. The tribe has been involved in important fishing-rights cases since the 1960s (Red Power) and has worked with state wildlife departments to save endangered rivers. Yakima attend Seven Drum ceremonies (Nez Perce) and maintain such customs as cradleboards for babies, long hair for men, and "wingdresses" for women. Many speak the native language, and some continue to make cornhusk baskets. Elders guide the community and govern as chiefs.◀

YAMASEE

- **LANGUAGE FAMILY: MUSKOGEAN**
- **LIFEWAYS: HUNTING**
- **LOCATION: NONE**
- **THEIR OWN NAME: YAMASEE**

The Yamasee were a northern Florida tribe of about 2,500 people. For protection, they allied with the Creek. In 1700 they moved to North Carolina to trade deerskins with the English. There they began killing and enslaving the Tuscarora. But Carolina slave traders also abused the Yamasee. In 1715, the Yamasee killed 90 percent of the traders. When the Cherokee defended Carolina settlers, the Yamasee fled south. They, together with refugees in Florida, formed a new tribe, the Seminole. There is no independent Yamasee tribe today.◀

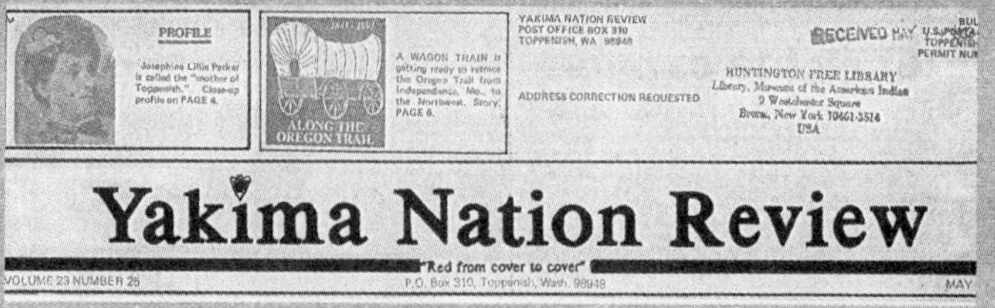

PROFILE

Josephine Lillie Parker is called the "mother of Toppenish." Close-up profile on PAGE 4.

ALONG THE OREGON TRAIL

A WAGON TRAIN is getting ready to retrace the Oregon Trail from Independence, Mo., to the Northwest. Story, PAGE 6.

YAKIMA NATION REVIEW
POST OFFICE BOX 310
TOPPENISH, WA 98948

ADDRESS CORRECTION REQUESTED

RECEIVED MAY

HUNTINGTON FREE LIBRARY
Library, Museum of the American Indian
9 Westchester Square
Bronx, New York 10461-3514
USA

Yakima Nation Review

"Red from cover to cover"

VOLUME 23 NUMBER 25 P.O. Box 310, Toppenish, Wash. 98948 MAY

Newspaper

The *Yakima Nation Review,* published in Toppenish, Washington, is a highly respected newspaper that is read all over the country. Its slogan is "Red from cover to cover," and it features local news as well as international affairs, which is rare in tribal newspapers.

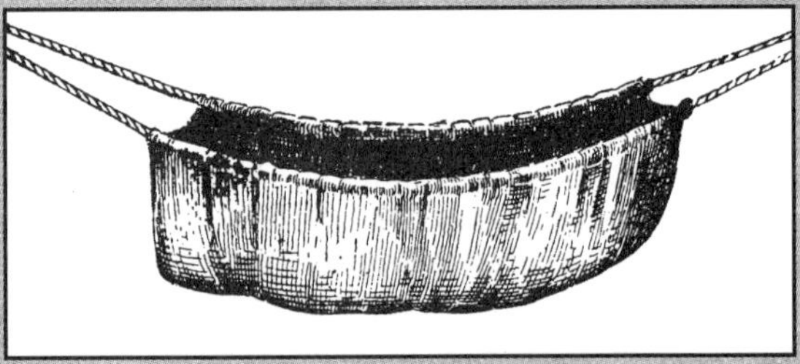

Cradle

Baby hammocks such as this one were generally made of cloth stretched over two cords. They were very common among Florida tribes. Hung between two trees, these cradles were used only for very young babies. Older children slept on a deerskin or on the ground.

Ishi

Ishi was the last surviving member of the Yahi band of the Yana Indians. When the rest of his people died, Ishi managed to survive by hiding in the wilderness. In 1911, white scholars at the University of California heard of Ishi and took him into captivity. He became a "living exhibit" at the university, where people came to stare at the "last Indian living in his natural state." Like most Indian people used as exhibits, Ishi died after only a few years, in 1916.

Yaqui Writer

Anita Endrezze-Danielson (born 1952) is of Yaqui and white ancestry. She has written several collections of short stories and poetry, and her work has been featured in such magazines as *National Geographic* and *Ms.* Her stories have been translated into Italian, Greek, Danish, French, and German. She lives in Spokane, Washington, with her husband and two children.

YANA

- **LANGUAGE FAMILY: HOKAN**
- **LIFEWAYS: HUNTING, FISHING, & GATHERING**
- **LOCATION: CALIFORNIA**
- **THEIR OWN NAME: YAHI**

Most of the nearly 3,000 Yana living in the northern Sierra Nevada Mountains were killed by white soldiers and settlers. In the late 1800s, whites considered California Indians "only diggers," and they could shoot them without fear of punishment. Meant as an insult, Digger referred to Indians who dug for edible roots. In response to the tragic losses, Yana chief Noreleptus built Ghost Dance earth lodges in the 1890s to protect his people from the end of the world (Great Basin). Other tribes sheltered the Yana, and some twenty people claim to be of Yana descent today. ◄

YAQUI

- **LANGUAGE FAMILY: UTO-AZTECAN**
- **LIFEWAYS: HUNTING & GATHERING**
- **LOCATION: ARIZONA & SONORA, MEXICO**
- **THEIR OWN NAME: YAQUI**

The Yaqui are a Cahitan-speaking people related to the Aztecs. Their homeland lies along the Yaqui River in southern Sonora, Mexico. Today they live on both sides of the U.S.-Mexican border.

Beginning in the early 1800s, the Yaqui fought a century-long land struggle with the Mexican government. In 1903 the Yaqui were finally defeated. More than 5,000 of them were sold into slavery for sixty pesos each. To avoid this fate, many crossed the border and settled in southern Arizona.

Yaqui ceremonies are a blend of traditional

199

beliefs and Catholicism. The Yaqui world of the spirits is called Huya Aniya. It is a timeless place where the powerful Little Animals live. The Little Animals—including deer, coyote, dogs, and goats—guide Yaqui dancers. Deer Dancers are serious, while Goat Dancers are clowns. Both kinds of dancers perform during the Catholic festivals of Easter Week.

The Yaqui worship Jesus but reject many other Catholic teachings. Yaqui priests, called maestros, have replaced missionaries. They lead prayers and hymns that were translated into Yaqui in the 1600s. The church is the most powerful force in Yaqui towns, but people do not go to church. Instead, the church comes to them. Easter festivals are held by host families. Church leaders and the congregation gather in the host's house for prayers, dances, and feasts.

Approximately 25,000 Mexican Yaqui live in eight towns in Sonora. Another 4,000 live on a 200-acre reservation near Tucson, Arizona. ◄

►Robert Mesta

Yaqui Robert Mesta is a scientist who works for the U.S. Fish and Wildlife Service. He has helped save many birds that were in danger of becoming extinct, including the California condor and the desert-nesting bald eagle. Mesta is grateful for the education he received. He advises young people, "Know what you want, persevere for it, and your education will play a big role in that."

YAVAPAI

- **LANGUAGE FAMILY: HOKAN**
- **LIFEWAYS: HUNTING, GATHERING, & FARMING**
- **LOCATION: ARIZONA**
- **THEIR OWN NAME: YAVAPAI**

SOUTHWEST

The Yavapai are a Yuman-speaking people. Their name means People of the Sun. Their homeland lies between the Salt and Williams rivers in Arizona. Before Europeans arrived, the Yavapai numbered about 1,000. After gold was discovered in their territory, they were placed on the San Carlos Apache Reservation in New Mexico. By 1910 tuberculosis had reduced the tribe to 550 people. Today, 150 Yavapai live on the Yavapai reservation near Prescott, Arizona, and 1,300 live with the Apache in Camp Verde, Arizona. ◄

►Carlos Montezuma

At the age of sixteen, Carlos Montezuma (1865–1923) was captured and sold to a white man. This man sent him to a university, where he studied medicine. Montezuma became a strong defender of Native American culture. He refused offers from Presidents Theodore Roosevelt and Woodrow Wilson to head the Bureau of Indian Affairs. Instead, he called for the abolition of the bureau, leading the fight for Indian rights by testifying before Congress and publishing a newspaper, *Wassaja*.

▶ Weaving

The Yazoo were villagers and farmers. They were also potters and weavers of baskets and blankets. This design (above) is typical of Yazoo art and was used to decorate woven crafts.

▶ In the Shade

This small, temporary structure was built by women seeking shelter from the sun. It is made of six arched poles tied together at the tips, stuck in the ground, and covered with loose brush or mats. Here, Mary Pohots, a Yokuts woman, works in the shade. She is grinding grain against the bedrock floor of the shelter.

YAZOO

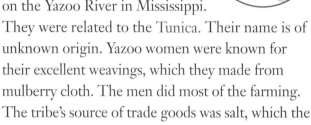

- **LANGUAGE FAMILY: MUSKOGEAN**
- **LIFEWAYS: FARMING & TRADING**
- **LOCATION: NONE**
- **THEIR OWN NAME: YAZOO**

SOUTHEAST

The Yazoo was a small tribe of about 1,000 people who lived on the Yazoo River in Mississippi. They were related to the Tunica. Their name is of unknown origin. Yazoo women were known for their excellent weavings, which they made from mulberry cloth. The men did most of the farming. The tribe's source of trade goods was salt, which the Yazoo mined and sold.

Sadly for the Yazoo, they got caught up in wars between the French and the Natchez. Having allied themselves with the Natchez, they were destroyed with them in the early 1700s.◀

YOKUTS

- **LANGUAGE FAMILY: PENUTIAN**
- **LIFEWAYS: HUNTING & GATHERING**
- **LOCATION: CALIFORNIA**
- **THEIR OWN NAME: CHUNUT**

CALIFORNIA

Before European diseases and war came to the San Joaquin Valley, about sixty bands spoke Yokuts. In the 1700s their population decreased by 75 percent, leaving only a few people. Today, 2,700 Yokuts are seeking federal recognition and trying to get their land returned to them. In the 1960s Yokuts leader Henry Jones helped form the Sierra Indian Center. The center is devoted to protecting the environment and restoring Indian culture, including reviving the Spring Dances (California).◀

YUCHI

- **LANGUAGE FAMILY:** YUCHI
- **LIFEWAYS:** HUNTING & GATHERING
- **LOCATION:** OKLAHOMA
- **THEIR OWN NAME:** YUCHI

SOUTHEAST

In the 17th century, about 2,500 Yuchi lived high in the Appalachian Mountains of North Carolina and Georgia. To protect themselves from Europeans, they allied with the Creek. The Yuchi name means Over Yonder in Creek.

Colonists often stole Yuchi livestock. Creek leader Tuskeneah said that when the Yuchi stole American livestock, the colonists "shot them down as though they were deer." The Yuchi were forced to Oklahoma with the Cherokee in the 1830s. Today, the two tribes live there together. However, the Yuchi maintain their own customs. ◄

YUMA

- **LANGUAGE FAMILY:** HOKAN
- **LIFEWAYS:** FARMING & TRADING
- **LOCATION:** ARIZONA & SONORA, MEXICO
- **THEIR OWN NAME:** QUECHAN

SOUTHWEST

The Yuma have given their name to a large group of Native American peoples of the Southwest United States and northwest Mexico who are related by the language they speak. The Yuma call themselves the Quechan, or People. They live along the southern part of the Colorado River. The Yuma used the waters of the Colorado to irrigate their farmlands. The river was an important transportation crossroads, putting the Yuma at the center of trade between California and Arizona.

In the early 1900s, the U.S government took

▶ Alligator Shield

This alligator shield was made by a Yuchi child. It is one of many traditional art objects made by Native American children that have been reproduced in the book *Four Circles of Learning*, a celebration of Native American culture.

▶ Quechan Yuma Man

Yuma children were required to perform physically and mentally demanding rituals as part of growing up. For example, eight- to ten-year-old boys had their noses pierced and were made to run many miles for four days in a row to test their endurance. This adult Yuma man underwent such a ritual and can be seen wearing a nose ring.

California Quail

Quail such as this one were once a staple of the Yuma diet. Lured from their nests by bunches of weeds the Yuma held in their hands, the birds were caught with slip loops or shot with tiny arrows. During the winter months, it was even possible to catch them by hand when they were cold and wet. The Yuma either cooked the quail in a stew or roasted them in coals. Their bones were ground up and eaten in gruel.

Tillamook Women

Two Tillamook Yurok women work on their basketweaving around 1890. The Salish-speaking Tillamook of southwest Oregon were a large band until the 1850s, when European diseases reduced their population of about 2,200 to less than 300 people.

much of the best Yuma land, then failed to follow through on its agreement to build the tribe an irrigation system in exchange for the land.

Today, the Yuma economy depends on agriculture. In recent years the Yuma have supplemented their farming by operating interstate truck stops. They have also opened a casino and set up trailer parks for long-term tourists.

The Yuma are strong believers in the equality of the sexes. Both men and women have served on the tribal council and as tribal presidents. The Yuma have also maintained much of their traditional culture. Most people on the Yuma reservation speak both English and Yuman.

Tribal dances such as the Bird and People dances are particularly popular today. But instead of traditional gourd rattles, the dancers are accompanied by music from tin-can rattles. Approximately 3,000 Yuma live on the Yuma reservation on the California-Arizona border.◄

YUROK

- **LANGUAGE FAMILY: RITWAN**
- **LIFEWAYS: FISHING & GATHERING**
- **LOCATION: CALIFORNIA & OREGON**
- **THEIR OWN NAME: OLEKWO'L**

CALIFORNIA

The Yurok are native to the lower Klamath River and adjoining Northwest Coast. Before contact with Europeans, about 2,500 Yurok lived there. In 1849, U.S. treaties created reservations to remove the Yurok from gold-mining sites. Battles resulted as miners attacked the new reservations, quickly reducing the tribe's population to 668.

In 1891 the Bureau of Indian Affairs (BIA) decided the Yurok did not exist. A narrow strip of land was provided to connect their land to the Hupa reservation. But timber companies were eager to make deals with the BIA to log Hupa land, and conflicts arose in the 1960s when only the Hupa were paid for the timber of both tribes.

The Yurok won a timber lawsuit in 1973 but will not receive any money until the BIA approves the tribe. More than 8,000 people have applied to enroll, electing a tribal council in 1993.

In 1988 the Yurok lost a lawsuit to stop a logging road from running through the sacred Siskiyou Mountains. The case was a test of the Indian Religious Freedom Act. Another problem the Yurok face is the use of the herbicide dioxin. Dioxin threatens human and animal health, as well as edible and medicinal plants. These plants are also needed for the Brush Dance, performed to cure sick children. Yurok Spring dances were revived in the 1960s (California). In 1990 the Yurok celebrated the survival of their culture by building a traditional redwood village in Patrick's Point State Park.◄

ZUNI

- **LANGUAGE FAMILY: PENUTIAN**
- **LIFEWAYS: FARMING & HUNTING**
- **LOCATION: NEW MEXICO**
- **THEIR OWN NAME: A'SHIWII**

SOUTHWEST

The Zuni live along the Zuni River in western New Mexico. The name Zuni is a Spanish form of the Pueblo word for the Zuni. The Zuni call themselves A'Shiwii, or Flesh. Like the Pueblo, the Zuni lived in villages of stacked adobe (clay-brick) houses. But the Zuni's origins are different from those of their Pueblo neighbors. Whereas the Pueblo are descended from the cliff dwellers—the earliest known inhabitants of the Southwest—the first Zuni probably came much later, around A.D. 700. It is likely that they migrated to present-day New Mexico

▶ Robert Spott

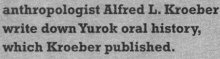

Robert Spott was decorated for bravery in World War I. Afterward, he helped anthropologist Alfred L. Kroeber write down Yurok oral history, which Kroeber published.

In a 1926 speech to the Commonwealth Club of San Francisco, Robert Spott said, "I did make up my mind in the war that I am an American and I went overseas to fight for this country. Then the officers came to me while I was overseas and they told me, 'You are all right. You fought for your country.' I just gave them a smile and I thought to myself, 'Where is my country when I get home?'"

▶ Rain Dance

The Zuni live in a very dry region where every drop of rain is precious. In their religious ceremonies, Zuni often invoke the *kachina* spirits of the rain. In this 1899 photograph, Zuni are performing a Rain Dance in which they impersonate the rain spirits. Behind the dancers is a Zuni pueblo.

Two Zuni Women

These two photographs of Zuni women show aspects of their culture and traditions. The woman carrying a bowl of water on her head—a typical Zuni practice—was photographed in New Mexico in 1940. The woman wearing an elaborate necklace of silver jewelry was photographed by Edward Curtis in southern California around the year 1900. The Zuni are expert silversmiths.

from southern Arizona and northern Mexico.

The Zuni name comes from the legendary Corn Maiden spirits who gave their flesh—corn kernels—to the Zuni. When the Zuni first received corn, they rejected it. The Corn Maidens were insulted and ran away, taking their corn with them. The Zuni starved until the Corn Maidens were convinced to return. Each year, in December, the Molowai Ceremony celebrates the gift of corn. Ten young girls represent the Corn Maidens and run foot races. The races symbolize the departure and return of the Corn Maidens.

DANCING AND FEASTING

From late November until the winter solstice—the first day of winter and the Zuni New Year—the Zuni have house blessings and Kachina dances. December ends with the ten-day Teshkwi fast. It is a time of quiet when no one works, smokes, travels, or lights outdoor lamps. Men, women, and children do not eat certain foods. Instead, they offer prayers for the year to come.

There were about 5,000 Zuni in the 1500s. The first outsider to visit them was Estevancio, a Spanish-speaking African. He was part of Álvar Núñez Cabeza de Vaca's famous "lost" expedition. Cabeza de Vaca believed he could help the Indians, but his expedition opened the way for other Spanish explorers in search of cities of gold (Southwest). The Spanish established missions in Zuni territory in 1629, but were chased out during a great uprising from 1672 to 1680.

Things changed with the coming of Americans in the 19th century. By 1900, epidemics had reduced the Zuni population to about 1,500. In the 1920s there was a struggle among different clans for control of the tribe. Since then, however, peace has reigned, and the Zuni have become increasingly self-supporting.

Today, many of the 6,000 Zuni support themselves as silversmiths. Almost 90 percent of the adult Zuni create jewelry that is world-famous for its beauty and craftsmanship.◄

TIMELINE OF THE AMERICAN INDIAN

This timeline shows some of the important events in Native American history from very early times to the present. Each event is marked with a symbol (shown on page 207) that indicates in what region the event happened.

Of course, this timeline is compressed, or squeezed. For the earliest dates, one inch equals thousands of years. For more recent dates, one inch represents only a few years. That's not because more things happened in the past few hundred years but because we know less about the events of very long ago.

Sometimes events are spread out over many centuries. Those events are indicated on the timeline more or less in the year they began, so it's important to remember that many events are contemporaneous—that is, they overlap each other in time. The heavy arrows beneath some events or cultures show that they continued for a long time after they are indicated on the timeline.

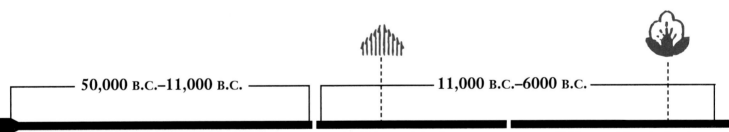

50,000 B.C.–11,000 B.C.   11,000 B.C.–6000 B.C.

c. 50,000 B.C.–11,000 B.C.: Waves of paleo-Indians arrive in North America from Asia, crossing the Bering Strait Land Bridge (Beringia). They eventually settle throughout the Americas.

c. 10,000 B.C.: The first medicine wheels—ancient spiritual sites constructed of rocks and boulders—are built in the Great Basin.

c. 6000 B.C.: After the last ice age, when the climate warms again, the Subarctic region is settled by migration from southerly regions.

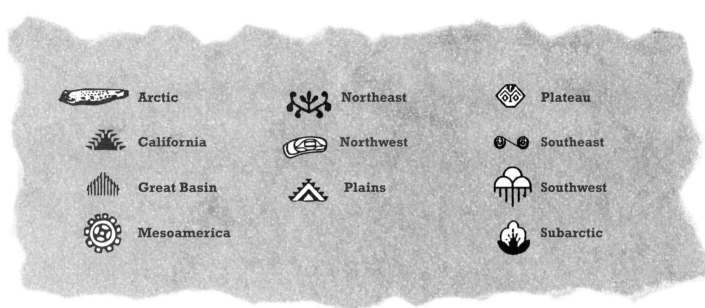

Arctic

California

Great Basin

Mesoamerica

Northeast

Northwest

Plains

Plateau

Southeast

Southwest

Subarctic

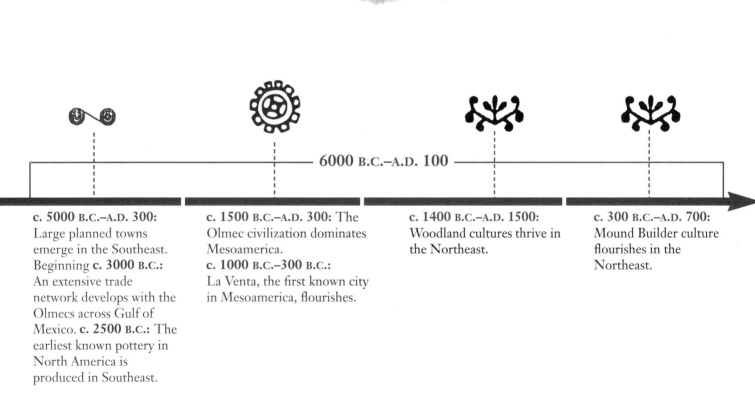

6000 B.C.–A.D. 100

c. 5000 B.C.–A.D. 300: Large planned towns emerge in the Southeast. Beginning **c. 3000 B.C.:** An extensive trade network develops with the Olmecs across Gulf of Mexico. **c. 2500 B.C.:** The earliest known pottery in North America is produced in Southeast.

c. 1500 B.C.–A.D. 300: The Olmec civilization dominates Mesoamerica.
c. 1000 B.C.–300 B.C.: La Venta, the first known city in Mesoamerica, flourishes.

c. 1400 B.C.–A.D. 1500: Woodland cultures thrive in the Northeast.

c. 300 B.C.–A.D. 700: Mound Builder culture flourishes in the Northeast.

Timeline of the American Indian

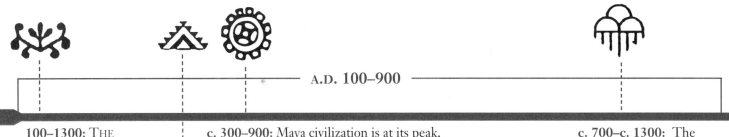

A.D. 100–900

100–1300: The Owasco, corn growers and ancestors of the modern Iroquois nations, live between Hudson River and Lake Erie in the Northeast.

c. 300–900: Maya civilization is at its peak, evidenced in such cities as Tikal, Copán, and Palenque and in sophisticated calendars and a written language.

c. 300: North Americans invent the bow and arrow and begin living on the Plains, migrating with the seasons.

c. 700–c. 1300: The Hohokan and Anasazi (cliff dwellers) cultures thrive in the southwest. **c. 800:** The Pueblo culture emerges.

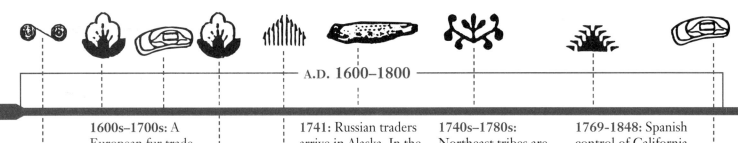

A.D. 1600–1800

1600s–1700s: A European fur trade opens in the Subarctic (and, later, on the Northwest Coast). Soon beaver, mink, and otter are hunted nearly to extinction.

1741: Russian traders arrive in Alaska. In the next eighty years, the local population falls from 18,000 to 1,500.

1740s–1780s: Northeast tribes are caught up in several European wars— King George's War, the French and Indian War, and the Revolutionary War. In the end, many flee to Canada after their homes and crops are burned.

1769-1848: Spanish control of California upsets the lifestyle of the native peoples, who are forced to abandon their settlements and adopt agriculture and Christianity.

Early 1600s: French explore and settle Mississippi River.
Early 1600s: The English settle Virginia. Some Southeast tribes, such as the Alabama, Apalachee, and Pombatan, fight with Europeans. Others, such as Creek and Cherokee, continue to thrive as farmers.

1600s: The French send missionaries to "civilize" the Subarctic tribes.

1700s: Great Basin tribes begin to hunt buffalo after horses are introduced to region.

Late 1700s: Northwest Coast society is changed when European and Asian traders arrive.

———— A.D. 900–1600 ————

c. 985-1014: Norsemen establish settlements in Greenland and the North American Subarctic. They encounter Native Americans, probably Micmac.

c. 1200: The first large "winter villages" are built on the Northwest Coast.

c. 1200-1700: An extensive trade, hunting, and slave-raiding network flourishes on Northwest Coast.

1400s: Aztecs conquer neighboring peoples to dominate Mesoamerica.

1519: Spanish conquistadors arrive and, in 1521, destroy Aztec capital, Tenochtitlan.

Mid-1500s: The Spanish bring first horses to the Southeast and the Plains. Wild horses quickly spread across the Plains and are tamed and used by Indians.

1500s: The Spanish explore and settle Florida.

———— A.D. 1800–1900 ————

1838: The Cherokee are forced to leave the Southeast and move to Oklahoma. So many of them die that the trip is called the Trail of Tears.

1804–1850s: Whites begin coming to the Plateau region, mostly passing through on their way to the Northwest Coast and California.

1848: Whites flood into California looking for gold. About 50,000 Native Americans are killed. By 1872, the native population had dropped from 300,000 to 30,000.

1854–1855: The Nisqually, Coast Salish, and Yakima tribes, having refused to surrender their lands, the northwest Coast attack city of Seattle.

1872–1873: In the Plateau, the Modoc and Nez Perce are defeated in Modoc War.

1877: After a 1,700-mile flight, Nez Perce under Chief Joseph surrender just short of the Canadian border.

1870s: After gold is discovered in the sacred Black Hills, war breaks out between Plains tribes and whites. **1876:** Indians defeat Custer at the Battle of Little Bighorn, but are soon forced to surrender.

1880s: The Apache surrender. They are the last tribe actively to wage war in the United States.

1885: The Cree, Ojibwa, and Métis rebel against the Canadian government.

1889: Paiute prophet Wovoka has a vision of the world returned to the old ways, before whites came. He reintroduces the Ghost Dance religion, which spreads among Indians. In 1890, hundreds of unarmed Sioux are massacred for practicing the Ghost Dance.

———— A.D. 1900–2000 ————

1930s: California tribes fight against discrimination and win the right to vote. But in the 1950s, many California tribes are terminated.

1930s–1970s: The Aleut and Inuit win self-rule in Alaska (1936). Large tracts of land are returned to natives in Alaska (1971) and in Canada (1994).

1950s–1990s: The Iroquois, Ojibwa, Menominee, and others fight for their treaty rights.

1992: Human rights activist Rigoberta Menchú, a Quiché Maya, wins the Nobel Peace Prize for her work against genocide in Guatemala.

Regions and Peoples

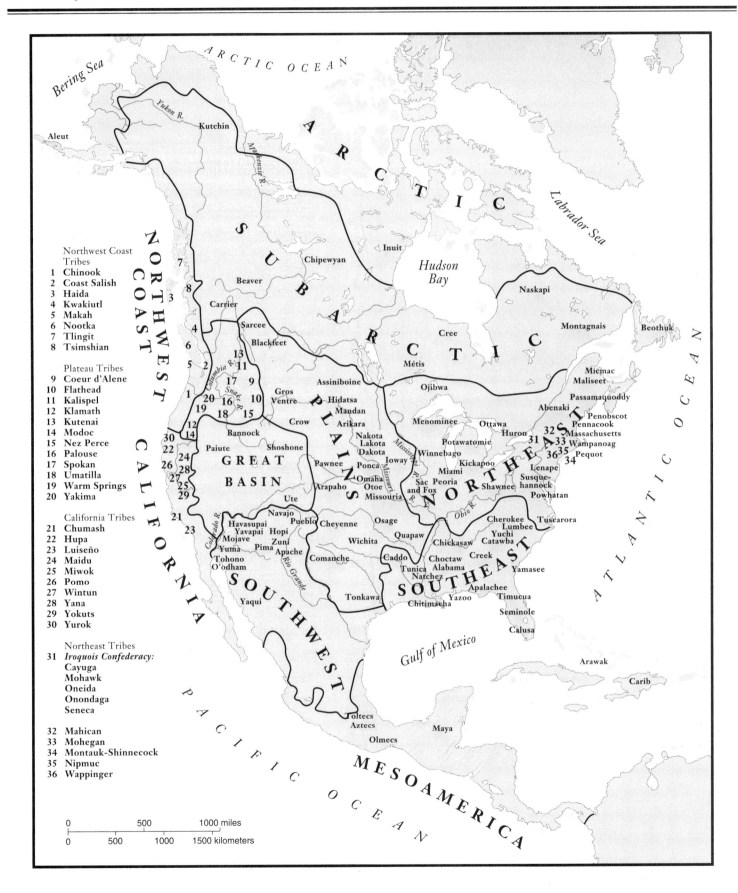

Northwest Coast Tribes
1 Chinook
2 Coast Salish
3 Haida
4 Kwakiutl
5 Makah
6 Nootka
7 Tlingit
8 Tsimshian

Plateau Tribes
9 Coeur d'Alene
10 Flathead
11 Kalispel
12 Klamath
13 Kutenai
14 Modoc
15 Nez Perce
16 Palouse
17 Spokan
18 Umatilla
19 Warm Springs
20 Yakima

California Tribes
21 Chumash
22 Hupa
23 Luiseño
24 Maidu
25 Miwok
26 Pomo
27 Wintun
28 Yana
29 Yokuts
30 Yurok

Northeast Tribes
31 *Iroquois Confederacy:*
   Cayuga
   Mohawk
   Oneida
   Onondaga
   Seneca

32 Mahican
33 Mohegan
34 Montauk-Shinnecock
35 Nipmuc
36 Wappinger

Language Families

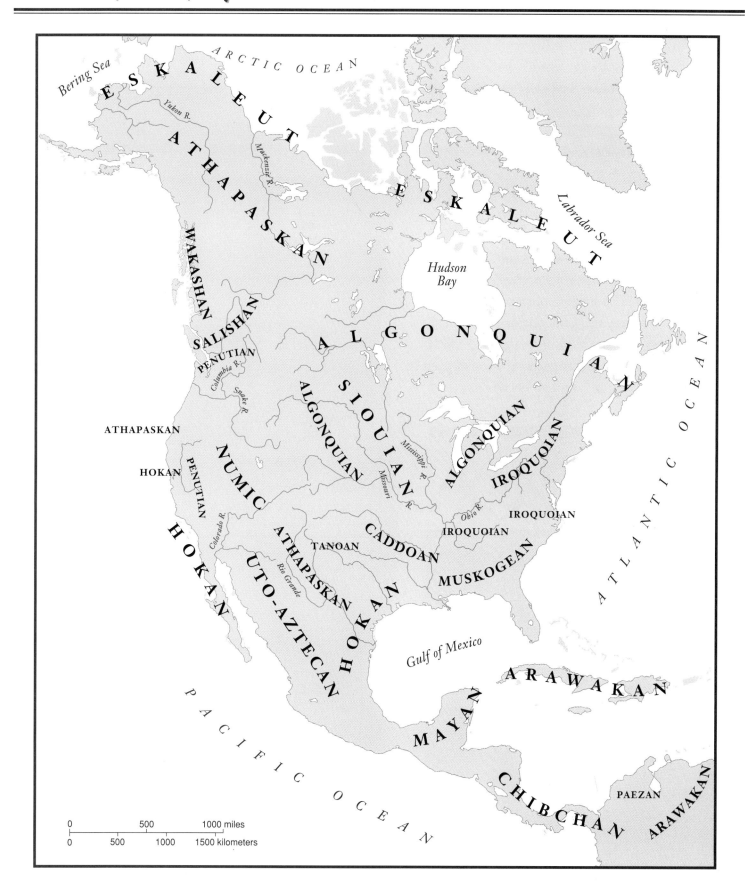

Bering Sea

ARCTIC OCEAN

ESKALEUT

Yukon R.

ATHAPASKAN

Mackenzie R.

ESKALEUT

Labrador Sea

Hudson Bay

WAKASHAN

SALISHAN

PENUTIAN

Columbia R.

Snake R.

ALGONQUIAN

SIOUIAN

ALGONQUIAN

IROQUOIAN

ATHAPASKAN

HOKAN

PENUTIAN

NUMIC

ALGONQUIAN

Mississippi R.

Missouri R.

ALGONQUIAN

IROQUOIAN

IROQUOIAN

Ohio R.

IROQUOIAN

ATLANTIC OCEAN

Colorado R.

HOKAN

UTO-AZTECAN

ATHAPASKAN

Río Grande

TANOAN

CADDOAN

HOKAN

MUSKOGEAN

Gulf of Mexico

ARAWAKAN

MAYAN

PACIFIC OCEAN

CHIBCHAN

PAEZAN

ARAWAKAN

| 0 | 500 | 1000 miles |
| 0 | 500 | 1000 | 1500 kilometers |

FORCED MIGRATION

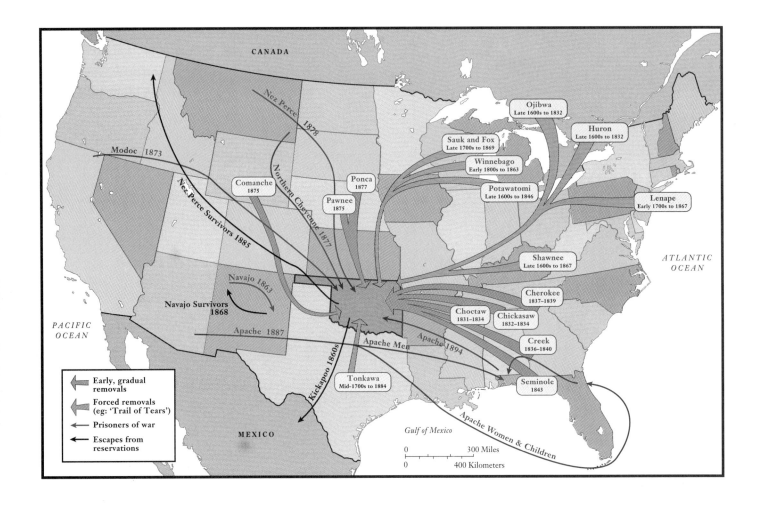

CANADA

Ojibwa
Late 1600s to 1832

Huron
Late 1600s to 1832

Sauk and Fox
Late 1700s to 1869

Winnebago
Early 1800s to 1863

Nez Perce 1878

Modoc 1873

Ponca
1877

Potawatomi
Late 1600s to 1846

Lenape
Early 1700s to 1867

Comanche
1875

Nez Perce Survivors 1885

Northern Cheyenne 1877

Pawnee
1875

Shawnee
Late 1600s to 1867

ATLANTIC
OCEAN

Navajo 1863

Cherokee
1837–1839

Navajo Survivors
1868

Choctaw
1831–1834

Chickasaw
1832–1834

PACIFIC
OCEAN

Apache 1887

Apache Men

Apache 1894

Creek
1836–1840

Kickapoo 1860s

Tonkawa
Mid-1700s to 1884

Seminole
1843

Apache Women & Children

MEXICO

Gulf of Mexico

	Early, gradual removals
	Forced removals (eg: 'Trail of Tears')
	Prisoners of war
	Escapes from reservations

0   300 Miles

0   400 Kilometers

THE LOSS OF LAND

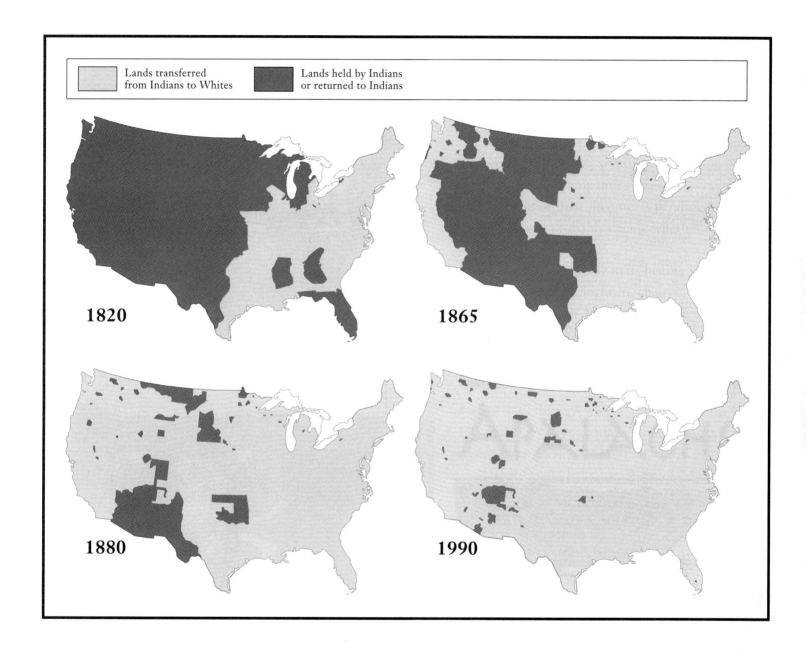

Lands transferred from Indians to Whites

Lands held by Indians or returned to Indians

1820

1865

1880

1990

PLACES TO SEE

The following museums and cultural centers feature updated exhibitions and educational programs on Native Americans. They are organized by region. Many of these centers are specially geared for school groups.

ARCTIC, NORTHWEST COAST

'Ksan Museum
PO Box 333, High Level Rd.
Hazelton, BC V0J 1Y0
(604) 842-5723
Museum is part of a reconstructed Indian village. Maintains a collection of Northwest Coast Indian artifacts, specifically Carrier (Gitskan).

Nana Museum of the Arctic
PO Box 49
Kotzebue, AK 99752
(907) 442-3301
Fax (907) 442-2866
Inupiat Museum of the Arctic houses land and sea mammal exhibits, arts & crafts, a technical diorama, and slide presentations. Eskimo dancers and a traditional Eskimo Blanket Toss. Maintains a multimedia interpretive program explaining traditional Inupiat skills and culture.

Southeast Alaska Indian Cultural Center
106 Metlakatla, PO Box 738
Sitka, AK 99835
(907) 747-6281
A collection of more than 4,000 artifacts; totem poles and chilkat robes; traditional native arts such as woodcarving, costume design, and metalworking.

WEST, SOUTHWEST

Cabot's Old Indian Pueblo Museum
California Indian Monument
67-616 E. Desert View Ave.
Desert Hot Springs, CA 92240
(619) 329-7610
A four-story Hopi-style Pueblo built by Cabot Yerxa as a tribute to the Indian cultures. Exhibits: Inuit collection, Sioux collection from the Battle of the Little Big Horn, Chumash & Pueblo culture collections. Special programs: Slide and lecture presentations to schools and organizations; sculpting for the handicapped; single artist exhibitions; art interview radio show.

Caddoan Mounds State Historic Park
Route 2, Box 85-C
Alto, TX 75925
(409) 858-3218
An archaelogical site of a prehistoric Caddoan village and ceremonial center, with three earth mounds occupied from 750–1300 A.D. Activities: School tours, teacher packet, outreach off-site presentations.

Denver Art Museum
100 W. 14th Ave Pkwy.
Denver, CO 80204
(303) 575-2256
Collection of North American Indian art; also, an ethnographic collection of Indian women's costumes, Navajo and Pueblo pottery, Hopi kachina dolls, Blackfeet ceremonial equipment, and wood carvings of the NW Coast. Special programs: Lectures; programs for children; annual Powwow; classes.

The Herd Museum
22 E. Monte Vista Rd.
Phoenix, AZ 85004-1480
(602) 252-8840
Fax (602) 252-9757
(602) 252-8848 (taped info; updates)
Anthropology and art museum exhibiting works by American Indians. Paintings, prints, sculpture, and contemporary craft arts are regularly on exhibit, as well as historic materials from the Southwest. Special collections: Hopi kachina dolls, and Navajo rugs and blankets. Special programs: Guided tours, lectures, workshops, annual Indian Fair and Market, Speakers Bureau, films, traveling exhibitions—Artist & Performers on the Road.

Museum of the Plains Indian
P.O. Box 400, Highway 89
Browning, MT 59417
(406) 338-2230
Presents historic arts created by the tribespeople of the Northern Plains, including Blackfeet, Crow, Northern Cheyenne, Sioux, Assiniboine, Arapho, Shoshone, Nez Perce, Flathead, Chippewa, and Cree. Displays the varied traditional costumes of Northern Plains men, women, and children in complete detail on life-size figures. Special programs: Film, "Wind of Courage," about the evolution of Indian cultures on the Northern Plains; series of one-person exhibitions; painted tipis on the grounds during summer; demonstrations of Native American arts and crafts techniques; tours.

Navajo Tribal Museum
P.O. Box 308, Highway 264
Window Rock, AZ 86515
(602) 871-6673
Exhibits approximately 4,500 objects relating to the history and culture of the Navajo and the prehistory and natural history of the Four Corners area. Special programs: Art exhibits/sales; Navajo information service; school and group tours.

San Juan County Archaeological Research Center
6131 US Highway 64
Farmington, NM 87401
(505) 632-2013
Contains exhibits of artifacts taken from the Anasazi-Salmon Ruin, including prehistoric Pueblo artifacts, replicated domiciles, and exhibits representing Navajo, Ute, Jicarilla, and Hispanic cultures. Also, an extensive on-loan collection of Navajo legends, myths, chants, and religious ceremonies; slides of rock art; oral history tapes; maps. Special programs: Educational programs and guided tours for student groups.

Southwest Museum
234 Museum Dr., Box 41558
Los Angeles, CA 90041-0558
(213) 221-2164
Collections focus on native people of the Americas, including 100,000 artifacts pertaining to the American Indian, Eskimo, and Aleut from prehistoric, historic, and modern times. Special collections on the Plains, California, Southwest, and Northwest Coast. Special program: Annual Festival of Native American Arts.

Ute Indian Museum
Ouray Memorial Park
17253 Chipeta Dr., Box 1736
Montrose, CO 81402
(303) 249-3098
Indian History Museum located on the site of Chief Ouray's 400-acre farm. Depicts the history of the Ute through the use of dioramas and objects made by the Ute, photographs and maps, and portraits of some Ute leaders. Activities: Exhibits artifacts, maintains botanical gardens of the plants used by Native Americans, changing exhibit gallery, lectures, and cultural fair in the fall.

NORTHEAST

American Museum of Natural History
79th St. and Central Park West
New York, NY 10024
(212) 769-5375
Special Collections: Eskimo exhibit and Indians of the Northwest Coast—Artifacts of the Coast Salish, Nootka, Haida, Tsimshian, Thompson, Bella Coola, Tlingit, and Kwakiutl; also, shamanistic regalia and ceremonial objects.

The Brooklyn Childrens' Museum
145 Brooklyn Ave.
Brooklyn, NY 11213
(718) 735-4432
Exhibits include Plains Indian material; also, Southwest, Eastern Woodlands and Northwest Coast artifacts.

Childrens' Museum
Museum Wharf, 300 Congress St.
Boston, MA 02210
(617) 426-6500
Collection includes Penobscot, Passamaquoddy, Iroquois, Ojibwa, Wampanoag, and Narragansett materials from both past and present traditions. Special exhibit: "We're Still Here—American Indians in New England Long Ago and Today."

Haffenreffer Museum of Anthropology
Brown University, Mt. Hope Grant
Bristol, RI 02809
(401) 253-8338
Exhibits tribal art in a collection of more than 10,000 ethnographic objects and 100,000 archaeological specimens. Extensive prehistoric Arctic collections, including Ipiutak and northern Athapaskan. Special programs: Education programs for schoolchildren; lectures and seminars.

Iroquois Indian Museum
Box 7, Caverns Rd.
Howes Cave, NY 12092
(518) 296-8949
A 45-acre nature park with educational trails

explaining the ethnobotany of Iroquois culture. Maintains an extensive collection of contemporary Iroquois fine art and craftwork; archaeological materials of the Northeast from the Archaic Period to the Contact Period (1700s). Special programs: A children's museum is designed to introduce children to the Iroquois people of today; educational programs; annual Iroquois Indian Festival (Labor Day Weekend).

Museum of the Hudson Highlands
The Boulevard, PO Box 181
Cornwall on Hudson, NY 12520
(914) 534-7781
Special Collection: Eastern Woodlands Indians—featuring more than 80 stone artifacts and 40 modern reproductions made by a group of Iroquois. Special program: Presentations to school groups, kindergarten to 4th grades. An Indian Loan Kit comprised of an Iroquois pack basket filled with artifacts and reproductions is designed for teachers to use to complement New York's 4th-grade history curriculum.

National Museum of the American Indian
Smithsonian Institution
3753 Broadway at 155th St.
New York, NY 10032
(212) 283-2420
One of the finest collections of Native American artifacts, ranging from Alaska to Chile and from the paleo-Indian period to the present. Special programs: Educational Department offers guided tours, visits with Native American artists, and a lecture series; The Film and Video Center researches and exhibits film and video productions.

Peabody Museum
of Archaeology and Ethnology
Harvard University, 11 Divinity Ave.
Cambridge, MA 02138
(617) 495-2248
Contains large collections of archaeological artifacts. Special exhibit: "North American Indian: Change and Continuity," dealing with the last 500 years of Indian-white relations.

Smithsonian Institution
Native American Museums Program
Office of Museum Programs
Arts & Industries Bldg., Room 2235
Washington, DC 20560
(202) 357-3101
Provides information services, educational opportunities, and access to resources to Native Americans and others. Special Program: Quincentary Programs—Various activities relating to the 500th anniversary of Columbus's voyages to the New World.

SOUTHEAST

Cherokee Indian Cyclorama Wax Museum
P.O. Box 398, Highway 19E
Cherokee, NC 28719
(704) 497-4521 (April-October)
(704) 497-2111 (November-March)
Presents over 300 years of Cherokee history in life-size wax figures depicting actual events. A large-scale electronically-lit map of the Southeast shows the original Cherokee Nation, covering over eight southern states, and compares it to the present-day Qualla Indian Reservation.

Historical Museum of Southern Florida
101 W. Flagler St.
Miami, FL 33130
(305) 375-1492
A depository of maps, manuscripts, and published materials of Southern Florida and the Caribbean; 28,600 artifacts, including Seminole objects. Programs: Folklife programs, research, off-site programs for all ages; annual Harvest Festival.

Indian Springs State Park Museum
Route 1, Box 439
Flovilla, GA 30216-9715
(404) 775-7241
Exhibits Creek artifacts that reflect stages of Indian civilizations. Special programs: Indian sign language, hunting techniques, pottery, basketmaking.

Jacksonville Childrens' Museum
1025 Gulf Life Drive
Jacksonville, FL 32207
Displays artifacts of the Florida Indians of the past and present.

Schiele Museum Reference Library and Center For Southeastern Native American Studies
P.O. Box 953, 1500 E. Garrison Blvd.
Gastonia, NC 28053-0953
(704) 865-6131
Maintains extensive holdings of Native American artifacts, clothing, utensils, rugs, pottery, jewelry, costumes, arts and crafts, etc.; collections of 12 major cultural areas in the U.S. and Canada; specialized collections on Southeast Indians, especially pottery. Special programs: Catawba Village Study-Tour Program designed for grades 4 and up; annual Native American Fall Festival in September.

MIDWEST

Cahokia Mounds State Historic Site & Museum
Box 681 (Site); Box 382 (Museum)
Collinsville, IL 62234
(618) 346-5160 (Site)
(618) 344-9221 (Museum)
Contains over 30 exhibits, including authentic artifacts from site and region; dioramas, graphics dealing mostly with prehistoric Cahokia Mound site. Outdoor reconstruction of late-Woodland pithouses and Mississippian wall, house, stockade, and garden; Woodhenge reconstruction. Special programs: Slide/tape presentations, guided tours, Native-American craft classes, lecture series.

Childrens' Museum
Detroit Public Schools
647 E. Kirby
Detroit, MI 48202
(313) 494-1210
Special collection: *American Indian Collection, including basketry, costumes, crafts, dolls, textiles, musical instruments, tools, and weapons.*

Childrens' Museum of Indianapolis
3010 N. Meridan Street
Indianapolis, IN 46208
(317) 924-5431
Collection consists of more than 2,000 objects representing the tribes of every region of North America.

Cranbrook Institute of Science
500 Lone Pine Rd., Box 801
Bloomfield Hills, MI 48303-0801
(313) 645-3260
Exhibits cover all major cultural areas of North America, especially the Northeast Woodlands and Plains. Activities: Special group program.

Historical Society of Wisconsin
30 N. Carroll St. (exhibit facility)
816 State St. (collections)
Madison, WI 53703/6
(608) 262-7700
Historic Wisconsin and Plains Indian artifacts and prehistoric archaeological artifacts from Wisconsin. Special Collections: H.P. Hamilton Collection, containing old copper implements of the Wisconsin and Plains Indians; the Titus Collection: features SW pottery. Special programs: Classroom lessons on Wisconsin Indian life; photograph, manuscript and tape collections.

National Hall of Fame for Famous American Indians
Highway 62, Box 808
Anadarko, OK 73005
(405) 247-5795
Outdoor museum containing sculptured bronze likenesses of famous American Indians, including Will Rogers, Jim Thorpe, Pocahontas, Chief Joseph, Sacajawea, Chief Quanah Parker, Charles Curtis, Osceola, Sequoyah, Pontiac, Hiawatha, etc. Special programs: Annual ceremony in August honors inductees; educational seminars regarding inductees' lives and contributions.

Pawnee Indian Village Museum
Box 475, Route 1
Republic, KS 66964
(913) 361-2255
Archaeology museum located on the best-preserved Pawnee earth-lodge site on the Plains. Displays describe Pawnee life on the Plains. Special Program: Pawnee Days Celebration in the fall. Main features are Pawnee Indian dancers and singers.

Sac & Fox Tribal Museum/Cultural Center
Route 2, Box 246
Stroud, OK 74079
(918) 968-3526/(405) 275-4270
Special Collections: The Frank Hanison Collection and Jim Thorpe Collection display pictures, treaties, documents, paintings, and artifacts by tribe members. Special programs: All-Indian Rodeo, Arts & Crafts Show, annual powwow.

Southern Plains Indian Museum
Highway 62 E., Box 749
Anadarko, OK 73005
(405) 247-6221
Focusing on arts of the tribespeople of western Oklahoma, including the Kiowa, Comanche, Kiowa-Apache, Southern Cheyenne, Southern Arapaho, Wichita, Caddo, Lenape, and Fort Sill Apache. Special programs: Annual series of one-person exhibitions; demonstrations of Native American arts and crafts techniques; events honoring Native Americans; tours and gallery discussions. In August, the American Indian Exposition features a week-long event of dance contests, and arts and crafts.

RESOURCE GUIDE

BOOKS

Nonfiction

Anderson, Joan Wilkins. *The First Thanksgiving Feast.* New York: Clarion, 1984.

Arnold, Caroline. *The Ancient Cliff Dwellers of Mesa Verde.* New York: Clarion, 1992.

—————. *City of the Gods: Mexico's Ancient City of Teotihucan.* New York: Clarion, 1994.

Indians of North America. 66 vols. Broomall, PA: Chelsea House, 1993.

Jenness, Aylette, and Alice Rivers. *In Two Worlds: A Yup'ik Eskimo Family.* Boston: Houghton Mifflin Co., 1989.

Jones, Jayne Clark. *American Indians in America.* Vol. II, *The Late 18th Century to the Present.* Minneapolis: Lerner, 1993.

Junior Library of American Indians. 30 vols. Broomall, PA: Chelsea House, 1993.

Kessel, Joyce K. *Squanto and the First Thanksgiving.* Minneapolis: Carolrhoda, 1993.

Let's Discover the Indians. Mult. vols. Broomall, PA: Chelsea House, 1993.

Monroe, Jean Guard, and Ray A. Williamson. *First Houses: Native American Homes and Sacred Structures.* Boston: Houghton Mifflin Co., 1993.

—————. *They Dance in the Sky.* Boston: Houghton Mifflin Co., 1987.

Moore, Reavis. *Native Artists of North America.* Santa Fe, NM: John Muir, 1995.

Morris, Richard B. *The Indian Wars.* Minneapolis: Lerner, 1993.

Native Americans. 4 vols. Brookfield, CT: Millbrook Press, 1993.

Native American Biographies. 10 vols. Mahwah, NJ: Troll Books, 1993.

North American Indians of Achievement. 24 vols. Broomall, PA: Chelsea House, 1993.

Sattler, Helen Roney. *The Earliest Americans.* New York: Clarion, 1993.

We Are Still Here: Native Americans Today. 6 vols. Minneapolis: Lerner Publications, 1992-93.

Wolfson, Evelyn. *From the Earth to Beyond the Sky: Native American Medicine.* Boston: Houghton Mifflin Co., 1993.

Yeu, Charlotte, and David Yeu. *The Igloo.* Boston: Houghton Mifflin Co., 1988.

—————. *The Pueblo.* Boston: Houghton Mifflin Co., 1986.

Fiction

Engle, Lorenz. *Among the Plains Indians.* Minneapolis: Lerner, 1993.

George, Jean Craighead, *Julie of the Wolves.* New York: HarperCollins, 1972.

—————. *The Talking Earth.* New York: HarperCollins, 1983.

Greene, Jacqueline, and Reteller Dembar. *Manabozho's Gifts: Three Chippewa Tales.* Boston: Houghton Mifflin Co., 1994.

Highwater, Jamake. *Anpao: An American Indian Odyssey.* New York: HarperCollins and Lippincott, 1977.

Hurmence, Belinda. *Dixie in the Big Pasture.* New York: Clarion, 1994.

O'Dell, Scott. *Black Star, Bright Dawn.* Boston: Houghton Mifflin Co., 1988.

—————. *The Serpent Never Sleeps: A Novel of Jamestown and Pocahontas.* Boston: Houghton Mifflin Co., 1987.

—————. *Sing Down the Moon.* Boston: Houghton Mifflin Co., 1970.

—————. *Streams to the River, River to the Sea: A Novel of Sacajawea.* Boston: Houghton Mifflin Co., 1986.

—————. *Zia.* Boston: Houghton Mifflin Co., 1976.

————— and Elizabeth Hall. *Thunder Rolling in the Mountains.* Boston: Houghton Mifflin Co., 1992.

Rockwood, Joyce. *To Spoil the Sun.* New York: Henry Holt, 1994.

Rumbaut, Hendle. *Dove Dream.* Boston: Houghton Mifflin Co., 1994.

Ude, Wayne. *Maybe I Will Do Something: Seven Coyote Tales.* Boston: Houghton Mifflin Co, 1993.

VIDEOS

Grade School

The Legend of the Bluebonnet. Irwindale, CA: Barr Films, 1990.

Lord of the Sky. New York: The Board, 1991.

Sacajawea. Hollywood, CA: Film Fair Communications, 1990.

Middle School & Junior High School

Foster Child. New York: The Board, 1988.

Mystery of the Maya. Evanston, IL: Wombat Film and Video, 1990.

Siskyaui—The Place of Chasms. New York: Electronic Arts Intermix, 1991.

Wind Grass Song, the Voice of Our Grandmothers. New York: Drift, 1989.

GLOSSARY

Adobe Sun-dried brick made of mud and straw. Adobe was widely used by Indians of the Southwest, particularly the Pueblo and Hopi, to build their houses.

Agency (see Bureau of Indian Affairs)

Allotment Act This law, passed by Congress in 1887, gave the president of the United States authority to divide Indian reservations into individual allotments and to sell the remaining land. By this law, reservation land was reduced from 155 million acres to 47 million acres in just a few years.

Altar A place of worship, where religious sacrifices and offerings are made and also where rituals are performed. Native American altars varied from tribe to tribe. Sometimes they were tables, sometimes clearings in the woods, or piles of rocks. For some Plains tribes, a buffalo skull served as a sort of altar.

Archaeologist A researcher who excavates, or carefully digs out, objects that have been buried by centuries of soil and rock. Archaeologists try to understand past cultures by examining the ancient objects, or artifacts, they find in the ground.

Band A group of Indians smaller than a tribe and usually from a single tribe. Bands were sometimes permanent units within a tribe, in which case they might be defined by marriage, birth, or membership in a particular clan. Sometimes bands were simply groups of Indians who followed a particular leader. These bands often broke up or changed when the leader died.

Black Drink A drink prepared from the leaves of the yopon plant, a species of holly that grows along the southwest coast of the United States. Many Indians of this region used Black Drink, which contained caffeine, in their ceremonies.

Bureau of Indian Affairs (BIA) The U.S. Constitution says that Congress will regulate trade "with foreign Nations…and with the Indian Tribes." However, while responsibility for treaties and relations with European and other countries was placed with the State Department, the War Department had responsibility for Indian relations. In 1824, the BIA was created as a division of the War Department. Its purpose was to "civilize" Indians and make them citizens of the United States, but many agents of the BIA were corrupt and took advantage of Native Americans. After many people criticized the way the military ran the BIA, the bureau was transferred to the Department of the Interior in 1849. The BIA is headed by the commissioner of Indian Affairs, who is appointed by the president. One or more Indian reservations is assigned to an agency of the BIA. (Large reservations have a single agency, while several small reservations usually share an agency.) The BIA agencies are the federal government's representatives on the reservations. In the 19th century, the agencies often served as a sort of police force to keep Indians on the reservation. Today, the BIA has offices in many big cities, and more than half of its employees are Native American.

Casino Since the 1960s several U.S. courts have ruled that because of Native American self-government, certain kinds of state and federal laws do not apply to reservations. This has enabled many Indian tribes to build gambling casinos in states where they are otherwise against the law. Many of these casinos have become important sources of income for Native Americans.

Census Every ten years the U.S. government counts the population of the United States. The count is used to calculate how many representatives each state has in Congress, to determine how much money will be allotted to each state, and many other things.

Clan A division within a tribe or across tribal lines. Members of a clan were sometimes closely related—a child was usually in his or her mother's clan, for instance. Sometimes clan members were simply believed to have a common ancestor in the very distant past.

Confederacy A political or social union of two or more tribes. This is a common form of government among whites, as well. After the American Revolution, but before the U.S. Constitution was written, the United States was governed by the Articles of Confederation.

Conquistador This Spanish word, which means conqueror, is the name given to Spanish explorers who came after Columbus. They mostly terrorized and often killed the native peoples of Mesoamerica, the Southwest, California, and Florida.

Cradleboard Flat boards onto which babies were laced so they could be transported. The baby was then carried on his or her mother's back or on the side of a horse. Or the baby might be leaned against a house or tree. In many tribes, cradleboards were handed down from generation to generation. Sometimes notches were carved in the cradleboard to show how many babies it had carried over the years.

Dances Dances are a very important part of Native American spirituality and culture. They are used to celebrate such things as the harvest and the new year, to give thanks to the creator, to prepare for war, and to commemorate special events such as birth, puberty, and death.

Depression (see Great Depression)

Dialect A branch of a language that shares some words and grammar with another dialect of the same language but is different enough that speakers of the two dialects would have trouble talking to each other.

Diseases Because their populations had been separated for thousands of years, Europeans and Native Americans had developed different diseases. Members of each group had developed immunities to their own diseases and were often protected from catching them—or at least from dying once they became sick. But neither Native Americans nor Europeans had any immunity to the other group's diseases. European diseases such as smallpox and typhus rapidly killed hundreds of thousands of Native Americans.

Dog Soldier Dogs were very important animals to Indians of the Plains, even after horses were introduced in the 16th century. The term Dog Soldiers usually refers to members of the Cheyenne Dog Society, warriors of proven bravery and daring. However, the Kiowa and several other Plains tribes also had Dog Soldiers.

Dust Bowl During the Great Depression, when most Americans had many economic troubles, there was also an important drought in the central Plains. Oklahoma, home to many Native Americans, had little rain for several years. Crops failed, farmers were ruined, and Oklahoma became so dry that is was called a Dust Bowl.

Enrollment Registering as a member of a tribe. In the 20th century, court decisions began awarding Indian tribes money in compensation for land that had been taken from them. It became important to know who were the members of these tribes, so procedures were set up to identify who was enrolled as a member of a tribe.

Epidemic When a disease spreads so quickly that nearly everyone in a particular area becomes sick or dies.

Federal recognition (see Recognition)

Giveaway feasts (see Potlatch)

Great Depression In the United States in the 1930s there was very high unemployment and very little production. Many people were forced to travel far from their homes to look for jobs, to wait in long lines for a little soup, or to beg in the streets. All Americans were hard-hit during this period, but Native Americans were among the poorest.

Guild A professional association of, for example, goldsmiths or potters. Its purpose is to advance the interests of its members, share information, and find good markets for its members' products.

Indian Religious Freedom Act Passed by Congress in 1986, this bill guaranteed First Amendment protection of freedom of religion for American Indians.

Indian Reorganization Act This 1934 act of Congress abolished the Allotment Act and returned to Native Americans the right to organize their own governments. It gave to the secretary of the interior the responsibility of returning "surplus" lands to the Indians and forbade the selling of Indian lands to non-Indians. The act also provided for hiring teachers to teach native languages in reservation schools and set up a scholarship and loan fund for Native Americans. (The bill did not restore Native Americans their rights to perform traditional religious ceremonies, however, and First Amendment protection was not guaranteed until passage of the Indian Religious Freedom Act in 1986.)

Indian Territory (see Oklahoma)

Jargon The specialized language of a group such as hunters, farmers, or doctors. Trade jargon is often an abbreviated way of saying things so that people who want to trade with each other but who do not speak the same language can understand each other a little.

Lodge This word is used to refer to all sorts of Indian dwellings—tipis, wigwams, wickiups—but it is more properly a permanent dwelling such as an earth lodge or grass lodge.

Masks Masks were very important to several Indian tribes. They were used in ceremonies and rituals and usually represented animals or gods. It was believed that the wearer of a mask assumed the traits of the character represented by the mask. When someone was wearing the mask of a god, he or she became that god for a moment.

Oklahoma (Indian Territory) The Indian Territory was organized in most of present-day Oklahoma in 1829. It was supposed to be a place to which various tribes would be moved and from which they could never be pushed out. However, in 1890, the Indian Territory was reduced by one-half. The other half was named Oklahoma Territory. In 1907, the two territories were merged and became the state of Oklahoma.

Potlatch This ceremony, which means "give-away," was particularly common among Northwest Coast tribes. Wealthy tribe members competed during potlatches, trying to give away more than anyone else.

Powwow This term has many meanings, but it is usually a gathering at which tribe members, or people from different tribes, can talk (often of political matters) and is usually accompanied by dances and other ceremonies.

Recognition (see Tribal status)

Serf A person who has to work on the land of an owner and who often has no right to travel without permission.

Status (see Tribal status)

Taboo Something that is not accepted by a society. Different societies have different taboos. In some cultures, for instance, it is taboo to eat with the left hand.

Taxes (see Tribal status)

Terminate (see Tribal status)

Totem In some tribes, the equivalent of a clan.

Tribal status The U.S. government periodically reviews the status of Indian tribes, deciding whether they have enough members to continue as a tribe. The government has to recognize a tribe for its privileges to continue. Sometimes, the U.S. government decides that a tribe no longer existed because there are too few tribe members. In that case, the tribe is terminated. In the past, these decisions were frequently made for political reasons. For instance, tribe members are not required to pay income taxes, and by terminating a tribe, the government could collect taxes from its former members. Or a tribe might have important natural resources on its land. If the tribe was terminated, that land no longer belonged to the tribe.

Vision quest A rite of passage in which a child goes out from his or her tribe to see a vision of the future and of what role he or she will play in the community.

INDEX